Bon Appétempt

Bon Appétempt

A Coming-of-Age Story
(with Recipes!)

Amelia Morris

GIC

GRAND CENTRAL
PUBLISHING

NEW YORK   BOSTON

Grand Central Publishing
Hachette Book Group
1290 Avenue of the Americas
New York, NY 10104

www.HachetteBookGroup.com

Printed in the United States of America

RRD-C

First Edition: February 2015
10 9 8 7 6 5 4 3 2 1

Grand Central Publishing is a division of Hachette Book Group, Inc. The Grand Central Publishing name and logo is a trademark of Hachette Book Group, Inc.

The Hachette Speakers Bureau provides a wide range of authors for speaking events. To find out more, go to www.hachettespeakersbureau.com or call (866) 376-6591.

The publisher is not responsible for websites (or their content) that are not owned by the publisher.

Library of Congress Cataloging-in-Publication Data

Morris, Amelia.
    Bon appetempt : a coming of age story (with recipes) / Amelia Morris. — First edition.
        pages cm
    ISBN 978-1-4555-4936-8 (hardcover) — ISBN 978-1-4555-4938-2 (ebook) 1. Morris, Amelia. 2. Morris, Amelia—Blogs. 3. Cooks—California—Los Angeles—Biography. 4. Food writers—California—Los Angeles—Biography. 5. Food—United States—Testing. 6. Coming of age—United States. 7. Cooking, American. I. Title.
    TX649.M67A3 2015
    641.5092—dc23
    [B]
                                                            2014013984

To Matt

Contents

Contents

"I feel that I have done everything, absolutely everything wrong, but perhaps something nice will happen anyway."
—Jane Bowles, in a letter to Libby Holman,
*Out in the World: Selected Letters of
Jane Bowles 1935–1970*

Bon Appétempt

Chapter 1

How to Toast a Cheerio

The movers left less than twenty-four hours ago, so it's not until I go to toast my Trader-Joe's-brand Cheerios, Joe's O's—perhaps a classy acknowledgment of the fact that they're blatantly ripping off Cheerios, right down to the bold yellow, oversize cereal box—that I remember I'd decided to put off cleaning out the refrigerator at our old apartment until tomorrow, and so the butter I need is sitting in our butter tray on the other side of town.

Not willing to give up so easily, I search through the previous day's takeout bag and find eight individually wrapped packets of Darigold butter. I tear back the foil and pop the contents of one unit into the frying pan, turn the burner to low, and watch the molded fleur-de-lis dissolve.

Toasted Cheerios in butter is one of the few snacks I remember my mom preparing for my brother and me when we were kids. I'd all but forgotten about them until a few weeks before, when I was surprised to hear her toasting the O's as we spoke on the phone; I'd assumed they were a treat she made only for us.

I'm making them now for the first time in my life, partly because I'm hungry for a snack, but mostly because my life is in boxes; because I've never handled transitions well; and I'd love a moment of food-induced nostalgic clarity—something like what Proust's narrator experiences after tasting the infamous lime-blossom-tea-soaked madeleine, during which "the other states of consciousness faded away."

I add a solid layer of Joe's O's to the melted butter and begin to stir. After a few minutes, I've avoided burning them, but they're not even toasting. I leave the heat on low and stir and wait. I stir and wait some more, and slowly but surely, a familiar nutty, buttery smell begins wafting up from the stove.

Within just a few more minutes, I find that my off-brand Cheerios have toasted up nicely. I slide them into a bowl and hold one between my thumb and forefinger. I pop it into my mouth, followed by another and another. I *sort of* remember the taste. But that's not how I would have eaten them as a child. I pour out an entire handful and throw back my head as I raise my hand to my mouth. And that's when the nostalgia hits me.

With a mouth full of buttered, toasted oats, I'm five years old, dressed in a loose-fitting unitard-esque pajama outfit. My mom is in a somewhat similar get-up—matching gray sweatpants and sweatshirt. Her short, dark blonde hair is pulled into the tiniest of ponytails with one of her colored cotton hair ties as she stands at the stove, stirring Cheerios in a hot pan. It's a strangely quiet, calming memory. My older brother, Billy, isn't anywhere around. My dad's not there either. It's just me and Mom, which is the exact opposite of another, much more dominant memory from that same year.

To recall that memory, I don't need any food.

In that one, I've swapped the unitard for a *leo*tard. It's navy blue and paired with opaque navy-blue tights. And if my white blonde hair hadn't been sticking out of my headgear in Beetle-juician tufts or I hadn't been wearing my older brother's hand-me-down wrestling shoes, which are a few sizes too big for me, you would think I might be on my way to ballet class, or maybe a Halloween party. But the video makes it quite clear: I'm at a wrestling tournament.

Yes, I guess it helps that I have this specific memory recorded on an ancient VHS tape labeled "Wrestling 1987 (Amy wrestling)," which I recently went to the trouble of transferring to DVD in order to watch it for the first time as an adult, curious to see firsthand what had become nothing more to me than an occasional dinner-party anecdote.

But watching myself wrestle twenty-five years after the fact isn't as fun as I thought it was going to be. Right before the match, I'm issued a red Velcro anklet, which the referee uses to direct points to the proper wrestler (e.g., two points, red). A green one goes on the ankle of my opponent, a little boy in a black singlet with red trim. Once the anklet is on, my five-year-old, round, pink face wears the expression of a little girl just now realizing what she's gotten herself into.

A woman whose face we can't see and whose gravelly voice and unrushed manner of speaking brings to mind so much of my rural Pennsylvanian hometown actually says to my dad: "Your daughter doesn't look too enthused."

My dad, perhaps suddenly realizing the same thing, calls out to me cheerfully, "Honey Bun!"

I turn and look at him/the camera with impatience, my young face telegraphing, "What do you want now, Dad?"

Dad. To describe him as "a wrestling fanatic with a day job as an obstetrician/gynecologist" doesn't quite cut it. His brand of fanaticism went so much further than the relatively passive act of attending matches and collecting memorabilia. No, Dad's love for wrestling required endeavors such as buying us a regulation mat for our basement, draining—via syringe—my brother's teammates' cauliflower ears in our kitchen, and journeying by train and rented van (Dad doesn't fly) to Seattle, Washington, from our home in western Pennsylvania in order to attend—as spectators—the wrestling portion of the Goodwill Games held there in 1990.

The tape cuts away so that in the next scene, I'm standing on the mat facing my competitor. The referee blows his whistle and within five seconds, the little boy has taken me down. In another few seconds, I'm on my back.

"Get off your back, Honey Bun!" my dad yells. And I'm trying, but there's something very sluggish about my movements. I seem dazed. This isn't how it went when I'd practiced at home on our regulation mat.

For most of the struggle, the referee is thankfully blocking the camera, but for a brief moment, he moves out of the way and you can see my face. I'm still on my back, attempting to bridge by shoving my chin into my chest, my face all scrunched up and red. I'm on the verge of tears. My expression doesn't say *athlete*, but rather a child thinking: *This is annoying. Get this kid off me!* And within a few more seconds, he will be. Because I'm pinned. The match is over.

I wish the story ended here, but it was a wrestling tournament, and for those of you who aren't familiar with the sport, most tournaments are double-elimination. So, I have to lose one more time before I can hang up my leotard.

When I step out on the mat for my second match, there's something notably different in my demeanor, in the way I hold myself. I know what I'm in for this time. This time, after I shake hands with a little boy in orange and before the whistle blows, I squat down as low as I can, my butt inches from the mat, a position that makes it harder for my opponent to take me down. And this time, I don't get taken down. Well, not immediately. This time, my opponent and I battle like true wrestlers, heads and arms interlocked, and instead of calling at me to get off my back, my dad is shouting, "Crossface! Crossface, Amy!" When I don't seem to get it, he tries to be more specific: "Cross *his* face!"

In this match, my dad isn't alone in his coaching. There's another man, a stranger, shouting advice at me. My brother's voice is there too, and at one point, he calls out, "Peterson roll!" with a laugh. A Peterson roll is an advanced move where, starting in the bottom position, you manage not only to sit up and roll out from underneath your opponent, but grab his leg in the process and wind up on top, getting back points. My dad laughs a little too. Of course, I can't hear these laughs at the time, but as I watch now it's clear that they're making fun of my rudimentary mastery of the sport.

The match is a tight one. With time running out in the third and final period, I'm just one point behind. "Get mean, Amy! Get mean!" my dad starts yelling.

But I don't. I lose 3–2, though it was so close that I don't realize this until we've shaken hands and the referee raises the arm of the other kid. Once again, you can see it on my face. *Wha? I lost?*

I do well enough that my present-day self momentarily wonders why it is that I quit. But we often underestimate what kids can pick up on. Even at age five, I had the sense that it was silly for me to wrestle. And beyond that, that even if I did well, I would never be able to compete with my brother, whose budding talent would consume the family. (Eight years later, when Billy threw his competitor to the mat in a move that took him to a fourth place finish at the 1995 state championships, I jumped up with such excitement that I slammed my shin into the seat in front of me, giving myself a nasty bruise that would take weeks to go away, which is all to say: I was deeply invested in my brother's wrestling career.)

After my second match, the tape cuts to one of Billy's from that same tournament. And as early as the age of seven, you can tell he's a natural. He's smart, self-confident, and at ease on the mat. He's also constantly looking up at the camera, at his coach, for advice—for approval.

And as I watch, for the first time I notice the electronic date in the bottom left-hand corner of the screen: 2-13-87.

It's jarring. It suddenly dawns on me that in five short months, reality will hit me with a much bigger blow than the fact that I'm not a very good young lady wrestler.

❊ ❊ ❊

People say you'll understand when you're older.

And for the most part, it's true. Take the classic film *Dirty Dancing*, which I first saw as a kid. When I watched it again in my twenties, I suddenly realized that what Penny wants is an *abortion*, and on top of that, there is this whole class-war element to it, e.g., Penny doesn't have the money to pay for the abortion, and guess who is *not* going to help with that? Robbie, the Yale-bound waiter, who casually says, "Some people matter, some people don't." I also realize the amazing conflict that's set up between Baby and her dad, who, in theory, is brimming with pride for his youngest, left-leaning, prospective

Peace Corps–joining daughter, until her open mind and open heart are turned toward Johnny, the blue-collar dance instructor, at which point, he is basically disgusted. (Also, though it may go without saying, adult me is surprised to realize that Patrick Swayze looks very good in his fitted black T-shirt and that I would definitely volunteer to practice the lift in a shallow lake with him, if, you know, I *had to* help the Kellerman dance staff out of a jam.)

* * *

People say you'll understand when you're older.

But sometimes, you won't.

In July 1987, five months after my wrestling debut, my dad's mistress, Dolly, gave birth to my half sister, Margaret.

At the time, my parents were living in separate houses, though they weren't yet divorced. They were also still working together in the same medical office in Meadville, our small town in western Pennsylvania; Dad as one of the two ob-gyns in town and Mom as one of the two pediatricians. In other words, if you gave birth to a baby at the local hospital—the Meadville Medical Center—my mom was going to know about it, one way or another.

But my mom didn't find out about Margaret's birth because my dad and Dolly decided to have the baby at home.

If you ask my dad about it, he will expound on the benefits of a home birth, especially if you have a licensed obstetrician-gynecologist there with you. But my dad was on call when Dolly went into labor—in fact, he was at the hospital delivering someone else's baby. So, instead of a licensed obstetrician-gynecologist, my soon-to-be stepmom called her neighbor friend over, and Dad came home in time to clean up. ("The placenta and umbilical cord were still attached," he tells me years later.)

I remember Dolly handing me the new baby to hold with a soft, "This is your sister." If we could play back the tape, I think my expression would be very similar to the one I had after losing my second wrestling match: head tilt, confusion. *Wha?*

At this point in the story, after the addition of this new family member, you would think Dad might be ready to confess that he's been having an affair, that he's gotten his mistress pregnant, and that actually, he became a father again just the other day.

But you would be wrong.

Instead, Dad asked Billy and me to keep our new little sister a secret.

The story goes that I lasted six weeks before telling my mom in the middle of one night: "Dad and Dolly have a baby." My mom woke up Billy to confirm the news. He did.

The divorce was finalized very shortly after.

* * *

This narrative is the one I grew up with: My dad was the bad guy; he didn't just cheat on my mom, he also had a baby with someone else; then he tried to hide all of this from her, forcing her to find out from her five-year-old daughter.

It doesn't hit me until very recently—as I am pacing around my living room on the phone with my dad, discussing his course of action (err, inaction) as openly and as matter-of-factly as we've ever done—what a weird and horrible plan this was. The moment Dad knew he was having a baby with someone else, why didn't he tell Mom and/or file for divorce? If not for the sake of Mom or Dolly and their feelings, at least for the sake of simplicity?

And for the first time in my life, I ask my dad what he was thinking: "I mean, you couldn't have kept Margaret a secret forever."

"Well, you never know, an asteroid could've hit the earth," he says in a jokey, Steve Martin kind of voice and laughs.

I don't laugh. I don't say anything, letting the silence fill the air between us.

I haven't been to the house he shares with Dolly in more than seven years, but I doubt it's changed much. I imagine him in his poorly lit, small rectangular office, speaking into the beige rotary phone that sits next to his computer, the screen of which is most likely displaying the current online chess game he's playing.

And then he adds, quietly, "Plus, I didn't want to hurt your mom." There's a rare sincerity to his voice. I believe him. And then, as I tend to do during most of our phone calls, I feel sorry for him.

Chapter 2

All of Them Had Hair of Gold

I'd always wanted a big, tight-knit family. The kind that might break out singing "We Are Family" on the dance floor at a wedding, or go on *Family Feud* together, or to Italian restaurants that serve giant family-style meals and then head home to watch a movie on *ABC Family* before going to bed, safe and sound in the comfort and security that only a cozy house full of family can bring.

My aunt told me I used to walk around with my forearm tightly wrapped around the necks of my dolls saying, "I'm going to have a big family when I grow up!" It was a deep yearning, so embedded that it still comes out from time to time now, most often and most embarrassingly while watching those horrible yet endearing Kardashian sisters on any one of their reality TV shows. *Wouldn't it be nice to have a brood of Armenian daughters?*, some part of me wonders.

I believe this desire for a big family originated with *Nick at Nite*, or specifically their re-airings of old episodes of *The Brady Bunch*. I particularly enjoyed the iconic one-minute opening sequence that explained in song how this mishmash of boys and girls somehow formed a family. The introduction culminated with your TV screen looking like a side of a

Rubik's Cube, only instead of different-colored squares, the squares were filled with different individuals.

And that's the way
we all becaaaaame
The Brady Buuunch!

✳ ✳ ✳

Have you ever held a puppy in your arms when it realizes that its owner has just pulled into the driveway after a long day at work? The dog is so excited and overwhelmed with emotion that when you go to set her down, her legs are already swimming through the air; she quite literally hits the ground running toward her owner. I imagine that was what I looked like when my mom took us to the Meadville Country Club pool in the summers during those golden, post-divorce years of joint custody.

My three main activities at the pool, ranked from most enjoyable to least enjoyable, were: jumping off the diving board, putting foodlike products from the snack bar (e.g., Strawberry Mentos and Flintstone orange-flavored push pops) on "our tab," and getting stung on the bottom of my foot by dying-but-not-quite-dead bees that were floating in puddles of water along the edge of the pool, the last of which was made not so bad by one of the young lifeguards who would carry me as a fireman might carry a child out of a burning building to the first-aid station where he or she would then tape up my foot and give me a few more Strawberry Mentos before releasing me back into the fun zone.

Here's the beautiful secret of joint custody: Nobody really has custody, so nobody's really in charge, especially when both of your parents are full-time, on-call doctors. Billy and I bounced from school over to Mom's house, where we were greeted by our nanny, Janice, who let us watch all sorts of television (including the movie *Dirty Dancing*), back to school, to Dad's house, or more than likely, to the doctors' lounge at the hospital, where he would be waiting to deliver a baby and where we would be allowed to watch all sorts of television, back to school, and so on, happy as clams.

⁕ ⁕ ⁕

The creators of *The Brady Bunch* got one thing right: They got rid of the other parents. Mr. Brady is a widower and Mrs. Brady is, *uhm*, well it's not clear. In fact, no mention is ever made regarding the circumstances in which her first marriage ended. But guess what? It worked. Because the important thing wasn't the status or whereabouts of the girls' biological father. It was that they were now a part of a new family, which consisted of a mom, a dad, six kids, and Alice—the housekeeper.

I watched episode after episode, on a TV anchored to the ceiling from the comfort of one of the doctors' lounge's twin beds, eating individually wrapped packages of saltines.

Little did I know that my family would soon be just one kid shy of *The Brady Bunch*'s six. Only my version would suck.

⁕ ⁕ ⁕

In our Brady-Bunch-esque opening sequence, the screen would be split into four rectangles: one for Mom, one for Dad, one for Billy, age nine, and one for me, age six. Billy and I would be smiling. Mom and Dad would look a bit underwhelmed.

Then, a fifth rectangle featuring Dolly would pop in.

And they knew that it was much more than a hunch.

Mom would then start looking at Dolly with a frown. But Dolly would look straight ahead, appearing relatively harmless, polite even.

In would come a sixth screen, newborn baby Margaret. Everyone would look a bit ill at ease. Perhaps we'd hear the screechy sound of a needle being abruptly lifted off a record. Then, Mom's rectangle would spin right off the screen altogether, like a tossed playing card.

In another moment, two new rectangles would pop up: one for Paul—Dad and Dolly's second child, born seventeen months after Margaret—and one for Travis, Dolly's twenty-something son from a previous marriage. I'm not sure if anyone would still be smiling at this point.

We would then have to quickly flash to black before showing a new screen, split between my mom and her new husband, Bruce. Mom would look like she was smiling after a good hard cry. Next, in would pop Billy and me again!

That this group would somehow form a family...

Or, to explain it to those of you who haven't memorized the theme song: Dad remarried the month after the divorce came through and became a stepdad to Dolly's son, Travis, while Dolly became stepmom to Billy and me. Soon after, Dad and Dolly had a second child together. And soon after that, Mom met and married a nice man named Bruce and moved back to her hometown of Pittsburgh.

Of course, one thing I really do understand now that I'm older is my mom moving two hours away. As a kid, I didn't get it. The two-hour car trip felt like a lifetime. Why couldn't Mom and Bruce live in Meadville or, better yet, in nearby

Saegertown, where Dad and Dolly resided? But it makes so much sense to me now. In Pittsburgh, she wouldn't have to live *and* work amid the swirling gossip of Dad's affair-avec-love-child. In Pittsburgh, she could be surrounded by people who loved her—her mom, dad, and new husband. In Pittsburgh, she had a chance at a fresh start.

And as far as fresh starts go, she couldn't have picked a better second husband. Whereas my dad seemed committed to doing whatever he wanted, no matter who he might hurt in the process, Bruce was focused on doing the right thing, to the best of his abilities, which were top-notch.

Bruce hadn't just played college baseball and college football at the Naval Academy. He had been drafted by the Baltimore Orioles (he turned them down) and played backup quarterback to Heisman Trophy winner Roger Staubach before becoming first-string quarterback himself in his senior year. And he wasn't just a Navy pilot, he trained under military instructors I've actually heard of, like John McCain, and could perform the kinds of aerial maneuvers I was previously only familiar with from *Top Gun*. And he didn't just serve in Vietnam. He went and nearly didn't come back. On a rescue mission, his helicopter (he could also fly those) was shot down in the jungle near the Laotian border.

He'd imagined a career in the Navy—becoming captain of an aircraft carrier was his dream—but his extensive injuries, which included a broken back, left him incapable of flying again and, therefore, of taking the kinds of jobs within the Academy he was most interested in. So, instead, he followed his faith. In typical Bruce fashion, he didn't go about this lightly. He received a PhD in theology, writing his doctoral thesis on Puritan preaching. He then worked for the Fellowship of Christian Athletes before pastoring churches of his own in Kansas City as well as Chicago. But to be closer to his ailing parents, he moved to Pittsburgh, where he stumbled into a job managing charitable trusts at a major bank. Of course, he made time for teaching an adult Sunday school class and also occasionally acted as a substitute or interim pastor at the various Protestant churches across town. It was there at one of these churches, the one my mom grew up attending, where he first met my mom.

Thus, the introduction of Bruce into our family brought with it the introduction of Christianity. Whereas Dad and Dolly went off to Canada, just the two of them, to get married in front of a judge, Mom and Bruce had a sizable church ceremony. I was eight and got to wear a puffy peach ball gown and blue eye shadow, and read a passage from the Bible, the one in First Corinthians about how love is patient and love is kind. And though I may have been too young to have cared about the details of Bruce's illustrious biography, I did know that the wedding was a good thing, that my mom was marrying a good guy.

But with Mom living two hours away, our joint custody schedule would no longer work; we couldn't bounce between the two houses every other day. Given all of the above information, it seems clear where Billy and I should've chosen to live.

Only by the time we sat down in front of a mediator at the courthouse, Billy was eleven—he would start seventh grade in the fall—and I was eight, and all we really knew was that our mom (who seemed to cry an awful lot for a grown woman) was moving far enough away that if we wanted to go with her, we would have to change schools, friends, lives, etc. So, instead,

Billy chose Dad, and though I don't remember, I'm told I said, "Whatever Billy's doing." Which makes sense given that I was so obsessed with my big brother, I probably also added, "And if there's time later, I'd love to talk to you about his wide range of talents. Of course, there's his wrestling, but have you seen him play Tetris?"

Chapter 3

A Tale of Two Cities

Dolly was pissed when Billy and I decided not to follow our mom to Pittsburgh. "I didn't sign up for Stepparenting 101, Bill!" we could hear her shout to our dad from the tiny laundry room she'd set up as an office for herself. I guess she had hoped we would disappear altogether, but I would argue that you kind of *do* sign up for Stepparenting 101 when you marry someone with kids.

By choosing to live with our dad, we thought we had chosen the path with the least amount of change, but, ironically, everything changed anyway.

Dolly and Dad lived in Saegertown (which had one stoplight and a population hovering around a thousand), and though the new custody agreement stipulated that I remain at the private Catholic school, Dad switched us to the Saegertown public schools anyway.

But most jarring was the new custody schedule. During the school year, we would spend the vast majority of time in Saegertown, only visiting our mom every other weekend. Then, during the summer, we would spend the majority of our time in Pittsburgh, with only two weeks in Saegertown. (Every other weekend, Mom picked us up in Saegertown on

Friday after school, and Dad came and got us in Pittsburgh on Sunday after dinner.)

In this way, my life was split in two.

Pittsburgh became summer and Saegertown winter.

Pittsburgh was a standard split-level house in the suburbs— with central air and my own room.

Saegertown was a one-hundred-year-old farmhouse with poor insulation, where, despite the new three-story addition, Billy and I shared a room in the old, alternately sweaty and cold part of the house while toddler Margaret and baby Paul enjoyed rooms of their own—Margaret's in the renovated and better insulated section.

In Pittsburgh, I biked to the bottom of the street, where I could flip down my kickstand, dash in between two of our neighbors' houses, and end up in the parking lot of a Togo's, where I might buy a cherry-flavored Slush Puppie with the one-dollar bill my mom had given me earlier that day for this very scenario.

In Saegertown, we drove. Our house sat on a two-lane country road that connected to Interstate 79. (Everyone drove. And if you weren't driving, it might be because you were working on your other car, the one you or your friend would drive in the big demolition derby that summer at the county fair.)

In Pittsburgh, we believed in God. The whole family— me, Billy, Mom, Bruce, and Grandma and Grandpa—went to church each Sunday we were in town as well as to Bruce's Sunday school class.

In Saegertown, religion was for the weak, or so our father made a point of telling us, especially during the long rides home from Pittsburgh every other Sunday night.

In Pittsburgh, cooking dinner and cleaning up afterward were a part of our daily routine.

In Saegertown, cooking and cleaning were chores. I washed the dishes, swept the dining and living room, as well as the front porch, and burned the garbage. That was supposed to have been Billy's chore, but since he was always at wrestling practice, it fell to me. (Have you ever tried to light a match and keep it lit long enough to catch something on fire in twenty-degree weather? With gloves on, it was impossible to grip the match properly. Without gloves but with frozen fingers, it was impossible to grip the match properly.)

In Pittsburgh, I ate food that I liked until I was full.

In Saegertown, I dodged food I didn't like and was constantly hungry.

Seemingly overnight, Billy and I had gone from eating our nanny's beloved Kraft macaroni and cheese and sliced hot dogs, to our stay-at-home stepmom's thick, white-sauced beef Stroganoff, which always inspired the unspoken question: Shouldn't beef Stroganoff be at least partially beef-colored? From our working mother's commendable frozen chicken cordon bleu that came out of the oven bursting with melted cheese, some of which may have even crisped up a bit on the surface of the pan, to our stay-at-home stepmom's hamburgers she cooked so beyond well-done that when you bit into them, the individual morsels of the ground chuck separated and scattered in your mouth like a thousand little pieces of rubber. (It's also worth noting that my dad has not eaten chicken since 1971 when he watched a video about how it's processed in factories, so when Dolly served something she called city chicken, the only thing we knew for sure was that it was not poultry.)

But mostly, Pittsburgh was where I was sure I was wanted. And Saegertown was where I was sure I was not.

Under the umbrella of Stepparenting 101 fell various tasks Dolly made clear that she hadn't signed up for either, like doing our laundry, making our school lunches, and/or allowing us to "infiltrate" her kitchen in the morning to make them for ourselves. We worked around these easily enough, though. Every other weekend, we returned from Pittsburgh with clean laundry and my sea foam green Eddie Bauer duffel bag loaded with granola bars, prepackaged Rice Krispies Treats, fruit roll-ups, and Dunkaroos, all of which I stored and often ate in the privacy of my bedroom.

What *had* Dolly apparently signed up for? Making sure we did our chores properly and that we finished our dinners. She was also on board with reminding Billy and me that she could never have *abandoned* Margaret and Paul the way our mom had *abandoned* us, and the occasional and straightforward "You're never going to amount to anything."

Unsurprisingly, my dad—the guy who put off disclosing the fruits (read: baby) of his affair to my mom until someone else did it for him—stayed out of the majority of these conversations, but on certain occasions, he couldn't help but react. Like the time I got 99th percentile on my Iowa Tests (of Basic Skills) and Dolly's response was that she'd gotten *99 pluses* when she was a kid. "There's no such thing, Doll," I can remember my dad saying as he walked away, laughing to himself. Or the time she said that Paul, age five, had been outside on the rings of the swing set doing *iron crosses*. As she said it, she held her arms outstretched perpendicularly, demonstrating the positioning of the extremely advanced men's gymnastics move there was no way a five-year-old could do.

My dad laughed, I think, not just because it was impossible, but because it really was funny the number of ways Dolly found to highlight how Margaret and Paul were special and Billy and I were not.

One of Dolly's many incongruities is that though she was (to say the least) the opposite of cuddly, her name was *Dolly*, *and* she made and sold stuffed dolls. She painted the faces and then dyed the fabric with tea to give them a worn-in, antiquey look, which she emphasized by attaching a little tag with an old-lady name on it: Constance, Prudence, Eleanor, etc. I never loved these dolls, but I remember thinking that she did know how to paint a face. In fact, I told her so during one of the two times our family met with a counselor together. We had to go around the room and say one good thing about each other. "You're good at drawing faces," I said.

"You're good at making Santas," Billy said. (In the winter, she also made papier-mâché Santa Clauses.)

What she said to us in return is a mystery. I can't remember; I can't even summon up a guess.

* * *

After our mom moved to Pittsburgh, I began to understand that the world was more complicated than I'd previously considered. I also began to understand (and believe) that with the good things in life must come an equal number of bad things.

My mom moving away was a bad thing, but school was a good thing. I was on the advanced track in all of my classes, always got As, and Jeremy Mesley—one of the most popular boys—would often ask me to hold his hand at recess.

Having to always get a ride with the Petersons to and from gymnastics because Dolly wouldn't drive me and because Dad was either working or picking Billy up from wrestling was a bad thing, but gymnastics itself was a good thing. I was one of the top gymnasts on my team, partly because every other weekend I practiced in an actual gymnastics gym in Pittsburgh, not the Meadville YMCA where class took place in the basketball gym, which meant we had to spend the first and last twenty minutes of each session setting up and breaking down the equipment.

As sixth grade turned into seventh turned into eighth turned into ninth, and I entered high school, the junior and senior guys asking for my phone number in the hallways in between classes became the good thing.

But coming home from school was always a bad thing.

A couple of years after the initial family merger, my twenty-three-year-old stepbrother, Travis, found a place of his own and Billy moved into his room, while I stayed alone in the one we'd shared. And when I think of Saegertown now, the first image that comes to mind is my room, and the floral wallpaper and the cobwebbed wooden rafters that paralleled the A-frame ceiling. It was where I spent the majority of my time, especially on the days I didn't have gymnastics practice. From the moment I got off the bus until dinnertime when Dad and Billy would come home from wrestling practice, the house was nonnegotiably *hers*. And during that time, Billy's room and my own were the only hospitable places.

I could only do homework and read for so long. So I entertained myself by wandering into Billy's room and snooping around in his stuff. He had this book of fatherly wisdom Dad had given him for his birthday. Each page held a quote by someone famous, and Dad had annotated some of the pages with his thoughts: "I've found this to be particularly true." And "I wish my father had told me this." I was taken aback by the intimacy of it, by Dad's handwriting itself. He'd never given me anything so personal.

Billy's room, like mine, was in the old part of the house, and so it had these old details to it like the little rectangular, decorative cast-iron grate in the floor. If you got on your hands and knees, you could see right through it to the kitchen below.

I spent a lot of time there, comparing the way my stepmom talked to Travis to the way she talked to Billy and me. When Dad was around, Dolly smoked only in the laundry room, but during these unencumbered hours, the two of them—mother and son—smoked openly and chatted as she cooked. It was a big farmhouse kitchen where the island in the center held a stovetop across from a wooden bar with room for three stools. So Travis would sit at the bar while she fried up ground chuck. I could tell how much she loved her firstborn, and it felt strange to watch, like seeing a villain in a movie do something kind.

During those afterschool hours is when I began keeping a record of every time I wished I lived with my mom. I knew that I hated living in that house, but I also knew how hard it would be to up and move, to change everything yet again, and I figured that it might help if I had proof of my daily moments of unhappiness. So, in the last page of my diary, I began adding hash marks for every time I thought about it. One for every time I went to bed hungry; one for every time she made me redo a chore I hadn't done properly; one for every time I woke up in Pittsburgh with a sense of dread on those Sundays Dad was set to pick us up; one for each time I had to wave good-bye to my crying mother from the backseat of Dad's van; and one for each time I flipped the lights on in my Saegertown bedroom only to find the century-old room still dark and gloomy.

By the end of the school year, the tiny hash marks filled the page.

* * *

Inertia is defined as "a property of matter by which it continues in its existing state of rest or uniform motion in a straight line, unless that state is changed by an external force." The key words there being *external force*. We feel we are too old to start over again, so we don't quit our jobs. We feel we waited too long, so we don't go back to school. We feel we missed the proper time frame, so we sometimes don't even buy wedding gifts.

Inertia kept me living in Saegertown for five years.

But the summer after my freshman year, I was tentatively proactive. I told my mom that I wanted to look into moving in with her full-time *just in case*.

I spent that summer entirely in Pittsburgh, forgoing the requisite two weeks in Saegertown. That summer, I was fourteen—old enough to begin to see the holes in my original theory that all the good things that happened to you had to equal the bad. I was old enough to see how desperately my mom wanted me to live with her. What if, I began to wonder, you didn't have to wait for things to happen to you, good or bad? What if all I had to do to live the life I wanted was open the door and step into it?

Chapter 4

Not So Terrific

Moving to Pittsburgh meant that I would attend one of the best high schools in the state as a sophomore. And just in case that's what I decided to do, at the beginning of the summer, my mom made an appointment for us to meet with the guidance counselor there to plan my class schedule.

And this is when I discovered that excellence in Saegertown translated to mediocrity-at-best in Pittsburgh. As it turned out, at my potentially new school, I would be a year behind the majority of incoming sophomores in both Spanish and science.

It was a bitter pill to swallow. In Saegertown, Billy was in the running for valedictorian (he would eventually graduate that year as salutatorian), and I had assumed I would follow in his footsteps. Unwilling to completely accept my new fate, I got a language tutor, and at the end of the summer, I took a test to skip a year of Spanish. I tried to do the same with science, but ultimately, I couldn't find a class or teacher willing to go over a year's worth of biology in two and a half months.

Although I suspected as much, I came to the same realization in terms of my beloved sport: that my high skill level within Meadville's YMCA gymnastics program equated to nothing special at the private Pittsburgh gym I attended, and a few weeks into the summer, I made the sad decision to retire my leos, or for the layman: quit the sport. This left a time slot open to focus more seriously on tennis, a game my mom loved and one we played often as a family.

Between Spanish tutoring, tennis lessons, the giant backyard trampoline I'd spent my entire life's savings on the previous summer, and hanging out with my one good friend, Emily, whom I'd met through the aforementioned Pittsburgh gymnastics school, summer flew by.

There was just one more hurdle to get through before I began my new life. I had to tell my dad that I wouldn't be coming home.

* * *

I waited until the last moment, a few days before school started in Saegertown and Dad was set to pick me up to take me back home to rejoin his family, as well as Billy, who'd spent most of the summer at his girlfriend's family's house. And though I knew it would be a difficult conversation to have, I also knew my dad. I knew he wasn't a fighter.

Or was he?

I don't think that loving people is an easy thing for my dad. At least it never appeared that way. To hug him is a thing of great awkwardness for all parties involved. His personality is tailor-made for the Internet age—he belongs alone in his office with the computer in front of him, communicating through message board forums on a chess site. He is not a father who calls you to check in. He is not a father who calls you *at all*. He is simply not someone who has made it a habit to show his emotions in any visible way, though when he does, he really does. I immediately think of a funeral my brother and I went to with him when we were young. It was for an eighteen- or nineteen-year-old kid named Adam who had died in a car accident, whom we all knew through the world of high school wrestling. We went to the funeral, the three of us, and Dad could *not* stop crying. It was the second time I had ever seen him cry—the first time being at the courthouse when Billy and I met with that mediator—but it made that first time seem like a fluke. This was not a quiet kind of crying. It was loud and unavoidable. People were staring, including me. His face was distorted. His skin was pink; his eyelashes dark black and shiny; his nostrils rounded and flared. "He was just a kid," he kept saying, over and over.

My announcement that I wasn't coming home unleashed this version of my father.

In those few days before school began in Saegertown, my dad called nightly and begged me to come home. I don't remember the exact details of these conversations as well as I remember the setting, the finished basement of our house in Pittsburgh, the so-called *game room*, where I'd sit on the beige, scratchy, tweedlike couch that Mom had brought from our house in Meadville, and cry.

It's hard not to do what your father tells you to do, especially when what he's asking is for you to come home. The only reason I was able to stand firm was because I knew that when I hung up, I would head up the stairs, which opened into the hallway that led to the kitchen, where Mom and Bruce would be sitting, and whose faces resembled what I imagine those of a couple waiting for the verdict from an adoption agency might look like.

* * *

Though school had yet to start in Mt. Lebanon, it had started in Saegertown, so I felt I was in the clear. Inertia was now swinging me toward my new life. So, when my paternal grandma, who also lived in Pittsburgh, called me and wanted to have lunch, I didn't think too much of it. In fact, I'm pretty sure I happily recommended Burger King, as they had a chicken Parmesan sandwich I really liked at the time.

Even though her age was only a few years shy of my maternal grandma's—Grandma Felt—Grandma Morris always seemed decades younger. Grandma Morris dyed her hair brown, while Grandma Felt had let hers go gray. Grandma Morris lived in an apartment with mirrored walls and a balcony. Grandma Felt lived in a home that always seemed to be collapsing in on itself. Grandma Morris went to Las Vegas monthly. Grandma Felt went to church weekly.

So when Grandma Morris picked me up and took me to lunch, she did it in her typical youthful way, whipping around the bends in the road, one hand on the wheel and the other resting on the open window ledge. I ordered my sandwich and should have known that something was up when Grandma didn't order anything for herself. There's something about going to lunch with someone who doesn't order anything that instantly puts the two of you at odds. Suddenly, you're not communing as equals but self-consciously consuming food while being watched.

And thus began my earliest lesson that just because she goes by the innocuous name of *Grandma* doesn't mean she has your best interests at heart. See, Grandma was there on business. Grandma did not understand why I hadn't returned to Saegertown like I had every other autumn. Yes, she understood I had a poor relationship with my stepmom, and yes, she agreed that I had been treated unfairly. But, did I realize that I was breaking my father's heart? Did I know that he called her crying last night? Why was I choosing to split up the family like this? And by the way, did I realize that his heart was *breaking*?

Truth be told, I *had* sort of felt like I was breaking my dad's heart. And, when I thought about it for a second, I was going to be starting high school the following week at a place four times the size of my last high school, where I had the sum total of one friend.

And so, at the pay phone stationed right outside of Burger King, with change provided by Grandma, I called my mom at work. The receptionist told me she was seeing a patient and asked if she could call me back. "It's kind of important," I said.

When my mom came to the phone, she was a bit out of breath, and I could hear the worry in her voice. "What is it, Sweetie?"

"I think I want to move back with Dad."

And then I heard something different in her voice, something very desperate. "Just wait until I get home. Just please don't make any decisions until I get home. OK? We'll talk about this tonight, OK?" I don't know what she thought—that I would call Dad and get him to pick me up before she even came home from work? But I did wait.

* * *

That night, once Bruce came home from work, we all discussed it, as a family. And away from Burger King and the dominating presence of my grandmother, the decision was clear. I was staying. School started on Tuesday, and I would be going—all five feet two inches, barely one hundred pounds of me.

Oh, and did I mention that I was a very late bloomer who had just gotten her hair cut boy-length short and who, since then was often mistaken for a young boy? Or, in the words of my homeroom teacher, "Welcome to your new school, Sir!"

In my mom's new life in Pittsburgh, she'd joined a practice with five other partners and was able to work less. This meant that she cooked much more often. And this meant that instead of frozen chicken cordon bleu from a box, she made it the old-fashioned way. She pounded the chicken breasts nice and thin, layered on the cheese and ham, and rolled up each one before breading, frying, and baking it to oozing-Swiss perfection.

It may not be the quickest recipe to prepare (in some ways, for Mom and me, it was years in the making). But it's completely worth it.

A few notes on the process: When Mom and I made this together recently, by the time she was finished butchering the three chicken breasts, she had six large slices of the breasts along with a couple of smaller (bonus) pieces that had detached themselves in the process, and which made for delicious mini chicken cordon bleus. For the bigger pieces of chicken, if you need to use a toothpick to secure the wrap closed, use it like you would a safety pin (instead of how you would skewer an hors d'oeuvre, which is what I did the first time I made this on my own, and which makes it difficult to pan-fry each side).

MY MOM'S CHICKEN CORDON BLEU

Serves 4

    3 to 4 large boneless, skinless chicken breasts (about 1½ pounds total)
Salt and freshly ground black pepper
6 to 8 ounces sliced Swiss cheese (about 6 slices)
4 ounces thinly sliced ham
1 cup all-purpose flour
Pinch of cayenne (optional)
¼ teaspoon garlic powder (optional)
2 large eggs
2 tablespoons milk
1½ cups panko breadcrumbs
1 tablespoon butter, plus more if needed
2 tablespoons olive oil

If the chicken breasts are large, you probably will want to slice them in half horizontally. In my experience, the thinner the piece of chicken, the easier it is to wrap up and the more delicious it tastes because the ratio of chicken to ham and cheese is almost equal.

Place the chicken between two sheets of plastic wrap, and using a meat mallet or rolling pin, pound each one out to ¼-inch thickness or thinner. You want to get them as thin as possible without tearing them.

Sprinkle each breast with salt and pepper, then top each with a layer of cheese and a slice of ham. Roll the breasts up as tight as possible, starting with the thinner side and working toward the thicker side. If necessary, secure them closed with a toothpick.

Preheat the oven to 350°F.

Place the flour in a shallow dish and season with salt, pepper, the cayenne, if using, and the garlic powder, if using. In another shallow dish, whisk the eggs with the milk and season with salt and pepper. Place the breadcrumbs in a third shallow dish and season with salt and pepper. Dip a rolled-up breast in the flour, shaking off any excess, then dip it into the egg and milk mixture and, finally, in the breadcrumbs. Transfer to a plate. Repeat with the remaining pieces of chicken.

Lightly oil a wire rack set on top of a large rimmed baking sheet.

Melt the butter in the oil in a large skillet over medium heat. Place the chicken roll-ups in the skillet and cook until they're golden brown on all four sides (it depends on the size of the chicken pieces, but it should take 2 to 4 minutes per side). Then, using tongs, hold each piece of chicken upright to fry each end briefly, 30 seconds to 1 minute.

Transfer the fried pieces of chicken to the wire rack on the baking sheet, place in the oven, and bake until the cheese is melted and bubbly and the chicken is cooked through, 10 to 15 minutes.

Chapter 5

September

$\mathbf{M}$att says that he first saw me at the *triangle*, which refers to a triangular-shaped grassy island in the middle of his street, which was also Emily's street. But I don't remember seeing him there.

In my memory, we first met at the Mt. Lebanon Lanes bowling alley during that last week of summer before school started. In retrospect, though, I'm not sure the word *met* quite fits to describe our interaction, as we didn't exchange a single word. But I certainly noticed him. It was hard not to. Emily and her friends were all in bands—punk bands, to be specific. They wore patched-up jeans, band T-shirts, and lace-up boots. Knowing this, I began to transition into this scene as best I could. I listened to the few punk bands I actually liked (Operation Ivy and Blink-182), acquired a pair of navy blue Doc Martens from a store downtown that specialized in punk-appropriate attire, and as previously mentioned, had my hair cut super short.

But Matt, I would soon learn, was a step ahead, already transitioning out of his punk phase and into a New Wave one. That day at the bowling alley, he was dressed in all black except for black-and-white-checked socks and a khaki trench coat, which he eventually removed to bowl. At six feet two inches tall, he towered over all of his peers and possessed a kind of relaxed self-confidence rarely found in boys that age.

I liked him immediately, and when it turned out that we had Western Civilization together, I made a point of getting to know him, finding out that he was in a band and "really into The Cure."

"Oh yeah? Me too," I said, lying. (That night, I asked my mom to take me to Sam Goody, where I bought The Cure's *Wish* album and began listening to it on repeat.)

I turned fifteen toward the end of September, just a few weeks after school began. It was a quiet birthday, as it fell on a weekday and I didn't yet know enough people to form a typical celebration. When I got home from tennis practice, there was a birthday card waiting for me from my dad. He wrote that it was the first birthday he wouldn't actually see me and told me how much he missed me. I went up to my room, listened to R.E.M.'s *Automatic for the People*, and cried.

I had been silently regretting my decision to move to Pittsburgh for the past three weeks. I'd done it to make my life better, but so far it felt far from it. My new school was enormous. I got lost on a daily basis, and despite the tennis lessons I'd taken all summer, I hadn't made the varsity team and was stuck on JV with a bunch of freshmen. In Saegertown, I was Bill Morris's little sister. I was *known*. In Mt. Lebanon, I was no one.

The following day, in a bit of a dramatic move, I passed a note to Matt in Western Civilization telling him I was considering moving back to Saegertown. I hadn't told anyone this, not even my brother, and I'm not sure why I chose to tell Matt except that perhaps I knew I would get the response I was hoping for.

Which I did. Matt wrote back saying he didn't think it was a good idea, saying he'd be sad if I left. It made me smile, at least for a few moments.

* * *

On the last day of September, I got a phone call from my dad. He sounded terrible. Travis, my twenty-seven-year-old step-brother, had committed suicide. He'd shot himself in the head.

I hadn't been back to Saegertown since I'd left the previous June, but I returned for the funeral.

I don't remember so much of that trip back. I don't remember if I slept in my old room or if I just went up for the day. I don't remember if my dad picked me up in Pittsburgh or if my mom drove me there. I just remember arriving at the funeral home, immediately seeing that the wake was open casket and being shocked. Dolly was standing in front of the casket receiving people. I don't remember waiting long. I don't remember waiting alongside Billy or anyone else from my family. I remember Dolly encouraging me to come forward, waving me toward her. I could see Travis's face as I approached her. He didn't look like he was just sleeping, like some people say. His skin looked fake and thick, like there was a layer of nude panty hose covering it.

I began to cry, and she reached for me. She hugged me tightly, trapping my arms between our bodies. I smelled the smoke on her. "I'm sorry," I told her. She grabbed me by the shoulders and we turned to face him.

"He loved you. You know that?" she said. I didn't know that, but I wanted to believe it.

I remember riding in the back of Dad's white Previa mini-van with Billy, Margaret, and Paul as we followed the hearse to the grave site. Dolly was in the passenger seat, and I remember her turning around to see all of the other cars that were following us. "If only he could've seen this," she said.

Afterward there was a reception. I think it was in the basement of a church. I remember the poor lighting, the metal folding chairs, and bad food—ham and cheese sandwiches on dry rolls. But mostly I remember that this is where my dad told me that he'd thought that perhaps I'd made the right decision to leave.

He didn't say anything more than that. He didn't need to.

I never considered moving back again.

Chapter 6

Giving Thanks, Sort of

After the divorce, holidays were divvied up. While Christmas alternated between Mom and Dad every year, Thanksgiving was firmly and perennially Mom's. Or should I say Grandma's? Even though the annual dinner took place at Mom's, there was never any doubt that Grandma was really the one in charge.

Grandma and Grandpa lived but a mile and a half away in the house my mom grew up in, and though they had always played an active role in Mom's life, now that I lived so close, they were playing an active role in mine—picking me up from practice if Mom or Bruce couldn't, taking me out to lunch after church, and slipping me the occasional ten- or even twenty-dollar bill.

Despite the potentially crushing setback of having my phone privileges revoked for a month because of a nonsensical prank call (with lots of yelling in the background) Emily and I had made, which brought two cops to my front door asking about a potential domestic dispute, by November, my new life in Pittsburgh was taking shape. I had made some new friends, had gone to the homecoming dance with one of them, and was simply enjoying living in a house with two people who clearly and convincingly cared about me.

And then came Thanksgiving.

Grandma's life was cooking for people: whether it was a church breakfast for a hundred, a dinner party for twelve, or later, after Grandpa died, a simple meal for herself and her dog.

And Thanksgiving was obviously no exception. Sometime in the early afternoon, our grandparents' car would pull into the driveway. And this is when Billy and I would do our best to hide, as what came next was a clown-car-esque removal of foodstuffs from Grandma's trunk and/or backseat.

The worst thing to get stuck carrying was the turkey, which Grandma transported in the roasting pan with all of the grease sloshing around in the bottom.

"But Grandma, *why* do you have to bring the grease?" I would ask, whining no doubt.

"How else are you going to make the gravy?"

The items she brought over didn't stop with dishes she'd prepared ahead of time, e.g., cranberry relish, ambrosia salad, and an assortment of pies. She would also bring ingredients, some of which weren't even Thanksgiving-related.

"The yellow cake mixes were on sale at Giant Eagle," she'd say to my mom.

And though there was no longer any free space in the kitchen for said boxes of cake mixes, Mom would simply nod. "Great."

In his late sixties, Grandpa had been diagnosed with type 2 diabetes, which meant that he could no longer eat much of what Grandma was cooking, or at least as much of it as he wanted. The bulk of my memories of Grandpa involve him sneaking food behind Grandma's back, and/or Grandma scolding him for having eaten something he shouldn't have, and/or the two of them bickering over how in the world his sugar could be so out of whack if all he had *supposedly* eaten that morning was oatmeal.

But Grandpa wasn't the only one having to watch what he ate. See, the thing about the trio of Billy, Thanksgiving, and high school wrestling was that they were completely incompatible. That year, Billy was a senior wrestling in the 134-pound weight group. And though he, too, was a late bloomer and still growing at age seventeen, any fool could see that Billy's body did not want to weigh 134 pounds. His cheekbones sunk into his face, and in his wrestling singlet, his hip bones protruded in a way that a female runway model would have admired. Therefore, Billy's presence at the Thanksgiving table was a sort of torture for him and a buzzkill for everyone else.

Relatedly, since quitting gymnastics, I'd undergone a bit of a growth spurt. Over the summer, I had worn a size zero, but all of a sudden, in a matter of months, I was buying clothes in a size two or even four. Of course, I didn't see it as a growth spurt at the time, and so I began to dabble in watching my weight as well. Emily and I together had decided to cut out soda, and because tennis wasn't half as exhausting as gymnastics practice had been, I'd taken to going on long runs, specifically to burn calories.

To talk about Thanksgiving, I must also talk about Christianity. Because of Bruce's leadership role in the church as a Sunday school teacher and occasional stand-in for the pastor, members of the church looked up to him. They came to him for help, for advice, for guidance, for friendship, and on

Thanksgiving, they came for dinner. At fifteen, I found these loners who didn't have families of their own and who usually had really sad stories behind their singular status to be major downers—even more so than Billy's perma-diet and Grandpa's diabetes.

And last, to talk about Thanksgiving, I must also talk about the way in which my mom and Grandma would both eat so much during the making of dinner that by the time we all sat down, they would be exhausted *and* full.

"Oh dear, I'm stuffed!" Mom would say, as she sat down at the table with outstretched hands, signifying we could now say grace.

And by we, I mean Bruce, who would then say a really long mini-sermon during which Billy and I, as a form of silent entertainment, would squeeze each other's hands as hard as we could. Once grace wrapped, we could finally eat. And since Billy and I had recently emerged from the game room downstairs, we were ripe for questioning from any and all of the out-of-touch Christian strangers at the table.

"What grade are you in, Amy?"

"Tenth."

"And what are you studying?"

"Just like the normal stuff."

"You don't have a major?"

"No, that's college."

"Oh. Well, any chance you'll go into medicine like your mother or the seminary like your father?"

"My *step*dad, and no, probably not."

And then to Billy:

"My, you aren't eating very much, are you?"

"No, I have to make weight."

"He's a wrestler," Mom would say.

"Oh."

At the far end of the table, you could hear Grandma scolding Grandpa: "Bob, that's enough."

And then, Mom sighing. "My goodness, I'm stuffed."

Chapter 7

The Saturday Boy

When you're fifteen, you don't call it "dating." You can't drive and you don't have an income, so you can't really go on a date. Luckily for Matt, he lived within walking distance of one of Mt. Lebanon's two malls *and* he had an allowance. Because, that winter, just a few months after we met, we went on a date.

It was a Saturday afternoon. I must have gotten a ride to Matt's house, or more likely, to Emily's house—as a way of not having to give my mom any extra, potentially embarrassing information—from which I walked down the street to Matt's, but once I was there, the two of us, him in his trench coat and me in my Gap peacoat, walked to the mall together. It wasn't snowing, but there was snow on the ground. I had to have known it was a date beforehand, but knowing you are going on a date and being on a date are two very different things, particularly for a fifteen-year-old girl. Suddenly, it was just the two of us on our own, with no friends nearby to ease the awkwardness. Suddenly, the idea that Matt *liked* me back was very clear and felt very weighty. And what did Matt have planned for our date? Lunch at China Gate, a sit-down, cloth-napkinned Chinese restaurant situated in a little nook on the top floor of the mall.

It's only now, as I write this, that I realize this was my first date of my entire life. For all of my flirting with my brother's friends in Saegertown, not one of them had ever taken me anywhere. And despite having danced a couple of slow dances with these boys at the homecoming dance, I hadn't actually kissed anyone before.

And so, as we entered the mall, I felt the intimacy of it and panicked. I told Matt I wasn't hungry. I told him I'd already eaten, in fact, and that maybe we should skip eating altogether. But he was already halfway up the weird annex-like stairs to China Gate. He was confident. He waved me on. He assumed I would chill out and at least order a wonton soup.

He assumed incorrectly.

I ordered nothing and ate nothing. But Matt remained undaunted, ordering himself a single egg roll and a bowl of hot and sour soup. Afterward, he led the way to the Godiva chocolate store two floors below and bought me the tiniest golden box with two perfect little truffles in it. I think most girls would have been completely won over at this point, but it was too much for me. I was getting an anxiety-induced headache and couldn't wait for the date to be over. We walked back—my hands safely in my pockets lest he tried to hold one—past Matt's house and directly to Emily's, where at last I could relax a bit in the comfort of the presence of a third person.

It didn't take long for our entire group of friends to find out that Matt had asked me out, and yet, we weren't *boyfriend and girlfriend*, and of course, to make fun of him for it. And while I know that this is just the first of many examples of how I made high school difficult for Matt, I also know that something amazing happened after this. Because after this, I cast Matt into the realm of *just friends*. And because we were just friends, I no longer had to impress him or feel the need to be perfect around him. Instead, I could be myself. I could actually have a real conversation with him—you know, one where if you don't hear the other person correctly, you can ask them to repeat themselves instead of just nodding and smiling and moving forward as if you'd heard because you're too uncomfortable to show even the smallest chink in your armor, even if it's not a chink at all.

And so, we were friends. Friends who watched *Party of Five* and then called each other after to discuss what Charlie or Bailey had done this time. Friends who tied up our parents' phone lines to such an extent that his mom or dad would inevitably jump on the line to say, "Time to wrap it up, Matt." Friends who made each other laugh so hard during Western Civ. that Mrs. Caskey, our teacher, had to separate us. We were friends who made mix tapes for each other. Well, mostly Matt made them for me. I listened to them on the long runs I would take through Mt. Lebanon's suburban streets, unable to ignore the fact that so many of the songs centered on the topic of unrequited love.

Junior year, we were friends who went to homecoming together, after which, when I ended up leaving with someone else, someone I had wanted to be more than friends with, we became friends who were *on a break*.

"We're on hiatus," Matt told me outside of our separate homerooms the following Monday morning before the morning bell.

It would be the first of many hiatuses. And of course I knew why, but I pretended I didn't. "Oh, c'mon! Really?" I was comfortable with this distance, when there was an obstacle in our way—though preferably an obstacle I was in control of. Later, it would bother me to no end when I heard that Matt was *hanging out* with someone else, especially when that someone was very pretty, very tall, and known to miss school for modeling gigs in Italy.

We were even friends who kissed, really kissed, one day after school, after tiring of the hiatus, after I'd been missing my monthly mix tapes, after I'd panicked that I might lose him as a friend forever.

In college, years later, the guys in my social circle would often ask me if I was high or drunk because of the way I was talking and/or joking, and when they realized I wasn't, that I was just being myself, they deemed me the "weird girl." And I think it would have offended me if it weren't for Matt, because those moments when I was apparently being my *weirdest* reminded me of how I was when I was with Matt. And the person I was when I was with Matt—apart from the times I really did hurt him—was my favorite person to be.

All I can say is that some people are ready at seventeen to start the rest of their lives with the person they love, but I was not one of them.

At our high school, for Valentine's Day, you could arrange to send someone a carnation with a little message attached, both of which would be delivered to your homeroom on the morning of the fourteenth. I didn't hold on to the carnation, but I do still have the message Matt sent me senior year. Perhaps in an effort to keep the messages appropriate, the school made them quite generic. "Happy Valentine's Day" it read at the top of a blue strip of paper, underneath which you were given five options—"Love, Friends, Crazy, Thank You, or Other"—and the directive to "circle one." But Matt hadn't circled any of these options. Instead, he had written in his own message and circled that: "I hate you," it said in the small printed handwriting I knew so well from all of our passed notes and mix tapes.

Though I'm no hoarder, I held on to this piece of paper for all of these years because, even though I couldn't digest it at the time, I think some part of me knew the feeling was mutual. That I hated him too—with my whole heart.

Chapter 8

A Major in Creative Writing with a Minor in Tortured Self-Reflection in One's Journal

At seventeen, I had no idea what I wanted to do with my life, let alone what to study or where. I only knew that I wanted to go to a *good* school that wasn't too close to home. I know the fact that Dolly had never left western Pennsylvania was a major influence in this latter part of my decision-making—sticking around your hometown your entire life seemed a sure recipe for unhappiness. And so, I ruled out any colleges in Pennsylvania, West Virginia, or Ohio.

Duke was my number one pick, as that's where my brother was. But when I didn't get in, I chose the next best *sounding* school on my list: Johns Hopkins University, a place I'd applied to merely because my dad had mentioned almost going there and a school Mom and I'd given a cursory, haphazard visit one late afternoon on a drive back to Pittsburgh from Durham.

But minutes after Mom and Bruce dropped me off at my freshman dorm, I fluctuated between feeling homesick and intimidated. All of my new classmates seemingly came from much cooler places than Pittsburgh—e.g., New York, Chicago, and Los Angeles—and arrived with declared majors in

International Relations, Political Science, and Economics. As for me, I was undeclared, having enrolled in classes that were basically a continuation of my senior year in high school: Calculus, American history, Spanish, and for fun, Introduction to Television.

I was e-mailing and calling my high school friends daily, including Matt, who was at NYU. I told them I wasn't impressed, that I was looking into transferring. And if it weren't for meeting a fellow freshman named Mary Anne during orientation, I just might have. Mary Anne and I hit it off immediately. We had so much in common. From our broken-up families to our stepsiblings to our Christian backgrounds to our loves of gymnastics. We even looked a bit alike.

By the end of September, according to our other new friends, we were "attached at the hip." And what we didn't already have in common, we quickly picked up from each other. Unfortunately for me, this meant speaking with a Midwestern accent, and more unfortunately for Mary Anne, this meant dieting.

By this point in my life, my focus on eating healthily had blossomed into a full-blown obsession; I had a food journal in which I would write down every item I ate along with its calorie count. And one day, while hanging out in Mary Anne's dorm room, I noticed that she had started to do the same. I laughed out loud at her list of foods and their corresponding calories:

banana, 7

licorice, 20

cheese and bean burrito, 150

"Seven calories in a banana?" I laughed. She clearly wasn't as well versed in this as I was. "I *wish!* Try a hundred!"

Later that year, she and I decided to do a three-day liquid diet together. (We were each five feet six and 125 pounds, which is technically underweight, but it's always nice to be thinner, right?) When our friend Liz heard of our plan, she looked directly at me and said, "Wait a second. Aren't you already on a diet?"

Mary Anne was majoring in Political Science and minoring in something called Writing Seminars, which through her, I discovered was basically JHU's liberal-arts term for creative writing. The following semester, I took one of the classes Mary Anne had taken: Introduction to Fiction and Poetry. The entire semester, all we did was read various pieces of fiction and poetry and then write our own. It was borderline shocking to me that you could receive a grade for something that didn't feel like schoolwork. And even more surprising that this could be my major. By the end of the year, it was decided. I was *Writing Sems.*

The one thing I could not emulate, as hard as I tried, was Mary Anne's relaxed approach to the other major part of college: partying. In high school, I'd gotten drunk just once, off of a few Zimas (remember Zimas?) just to see what it was like. And I did so at the end of senior year, in the controlled environment of the basement of my friend's house with her and her fraternal twin so that I could be sure to neither get date-raped nor make an ass of myself in front of a bunch of people.

So, it may go without saying that I was a bit of an outlier freshman year. While my classmates reveled in their newfound freedom, getting drunk, hooking up, and steadily gaining their freshman fifteen, I cautiously sipped on diluted drinks, dated a couple of guys, studied, made sure to get in a four-mile run five times a week, and went to church on Sunday mornings, *with* Mary Anne of course.

But at the beginning of sophomore year, Mary Anne met a senior named Cliff, who quickly became a serious boyfriend, and all of a sudden, I had all this time to myself. I remember deciding: I need a boyfriend too.

As goal-oriented as always, I was dating one of Cliff's fraternity brothers, David, within a few weeks. David was a junior with brown, curly, skateboarder-like hair. He was not your classic fraternity bro. He was quiet, soft-spoken, the kind of guy who, at a party filled with dudes calling "Next!" at the beer pong table, would be content leaning against a wall sipping on a beer all by himself.

Before he even tried to kiss me, he took me on a date to the Baltimore Museum of Art and then cooked me dinner back at the row house he shared with three other guys. Was the house rodent-infested, the chicken overcooked, and the accompanying rice sourced from a Rice-A-Roni box? Yes. But it was *college*. Guys didn't cook girls dinner, at least not before they'd even made out with them. David was one of the good guys. And it didn't take long before he and I were the ones spending every minute together.

* * *

Junior year, I studied abroad in Madrid for the fall semester, and though Mary Anne was still my best friend and David still my boyfriend, without either of them by my side, I had to rely on myself. I handled this mainly by obsessively writing in my journal, my main topics being my need to be a better Christian, my increasingly conflicted feelings over my relationship with David, and of course, my diet, which at this point was strictly vegetarian (a choice not inspired by a particular love for animals but rather because it seemed easier to eat healthily by cutting out a major food group). It was also not supposed to go over 1,400 calories per day.

Ironically, the farther away I got from Mom and Bruce geographically, the more into Christianity I became. The year before, Mary Anne and I had even joined JHU's Christian Youth Group, occasioning their weekly Bible studies. But while Mare's relationship with God seemed easy and stress-free, to read my journal, which interspersed Ani DiFranco lyrics with passages from the Bible, is to encounter the thoughts of one very confused twenty-year-old.

My casual, hesitant drinking freshman year had blossomed into a handful of very drunken nights sophomore year, which I'd found to be both extremely fun and a major source of stress for me. My body was a temple, right? And downing shots and smoking cigarettes was no way to treat such an edifice. Plus, as an underage sophomore, it had been illegal (a fact that didn't seem to bother anyone else on campus). But now I was in Spain where it wasn't. And yet still, I gave myself a hard time. Or, to quote my journal: "I'm an idiot. Drunk again."

Similarly, as a Christian, I knew I should be *dating* a Christian so that I could marry a Christian, and though David grew up Catholic, it was much more of a cultural identification for him. On this topic, I wrote a lot, most of the time not very coherently: "I don't know what my problem is. I do kinda. I feel like I need to chill with my Christian friends more. Where are they?"

Occasionally, I made a bit more sense: "I need God in my life more and David just...Sometimes I feel like it's hard enough trying to figure myself out and what I want to do, let alone have a serious relationship."

And as for my never-ending diet? Well, as fate would have it, my randomly assigned roommate in Madrid had had great success with Weight Watchers. Within days of living with her, she pulled out the Weight Watchers literature from her backpack and taught me how to *count my points*. For good measure, on the last page of my journal, I copied down a long list of foods and their corresponding point equivalent, e.g.:

ice cream (light) = 3
(fat free) = 2
(regular) = 4
(cone) = 1

This kind of monitoring left little room for flan and chocolate and churros, although I did make an allowance for tortilla española, clearly unaware of how much olive oil is used in the Spanish classic.

Despite the fact that I was living in Spain and took weekend trips to Paris (where Mary Anne was studying for the semester), Dublin, and Florence, I didn't return to Hopkins very culturally enlightened or rejuvenated. Rather, the extra independence had left me in a peak state of mental turmoil.

Mary Anne and I, along with our mutual friend Sonya, found an off-campus apartment with three bedrooms, three bathrooms, and a gigantic balcony. It should have been a happy time—my first apartment! But instead, I spent the first month back in town isolating myself and breaking up and making up with David. Meanwhile, Sonya and Mary Anne spent it like two normal college kids, studying together during the week and going out on the weekends. They even cooked together, making balanced dinners of rice, broccoli, and pan-fried chicken breasts. And though they always invited me to join in on whatever it was they were doing or cooking, I never did.

"I'm good," I'd say, pouring myself another bowl of cereal, convincing myself that I was somehow healthier.

Sonya had even brought an appliance with her—a rice cooker—and always made sure to cook more than enough rice for dinner so that in the morning she could use the leftovers to fry up one of the dishes taught to her by her Filipina mother: rice and eggs.

But that year, I truly cannot remember making anything for myself to eat apart from cereal, microwaved oatmeal, or baked tortilla chips and guacamole. By March, however, exhausted by my own thoughts, I began emerging from my cocoon to go out with them on weekends. And since I had typically eaten nothing of substance for dinner, I would get drunk before we'd even left the apartment to meet up with the rest of our friends. And despite my so-called vegetarianism, at the end of these nights, without fail, I would buy a foot-long turkey hoagie with all of the fixings, which I'd eat in the living room of our apartment while rewatching our VHS copy of *Far and Away*.

To add to my list of internal conflicts, as part of his spring break, Matt came to visit me that semester during one of the weekends that David and I were back together. Mary Anne, Sonya, and I took him to a fraternity party. It was a horrible decision. Matt didn't belong in this world of beer pong and flip cup, and it wasn't just strange to see him there, it was painful. Of course, what was even weirder was going home at the end of the night and setting up a bed for him on the couch while David and I slept in my room. So weird that I apparently couldn't even wait until the next day to write about it in my journal: "Matt Bookman and David are out on the balcony talking right now. What?!"

By the end of the semester, much to my disgust, I had finally gained my freshman fifteen. (I'd just done so as a second-semester junior.) Hardly any of my clothes fit me, and I hated myself for it. I had lost control of this thing I thought I had a tight grip on, and on top of that, I was embarrassed that I cared so much, that being thin was such a priority in my life. I cried to my mom so much without giving her the reason why that she offered to pay for me to see a therapist. When a few weeks later I was finally able to tell her that the reason I was so upset was because of all the weight I'd gained, I was hoping she might tell me that I was being silly, that I looked great. But I should have known better. My mom is someone who takes back-to-back spinning classes and who clearly has her own bevy of body image issues. No, instead, she said, "You're not *fat*. You're not *skinny* either," before offering to set me up with a personal trainer, a "friend of mine from the gym." I agreed.

And it worked. While Sonya and Mary Anne stayed in Baltimore that summer, commuting into D.C. daily for their internships, I went home, got a job at a record store, and met with a personal trainer twice a week.

I entered senior year thinner than I was at the beginning of junior year, on antidepressants, and finally, firmly broken up with David—thanks in part to all of the phone calls to

Matt (who had spent his summer interning at a production company in Los Angeles) and to whom I wouldn't necessarily explain the situation but who made me laugh and feel normal for at least the duration of our call. But back at school, I had a new problem. I had to figure out what I was going to do next year, *after* college.

That fall, I turned twenty-one, the last of my friends to do so. And before we all headed out to a bar to celebrate, I fielded a happy-birthday call from my dad, who used this as an opportunity to remind me that it all went downhill from there. "College is the best it gets. You may not realize it now, but you will, *you will*," he said in his standard, quiet, melancholic phone voice.

"OK, well, thanks for calling!"

That night, I met a guy named Danny who didn't go to Hopkins and who I would end up seeing for the next couple of months. He was a few years older, sang in a band, wore thick-rimmed glasses and skinny jeans, and worked in a tattoo parlor—an original hipster. Across his stomach read the words: *HELL BENT* in gothic-styled block print, because he was, as he told me, "hell bent and heaven sent."

So while the vast majority of my friends applied to graduate school and/or office jobs with health plans and retirement accounts, I went to Danny's shows, hung out with his friends, and took my dad's advice, making the most of my last year as a college student. I drank a lot, smoked a lot, and stopped going to church and youth group altogether. (I also went ahead and got my nose pierced.)

I was on a mission to self-destruct, though at the same time, I couldn't go through with it fully. I mean, I was still the girl who had experimented with alcohol for the first time by drinking three Zimas on a full stomach. Though I contemplated it, I couldn't go through with getting a tattoo from my tattoo artist boyfriend. I also couldn't blow off my writing classes. (I was at work on a novel that my favorite professor found "very promising.") Plus, the previous year, as part of a criminal justice class I had to take for distribution credits, I'd read *The Corner*, a nonfiction account of life on the inner-city streets of Baltimore by David Simon, the creator of *The Wire*, which affected me so much that I promised (aloud and on multiple occasions) never to do drugs because I didn't want "to contribute to that world in any way, shape, or form." So as drunk as I would get, if anyone pulled out cocaine at a party, I would make a point not to participate. "Geez, guys. Have none of you read *The Corner*?"

By year's end, I had come up with my own idea of what it was to be a writer. Writers *wrote*, I concluded. And most of them did so while living life just above the poverty line and somewhere in between states of drunkenness and sobriety.

Inspired by the title of George Orwell's memoir, *Down and Out in Paris and London* (which, to be clear, I never actually read) and naïve enough to think that my experience in Madrid, where my housing and meals had been not only set up for me, but also paid for by Mom and Bruce, could somehow be replicated in the real world, I decided that after graduation I would travel. And of course, write. *Down and Out in Paris and London*, here I come!

Only I'd already been to Paris and London. This time, I wanted to go to Central or South America. When I said as much one day over winter break to my family, Bruce told me he could put me in contact with friends of his who ran some sort of Christian outreach program in Costa Rica. Even though I'd begun to distance myself from all things Christian, I was still up for a trip to Costa Rica. And at the time, so was Mary Anne, whose plan was to defer a year before enrolling in a graduate program in Scotland.

Five months later, however, at graduation, Mary Anne and I were hardly speaking to each other. At the time, I'm sure I didn't see it this way, but now it's clear to me what happened between us. I'd gained back all the weight I'd lost that summer and more. Plus, after breaking up with Cliff, she quickly fell into a new relationship, while I was boyfriendless for the first time in three years. Essentially, I resented her for detaching herself from my hip, for no longer being on the same page as I was—basically, for not being *depressed* along with me.

It was clear that we were no longer going to be traveling together, yet if I didn't go on this trip, my post-graduation plans would begin and end with returning to Mom and Bruce's house in the suburbs of Pittsburgh, just like I'd done the summer before. Not able to accept that as my fate, I decided to go to Costa Rica by myself.

My college friends who watched me pour bowl of cereal after bowl of cereal find it ironic that I now derive so much pleasure from cooking and writing about food. And, of course, I do too. I started cooking Sonya's rice and eggs dish based solely on those three words, rice and eggs, as I have no recollection of ever eating her version. I have no idea how much my dish resembles the original, but I do know that cooked rice lightly coated in garlicky olive oil with a fried egg (and a runny yolk) on top is an absolute delight. Serve it with some manner of steamed or sautéed green vegetables and sriracha, and who knows? You may even like yourself by meal's end.

RICE AND EGGS WITH BROCCOLINI AND SRIRACHA

Serves 2 generously

  2 cups sushi rice (short-grain white rice) or, even better, about 4
    cups leftover already-cooked rice
  2 or 3 eggs
  1 bunch broccolini, rinsed
  Salt
  2 tablespoons olive oil, plus more if needed
  3 cloves garlic, chopped
  Freshly ground black pepper
  Sriracha sauce

If you don't have leftover already-cooked rice on hand:

Rinse your rice. (This is one of those tasks that as a beginner cook I skipped but that I never ignore now, as I know it leads to better rice—rice where each grain seems to hold its own, resisting clumpy mushiness.) Put the rice in a bowl and cover with cold water. Using your fingers as a dam, pour out just the water and repeat two more times.

If you have a rice cooker, cook your rice in it. If you don't have a rice cooker, I'm sorry! (I also really think you should get one. I'm not usually an advocate for kitchen gadgets, but if you make rice fairly often, a rice cooker is *so* worth it. Plus, whenever I make this meal, I always prepare extra rice so that the next day, I can take a tortilla-size sheet of nori, put some leftover rice on top, put some sliced avocado on top of that, maybe some cucumber too if I have it, roll it up, and eat it like a taco—dipped in soy sauce, of course.)

If you don't have a rice cooker, put your rinsed rice in a large saucepan and add 3 cups water. Bring to a boil, then reduce the heat to a simmer, cover, and cook for 20 minutes. Turn off the heat. If you have time, let your rice hang out in the pot with the lid on for at least 10 minutes before frying it.

Place the broccolini in a skillet, give it a couple pinches of salt, and add about an inch of water to the bottom of the pan. Cover the pan and heat over medium heat, checking on it after a few minutes. You want the water to be simmering but not boiling. Once it's simmering, it'll only need about 5 more minutes. You want the broccolini to be *just* tender. Once it is, drain and set aside.

Grab a large nonstick skillet. (Cast-iron works really well here because I typically use this same pan to fry my eggs.) Add the oil and heat it on low to medium heat, making sure it covers the surface of the pan. (You can always add a bit more olive oil if it doesn't.) Add the garlic and a pinch of salt. Stir until it's fragrant, 2 to 3 minutes, then add the rice. Turn up the heat just a tad and mix the rice all around in the pan until each granule is coated. Give it a few more pinches of salt as you stir. This should take 3 to 4 minutes.

In the interest of fewer dishes to clean, I like to divvy up the rice between two plates at this stage and fry my eggs in the same pan I just used. If the pan looks dry, add a bit more olive oil (it's OK if there's still a bit of rice stuck to it). Crack the eggs into a separate bowl and then slide the eggs into the pan. Reduce the heat to low and cover. The eggs are done when the whites are set but the yolks are still runny. This can take anywhere between 2 and 4 minutes. (But remember, runny yolks are key here!)

Once they're done, place the eggs on top of the rice. Season the eggs with a bit of salt and pepper. Add the broccolini to the plates. Make sure to serve with sriracha. (The best bites include a mixture of rice, egg, broccolini, and a touch of sriracha.)

Chapter 9

The Wrong, Long Path

While I was away at college, Mom and Bruce downsized to a two-bedroom condo, and so it was from Bruce's newly set-up third-floor office where I hesitated for a few minutes before finally purchasing the round-trip ticket to San José, Costa Rica, leaving Pittsburgh in mid-June and returning six weeks later. I hesitated not only because I was going alone but because my plans included nothing more than spending some time in the city, volunteering, maybe making a friend or two, and traveling to the coast. It scared me, but what was scarier was *not* going. Because if I took away Costa Rica, all I was was an unemployed liberal arts graduate.

I arrived in the capital with the bare minimum: a backpack full of clothes, my journal, a Costa Rican guidebook, the address of a hostel, and the phone number of Bruce's Christian friends. But the minute the taxi dropped me off at the hostel, I knew I'd overestimated myself.

The hostel in San José issued me a twin bed, which was part of a bunk bed, which was in a room with five other bunk beds. As far as I could tell, I was the only one traveling alone. Wasting no time, I retrieved the notebook with the phone number of the Costa Rican Christians from my backpack.

But when I called, I got a Spanish recording telling me to hang up and dial again. I figured I was doing something wrong, like not using the proper city code. I tried the number again, slightly differently. Still nothing. I tried again and again, finally asking the person working the front desk for help. Still, I couldn't get through. In the common area, I logged on to one of the computers and sent an e-mail to the address Bruce gave me, explaining I'd arrived and that the phone number I had for them didn't seem to be working.

In the meantime, I tried casually hanging out by the pool with a book in hand, pretending to be OK with the fact that I was there alone, as if I hadn't just spent an entire semester at college drinking too much in order to avoid feeling a moment of such loneliness. I lasted maybe a half hour.

In need of some cash and food, I decided to venture out. A couple of blocks away, I found a bank, withdrew some *colones*, picked up groceries, and got whistled at by various passengers in cars driving by. Back at the hostel, I ate my dinner by myself and checked my e-mail. There was nothing waiting for me.

From the semi-comfort of my twin bunk bed that night, I put together a plan B. According to my guidebook, I could take a bus to any one of the beach towns. I decided that's what I would do if I didn't hear anything from the Christians in the morning. After all, if I was going to be alone, I might as well be alone at the beach, right?

But in the morning, before I even checked my e-mail to see if anyone had responded, I realized that I didn't have my bank card. Instantly, I knew I'd left it in the ATM machine. And instantly, I knew the jig was up. Within the half hour, I packed up my things, checked out of the hostel, and hailed a cab to the airport where I paid a 125-dollar fee to change my return ticket to the very next flight out of San José.

Of course, I could have gone back to the bank and tried to retrieve my card. I also had a credit card I could have used. Basically, if I'd wanted to make it work, I could have. But that's the thing. I didn't. In fact, the relief I felt upon changing my ticket and knowing I was going back home was overwhelming.

When I think of the mishap now, I can't help but think of Freud's theory on such mistakes, how they are manifestations of unconscious thoughts and impulses. I wasn't ready to jump to this conclusion at the time, but the truth was that I simply wasn't the kind of freewheeling, laidback, outgoing person who could travel around a foreign country by herself. I didn't want to take a bus to the coast so that I could be alone at another hostel even if it was near the beach; I didn't want to volunteer with Bruce's Christian friends even if they did get in touch with me. The truth was that I didn't want to be there, period.

At the Pittsburgh International Airport, I called my mom from a pay phone. It was late, and I could tell from the way she answered that I'd woken her up. I tried to sound sick. I told her I was in Pittsburgh, that I hadn't been able to get in touch with Bruce's friends, that someone from the hostel must have *stolen* my bankcard, and that I'd gotten food poisoning. I told her I hadn't known what to do so I'd gone to the airport and gotten on the first flight home.

"So, you're here? In Pittsburgh?"

"Yes."

"OK, I'm coming," she said. "See you soon."

Epic failure that it was, the trip was still my graduation gift from my mom and Bruce. And now that it was over, it was time to properly introduce me to the real world. The day after I arrived back home, Bruce knocked on my bedroom door. In his hands were my car insurance and cell phone bills. Two things that were now mine.

By midsummer, I'd gotten a job waiting tables at Aladdin's Eatery, a casual Middle Eastern restaurant located in what is referred to as *downtown* (suburban) Mt. Lebanon. Not only did I get a cursory education in Middle Eastern cuisine (*kofta* is like a meatball, whereas *shawarma* is shaved meat) from Jessica, the twentysomething restaurant manager, I also quickly learned about the specific kind of exhaustion that comes from having a job where you're on your feet for eight hours a day.

It was a family-operated restaurant with two other better-established locations. The patriarch of the family oversaw all three, leaving his son, Fady, an ex–football player and a giant of a man, in charge of this one. Most nights, I closed with one other server and Jessica, whose idea of supervision was to smoke a cigarette with you before locking up. But some nights, Fady closed the restaurant, and you had to do everything on the closing checklist, e.g., vacuuming, cleaning the bathrooms, restocking the takeout containers. If he found something you'd missed—usually a few grains of rice on the carpet—he'd point it out, reciting something his football coach used to tell him, "You do it right. You do it light. You do it wrong. You do it long."

More often than not, I had done it wrong and, consequently, long.

In between lunch and dinner shifts, while eating my daily dose of employee-discounted hummus, pita, and Lebanese *salata*—a salad consisting of chopped red onion, tomatoes, cucumber, and parsley tossed in a dressing of lemon juice and olive oil—my idea of what it was to be a writer changed. Writers write, I still believed, but they probably wrote a lot more if they didn't feel like total losers because they were waiting tables in the town they grew up in and living at home with their parents.

Suddenly, being a student, an idea I'd snubbed my nose at just a year earlier, no longer seemed like a bad idea. I decided to apply to MFA programs in creative writing. Applications were due in December and January, but school wouldn't start until the following August or September. I knew I couldn't spend an entire year living with Mom and Bruce, sneaking glasses of red wine up to my room each night and then having to walk down the street to smoke one measly cigarette only to return and hear my mom shout, from two rooms away, "You smell like smoke!"

Expensive lesson that it was, Costa Rica did teach me one thing: that I was a person who, if going to travel by herself, needed some type of structure—a group or a job or even a family.

So, I applied to an English teaching program at a university in Argentina, which paid a small living stipend and offered free housing with local host families. When I was accepted at a school in Rafaela, Argentina, a medium-size town about a five-hour drive northwest of Buenos Aires, I formulated a plan to go there for the spring semester; while there, I would find out which MFA programs I got into, then, come July, after some traveling through South America, I would return home, pack up my things, and start graduate school in August. I'd applied to schools in New York, California, and England, so I also decided to sell my car, since I wouldn't need it in any of those places. At last, I had a plan *and*, bonus, a sizable savings account.

Before I left, my coworkers at Aladdin's wanted to buy me a few drinks at the bar just one door down from the restaurant. Matt, who happened to be in town from New York, where he'd been crashing with friends and looking for a job ever since graduation, came as well. We all got along great, though Jessica didn't seem to understand my relationship with Matt.

"I don't get it. Why aren't you dating him?" she asked me while he was in the bathroom.

It was a question I had fielded so many times over the years I could respond without thinking. "We're just better as friends."

* * *

I arrived in Argentina in the spring of 2004. And as I would soon discover, the country was very much still in recovery from a major economic crisis. I had known nothing about this beforehand but almost every Argentine I spoke to, beginning with the gentleman I sat next to on my flight from Buenos Aires to Rafaela, would bring it up to me in some way.

"Ah, you're a Yankee," he said to me after hearing me speak Spanish with my American accent, before launching into an explanation of how their peso used to be equal with the dollar.

"We used to be one to one," he told me with pride, holding up his two pointer fingers, clearly unhappy with the current exchange rate, which at the time was closer to one to three, as in one dollar equaled three pesos, as in a cup of delicious espresso at the airport cost me just thirty cents.

My host family consisted of the matriarch, Silvia, and her

three sons, Adrian, Fabian, and Hernán, who ranged in age from sixteen to twenty-three. And when I arrived at their humble two-bedroom, two-bathroom house, accompanied by the program director, who had picked me up at the airport, they were in the middle of throwing a big dinner party in my honor. As part of the celebration, they'd invited at least ten of their close friends, so that, after my twenty hours of travel, I got an introduction to the way Argentines greet one another, with a heartfelt hug and cheekbone-crushing kiss, about twelve times in a row.

Any of my friends will tell you that I'm a bad hugger. According to them, I tense up as they approach with arms outstretched, don't hug back properly, and pull away too soon. So I can only imagine what my Argentine host family thought during this extended meet and greet. But it was a perfect precursor to what was to follow. Because as much as I would try to be my regular, non-hugging, fairly isolated, non-meat-eating self, for the next five months, it was hardly an option.

After meeting everyone, Silvia showed me to my room, which was also her room. They had set up a twin bed for me in the corner. So there went any opportunity to hole myself up and write in my journal for hours on end.

Because of a questionnaire I had filled out as part of the application process, Silvia knew that I was a vegetarian whose favorite breakfast was cereal and milk. At dinner that first night, she kept pointing to dishes, nodding as she said, *"sólo vegetales."* And in the morning, she told me that she'd bought me some cereal. She opened a cupboard and retrieved a plastic produce bag filled with about a cup's-worth of what looked like puffed rice. I thanked her, eating it with a bit of milk poured on top, but as soon as I saw what my Argentine brothers were eating—thick slices of toast with dulce de leche spread on top—I told her that I liked toast too. And after a few days of salad and vegetables for dinner as the rest of the family ate ham and cheese empanadas and steaks off the grill, I wasn't just hungry, I also felt rude.

And so, at the end of the week, I told Silvia that I wanted to experience Argentina properly, and if that meant eating meat, I was up for it. Her face lit up immediately, and I braced myself for one of the top-ten strongest hugs of my life.

Silently, though, I reassured myself that this was all just temporary. And as soon as I got back to the States, I could resume my vegetarian diet. Because, just like with Madrid and Costa Rica, I hadn't necessarily signed up for an adventure. I had signed up for the opportunity to better my Spanish, to be able to put something on my résumé, and mostly, to have a place to lay my head that wasn't the suburbs of Pittsburgh until graduate school started.

But then, just a few weeks later, I got the news that I hadn't been accepted into a single MFA program I had applied to. The decision letters arrived at Mom and Bruce's, but I'd asked specifically that my brother be the one to relay the news to me. And he did so gently over e-mail. *Are you sure?* I wrote back, as if he might've read the letters incorrectly.

Yeah, he wrote. *I'm sorry.*

Once again, I needed a new plan.

❋ ❋ ❋

My host mom, Silvia, was the opposite of both my parents in so many ways.

My dad started smoking in his late thirties, I assume around the time he started seeing Dolly, since he was *not* a smoker while with my mom.

When I still lived in Saegertown, if I needed to talk to him, I would knock on the always-closed door to his study and call his name.

"One minute!" he would say before opening the door, coming out, and shutting it behind him. "Yes, Honey Bun?"

Of course, I could smell the smoke. I could always smell it, but it wasn't until I'd found a pack of Marlboros in his leather coat pocket during the last year I lived there that I knew for sure Dolly wasn't solely to blame for the pervasive stench. And though I was confused and upset, I never approached him about it. Not once.

Silvia, on the other hand, had smoked since she was a teen-ager, and though her sons didn't like the habit, she did so openly and unapologetically throughout the house.

On the days my mom worked, she would come home deflated and exhausted, annoyed that Bruce hadn't done anything for dinner, not even called for pizza to be delivered, whereas Silvia came home from work almost joyfully with an armful of gro-ceries, which she would set down before pouring herself *un Gancia*—her favorite brand of vermouth—turning on some music, and dancing around the kitchen as she began to cook. Inevitably, as she danced, she would raise her arms above her head, revealing her tanned fifty-year-old belly, a small act but one that always surprised me sheerly because of its lack of self-consciousness. (As far as I knew, my own mother had no midriff.)

While my dad was an outspoken atheist and Mom and Bruce were outspoken Christians, Silvia was neither. She didn't go to church; she didn't talk about God, yet every night, she slept beneath a giant crucifix, which hung on the wall above her bed. (This bed, by the way, was located a mere four feet to the left of my own—a proximity I got used to only because of how comfortable Silvia was with it: she undressed each night right in front of me and climbed under the covers with a sleepy *"Buenas noches, hija."*)

And while communicating was not a high priority in my family, Silvia was a *sharer*. She told me about her divorce, her current boyfriend, about her sons and their girlfriends. And when I became interested in the recent economic crisis everyone seemed to make a point of telling me about, she told me story after story; how she would be shopping at the grocery store and the price for milk would be changing *as* she shopped, how despite having a good job as a professor of engineering at a nearby college, she couldn't plan for the future, how the government had frozen everyone's bank account so that she couldn't withdraw more than $200 dollars a week, and how she had no choice but to start living day by day—*día por día.*

The longer I lived there, the more this kind of approach to life rubbed off. Because without making a conscious effort, I began to relax about my future, about the fact that my plans began and ended in Argentina, that I had nothing lined up and no school to enroll in once I got back to the States.

And what do you know? Relaxing suited me. Because unlike my tense time in Madrid, during which I hardly added one new word to my Spanish vocabulary, a few months into my stay in Rafaela, I was speaking Spanish with ease—sometimes even writing in it in my journal. And unlike how I was in college, seemingly unable to date someone without thinking about our potential as a long-term couple who shared the same religious beliefs, I casually dated a few Argentine guys, one of whom drove me around town on the back of his motorcycle.

Most shockingly, also without making a conscious effort, I finally stopped counting the calories I consumed each day. Perhaps it was because I couldn't begin to fathom how many were in Silvia's *milanesa* or her vanilla cake with dulce de leche, or the tiny buttery biscuits my youngest host brother, Adrian, and I snacked on together around four o'clock each day. Or perhaps it was because I was enjoying myself too much to ruin it with round-the-clock tabulating.

But whatever the reason, the result remained the same: I left Argentina much less confused, with a stronger sense of self, and, ironically, with looser-fitting clothes.

In fact, I had assimilated so well that at the end of the semester, when the program director asked me to stay on for the summer, I came very close to saying yes. But in the end, I had to admit that I missed my life in the States. Or, rather, I missed the life I could potentially have in the States. Matt was back in Pittsburgh. He and I had been writing letters to each other for the past few months, so I knew that he'd given up on finding a job in New York, but that as a young up-and-coming director "to watch," *Esquire* magazine had chosen him to shoot a short film based on a story they owned the rights to, that he was being featured in the magazine, and was planning on moving to Los Angeles in the fall.

Most of all, I knew I wanted to see him before he left.

*　*　*

I may have come home with an Argentine frame of mind, but logistically, I was in the same place I'd started over a year earlier: the guest room of my mom and Bruce's townhouse, and yes, waiting tables at Aladdin's.

No, that's not entirely accurate. Things were worse.

Having sold my car before I'd left, now I rode my orange mountain bike through the August humidity and the notoriously hilly streets of Pittsburgh to the restaurant and back, dressed in my polyester black work pants.

In fact, things were *much* worse. While I was away, as it turned out, Matt had begun seeing Jessica, the manager at Aladdin's Eatery—*my* manager. And while Matt's and my bizarre seven-year courtship had occasionally included a third wheel, never before had the third wheel been me.

Down and Out, Period. That was the current title of my Orwellian memoir.

But there is a clarity that comes in hitting rock bottom—perhaps a very desperate kind of clarity, but a clarity nonetheless.

I set three goals for myself.

1. Make active steps toward becoming a paid writer.
2. Get Matt back.
3. Move out of my parents' house once and for all.

While in Argentina, I had devoured Rainer Maria Rilke's *Letters to a Young Poet*, a collection of Rilke's letters giving advice to an aspiring young writer and fan of his who had contacted him seeking just that. Very much inspired by this idea and in the service of goal number one, I decided I would send postcards, thirty of them in thirty days, to be exact, with thirty different comedy sketch ideas to *Saturday Night Live*'s head writer, Paula Pell. Who knew? By the end, maybe she would offer me an internship or something.

The whole thing makes me cringe now: the fact that at least some part of me thought this stunt was clever enough and that I was funny enough to bypass all of the hard work that comes along with becoming a comedy writer; my strategic choice to send the postcards to Paula Pell rather than Tina Fey (as I reasoned that Paula would have less fan mail and thus might be more affected by an aspiring writer looking to her for guidance); and, not least of all, the individual postcards themselves, some of which weren't even sketch ideas but rather made-up, absurd accounts of what I'd done that day.

After the very last one, I sent her a cover letter and my résumé inside a standard business envelope.

Matt was having a better go of it: *Esquire* had chosen his film as one of their three finalists and would be throwing a party in New York, where they would screen all three and announce a winner. And as the date of this party fell on the weekend of my twenty-third birthday, I convinced Matt to take *me* as his date instead of Jessica. And though Matt didn't win the contest, the trip was a success for me, standing forever as the marker of the beginning of our relationship as adults.

And as for getting out of Dodge?

Well, the good people at *Esquire* had found it in their hearts to have a West Coast celebration as well. And since a few agents in Los Angeles had expressed interest in representing Matt, he planned to drive out there in time for the party, and then to stay in Los Angeles and see if he could find work as a writer/director.

I didn't love the idea of following my brand-new boyfriend to Hollywood, but I also knew I wasn't going to become a comedy writer living in the suburbs of Pittsburgh, even if Paula *did* get back to me (a scenario I'd yet to rule out). So, I made the not-so-tough decision to hang up my hummus-stained apron (once again), hop into Matt's Hyundai hatchback, and hit the road.

Down and Out in Hollywood? No way.

Silvia would make this cake for no reason other than because she wanted cake. She always made it in a sheet pan, spreading store-bought dulce de leche on top. But since dulce de leche is hard to find here, I make my own by simmering a can of unopened sweetened condensed milk in water for two hours. It's strange, but it works, and it's highly satisfying. I've also changed the form from a sheet cake to a layer cake. But I still think you should make it "just because," in the middle of the week, in honor of Silvia, my Argentine mom, who unwittingly taught me to *chill out*.

SIMPLE VANILLA CAKE WITH DULCE DE LECHE

Makes one 9-inch layer cake

For the dulce de leche:

1 (14-ounce) can sweetened condensed milk

For the cake:

¾ cup (1½ sticks) unsalted butter, softened, plus more for buttering the cake pans

2½ cups all-purpose flour

1 tablespoon baking powder

½ teaspoon salt

1½ cups sugar

4 large eggs

1 cup whole milk

1 teaspoon pure vanilla extract

Remove the paper label from the can of sweetened condensed milk and submerge the unopened can in a large, deep pot of water. Bring to a boil. Reduce the heat to low and simmer for 2 hours, adding water as needed to keep the can completely underwater.

While the can is simmering, make the cake.

Preheat the oven to 350°F. Butter two 9-inch cake pans, line the bottom of each with parchment paper, and then butter the paper as well.

In a large bowl, whisk together the flour, baking powder, and salt.

In the bowl of an electric mixer, beat the butter and sugar on medium speed until well combined, 2 to 3 minutes. With the mixer on low speed, add the eggs one at time, letting each one fully absorb before adding the next. Scrape down the sides of the bowl and mix for a bit longer. Keep the mixer on low and gradually add the flour mixture until it's completely combined. Add the milk and vanilla and beat the mixture on medium speed until just combined.

Divide the batter between the two pans. Smooth the tops with the back of a spoon. Bake until golden and a toothpick inserted in the center comes out clean, 28 to 32 minutes. Let the cakes cool in their pans on wire racks for about 15 minutes, then turn them out onto the racks to cool completely.

When the can of sweetened condensed milk has simmered for two hours, use tongs to remove it carefully from the simmering water and let it cool for about 10 minutes. Carefully (again), open the can and scoop the dulce de leche into a bowl: It should look like creamy caramel. Whisk until smooth.

Ideally, you want to move straight into assembling the cake at this point. (You want the dulce de leche to still be fairly warm so that you can pour it onto the top cake layer and get some pleasing drips along the side of the cake. The goal is for it to look *rustic*. But if the dulce de leche is too cold to form proper drips, no worries! Just spread it over the top with a butter knife in a nice thick layer.)

To assemble the cake:

Place one cake layer on a platter. Spread a layer of dulce de leche over the surface. Top with the second cake layer. Finish by topping with the remaining dulce de leche.

Chapter 10

Parasites in My Eyes

You can use your Spanish!" my mom said, wide-eyed, after I told her about my plan to move to Los Angeles. She and Bruce are practical people, and though I majored in *both* Creative Writing and Spanish, my mom liked to focus mainly on the Spanish.

I nodded and smiled. "Totally."

Of course, my plans didn't include using *my* Spanish. My plans included finishing my novel, enrolling in improv classes, and getting a job waiting tables. My friends, who as recently as two months ago, received letters from me from Argentina quoting long passages from *Letters to a Young Poet*, worried that I was going to find Los Angeles vapid and superficial, but when I told them how cool the *Esquire* party in New York was, and how famous the judges of the short film contest were, they seemed to get it. *Oh, Matt is on the verge of super success? In that case, God bless and have fun counting the money!*

* * *

Within two days, we are in the highway town of Shamrock, Texas, and have listened to enough Counting Crows, *Les*

Misérables Original Broadway Recording, and Built to Spill to confirm our standings as suburban, upper-middle-class, white people who came of age in the nineties. As far as we can see, there are two hotels and not much else in Shamrock. We choose the Shamrock Inn. (When in Rome, right?)

The abundant images of green shamrocks on the hotel's various signage cannot hide the fact that we are in *Texas*. Our car is the only non-pickup truck in the lot, and a man donning a cowboy hat unself-consciously checks in right before us. In the lobby, a banner touts a *Free Hot Breakfast!* and in the morning, we're treated to mediocre but *Free Hot* grits, sausage, bacon, and eggs.

We take I-40 west through the Texas panhandle and into New Mexico before heading north to Taos, where we've planned to stay with my aunt and uncle for two nights. We arrive at their sprawling adobe house and are welcomed by two grown Goldendoodles and seven of their recently born puppies. My aunt, uncle, and their son, Dylan, have just moved there from Boston in order to expand their business— a book publishing and distributing company focusing on holistic medicine and healing. They are a hippie success story for the books. (And yes, Uncle Bob, my mother's brother, has a ponytail.)

With all of the space their new southwestern home affords them, my aunt has created the garden of her dreams, from which she has plucked many an ingredient for the night's dinner. We eat and talk politics—the 2004 presidential election is just a month away—while eleven-year-old Dylan, named after both Bob Dylan and Dylan Thomas—occasionally chimes in with his own two cents, e.g., "Conservatives are killing America!"

Speaking of conservatives, my mom has told my aunt and uncle that Matt is "just a good friend of mine," but they instantly know better. They set us up in the guest room together, and before wishing us good night, give us one simple rule: We are not allowed to smoke cigarettes, though we are allowed to smoke weed. We aren't "holding," so don't take them up on the offer, but thank them all the same. In the morning, we wake up to the puppies, all of which someone has loosed into our room. Matt swiftly picks them up and places them on the bed with us. It's a good start.

Though my aunt Martha is a soft-spoken, extremely thin, kindhearted product of Haight-Ashbury in the sixties and has always been incredibly sweet to me, she is not someone I would want to get in a disagreement with. So when she tells me that she's set up an appointment for me to get my eye read in order to help with the migraine headaches I sometimes get, even though I have no idea what she means, I say, "OK."

And so after spending the morning exploring Taos, Aunt Martha, Matt, and I arrive at my eye appointment, in another simple adobe-style house, separated from its nearest neighbors by maybe half a mile.

Within minutes, a woman sitting on a stool, her legs straddling one of mine, leans into my face like she's about to kiss me and looks deep into my left eye with some sort of magnifying glass. At this point, I'm assuming that this is akin to having your palm read, and so half-expect her to pull back and tell me that I'm embarking on an amazing adventure. But instead, she says, "You have a sensitive digestive system and more parasites than normal."

I nod understandingly.

She prescribes me an herbal remedy that will hopefully

help with this. I thank her, and forever after, when Matt looks into my eyes, he tells me that he sees parasites—many, many parasites.

In the morning, we're anxious to get back on the road. Not because we're ready to leave Taos, but because Las Vegas, a city I've never been to as an adult, awaits.

During the twelve-hour drive, Matt gives me an education in everything I need to know about blackjack. At points, I have a deck of cards and am dealing us hands, balancing the cards on the tops of my legs. But nothing can really prepare you for Vegas.

I'm initially most impressed by the ease of the city. You are driving along this empty desert highway and then, out of nowhere, you are in a city driving directly underneath towering hotels and their neon lights.

In another moment, we have parked free of charge in the garage of the Bellagio and are taking the elevator to the casino floor, but first, Matt wants to show me the Chihuly glass sculpture hanging from the ceiling in the lobby. "Isn't it cool?" he asks, whisking me outside, where he shows me the giant fountain spouting water in choreographed ways in the middle of a lake in front of the hotel.

But then he can't wait any longer; it's time to play some blackjack. And so, with the confidence and fluidity of an experienced expert, Matt is suddenly exchanging two-hundred-dollar bills for a not-so-big stack of chips. He's sitting on a stool in a semicircle of other blackjack players, all facing the dealer. I'm standing behind him so he can't see my mouth drop. Two hundred dollars? All at once? What is he thinking? I pinch his shoulder and whisper into his ear, "What are you doing?"

"You have to start with that much. You've got to get into a rhythm."

I stand back and close my mouth. The minimum bet at this table is ten dollars, which I will soon find out is as low as the minimum ever gets at the Bellagio and is the reason why this particular table is full, as the one across from us, with a minimum of fifty dollars, has only one player. So, what is Matt doing betting twenty-five dollars on the first hand? He doesn't even *have* to bet that much. I cross my arms and grip into them with my fingers, watching as he's dealt a jack and a ten. The dealer has seventeen. And just like that, Matt has won twenty-five dollars. He looks back at me and smiles. I loosen my grip a little.

In less than ten minutes, he goes down a hundred dollars and then up a hundred dollars. I pull at his elbow and tell him to take a break, but he's ordered a free drink with the cocktail waitress and wants to wait for her to return. Waiting for his cocktail, he loses another seventy-five. I dig my fingers back into my arms.

Matt looks back at me and raises his index finger. "One more and then we'll go."

I nod and watch as he places twenty-five dollars on his next bet. He's dealt two eights. The dealer shows a six. From the morning's blackjack training, I know that Matt is assuming the dealer has sixteen and that even if she doesn't, there's a high likelihood she'll bust. Matt then splits his hand, which I also know from my training means he now has two hands and must put down another twenty-five dollars. His next card on top of the eight is a face card. He stays. But the next card on the other eight is a two. He doubles down, which means he must put down another twenty-five dollars and then he can only receive one more card from the dealer. On one hand alone, he's bet seventy-five dollars—a night's worth of tips at the restaurant where I was still working just five days before.

"C'mon! Big card!" Matt shouts and claps his hands together. I look at him as if he's a stranger.

But when the dealer flips the card over and it's an ace, I'm the one jumping up and down and clapping. Twenty-one!

The dealer busts, and I can hardly contain myself, fighting the urge to pick Matt up onto my shoulders and parade him around the casino floor like my own personal Rudy.

I beg him to quit while he's ahead, and as soon as he does, I try to get him to spend the winnings. But Matt has an idea. The Bellagio VIP room, where all the VIPs go to check into the hotel so that they don't have to wait in line with all of the *normals,* is an unassuming little annex behind two large doors with a gold sign that reads: VIP SERVICES. Most people probably don't even notice it, but on his last trip here, Matt did, realizing that today's VIPs *look* just like the two of us, a young couple dressed in jeans and T-shirts who just spent twelve hours in a car. And if you act like you know what you're doing, everyone just assumes you know what you're doing. *And* the last thing any casino employee ever wants to do is offend a VIP by asking whether or not you do, indeed, belong in the VIP services lounge.

The services for the very important people include a help-yourself buffet-style bar. And we do help ourselves—to a couple of gin and tonics in sizable lowball glasses. There are snacks too: fresh strawberries, dried mango, chocolate, crackers, cheese, and a wide assortment of nuts. As we step back out onto the casino floor, I can already feel the gin working its way through my system. The world is our oyster; the future is bright. Apart from my sky-high eye parasite levels, I am the luckiest girl in the world.

"Should we find a blackjack table?" Matt asks.

I smile and nod. "Yes, please."

Chapter 11

The Road to Vons Is Paved with Pavement

The *Esquire* party is held at the Beverly Hills mansion of NFL superstar Keyshawn Johnson. We valet Matt's Hyundai, accept a couple of passed drinks, sip them by the pool, and gawk at the sweeping views and sweet C- and D-list celebrities we know so well from *The Real World* and *Road Rules*. (Randy from *American Idol* is there too.)

We wake up in the morning in the two-bedroom condo on the west side of town that we're subletting for three months. The owner of the place is a working actor in his forties who is giving us a deal because he is most concerned about the well-being of his two cats, one of whom is eighteen years old and has a hard time with any activity involving moving or eating. We have no job leads and no place to report to.

I'm ready to start looking for a waitressing gig, but Matt's friends encourage me to send my résumé to a particular temp agency that helped them get good assistant positions within the entertainment industry. But even after the multiple job interviews the agency has found me, no one has hired me. At the same time, the talent agent who was interested in Matt has stopped returning his calls. He resorts to sending his résumé to the same temp agency. He also applies to every entry-level job within *the industry* he can find and sends his short films out to every contact he has and even ones he doesn't.

But by early December, we've been here for two and a half months, and we've just about given up on finding jobs before the town shuts down for the holidays. (When celebrities go on vacation, everyone who works for them does too.) It's set to be a bleak Christmas for us. We don't have enough money to fly home, nor do we feel we can, since, uhm, we just got here.

And then I get a call from Julian, my white-haired temp-agency agent.

"I've got an assignment for you at CAA," he says.

CAA stands for Creative Artists Agency, which is the best-known talent agency in the business. I'd been there the previous month for an interview for a second-assistant position—basically the assistant to the assistant—during which I doubt my jaw closed once. The place exuded money and success, from the valet parking for guests to the giant Lichtenstein in the lobby to the twenty-two-year-olds dressed in slim-fitting suits. "It's a temporary position, but with the right attitude, it could lead to more."

"Sounds great."

"Now, can you gift-wrap?"

"Sure!"

I start the next morning.

That night, Matt and I are still in unemployed mode, and so when we get a craving for ice cream at eleven-thirty p.m., we walk to the nearby Vons grocery store to pick up a pint of cookies and cream as we have done on so many other nights. Only, this night, I'm wound up. I'm running and jumping onto Matt's back for a piggyback ride. To make it extra fun, he is dodging my jumps. After one such jump, I am rebounded off his body, and my foot hits the pavement at a weird angle. I stand up and know something's wrong, but Matt thinks I can walk it off, and I try. I make it to the frozen-foods section before sitting down on the cold grocery store floor and taking off my shoe and sock to see what I've done.

The side of my foot has swelled up into into an odd-looking mound. I instantly start crying. It's broken. I'm positive.

But I call my mom anyway to see if she agrees with my diagnosis. It's almost three a.m. on the East Coast. She picks up the phone, half-asleep.

"I just broke my foot," I tell her.

But once she wakes up a bit more and gets the whole story, she isn't so sure.

"There are so many bones in the foot, Ame. Why don't you go home and sleep on it and see what it looks like in the morning."

But the mound is growing by the minute. Plus, in high school, my brother famously walked on a broken foot that both of my doctor parents said wasn't broken for a solid week before finally taking him to get X-rays and confirming that yes, in fact it *was*.

"No, Mom. I wanna go to the ER."

She sighs. "Fine." And then right before I hang up, "Thank God I got you health insurance!"

Matt and I go to a nearby emergency room, get X-rays, and return home at three in the morning with an officially diagnosed broken foot, a pair of crutches, a prescription for Vicodin, and the name of an orthopedist who can put a cast on it tomorrow.

* * *

Hanging on the walls in the guestroom of our subletted condo are posters from many of the Broadway shows the owner has been in—it appears he had a good run as the lead in *The King and I.* When he gave us his keys, the three of us chatted for a while, getting to know one another a bit. He told us about his most successful role to date: a scene he shared with Viggo Mortensen in the Disney movie *Hidalgo.* He seemed so proud, and rightly so.

And one day, a week or two into our stay there, when we had sent our résumés out to a couple of places and had nothing to do the rest of the day, we put his copy of *Hidalgo* into the DVD player. Neither of us had seen it before, so we turned the lights down, made some popcorn, and allowed ourselves to be entertained. And we were. It was exciting, too, when we saw someone we knew from real life on our television screen. But the scene was so short, maybe two minutes long. And I remember thinking that what you really remember from the scene and from the movie on the whole is the ruggedly handsome Viggo Mortensen. Mortensen was the star of the show. But more important, what I remember thinking was: Matt and I are going to do better than this nice man and his two-minute spot in a Disney movie. Sure, he's done well for himself. He owns a condo in California with a little back patio and a community pool. But Matt and I are headed for bigger things, and more quickly too.

* * *

The following morning, Matt drives me to CAA. My crutches are in the backseat and my throbbing foot is in a Velcro and plastic boot they'd issued me last night in the ER. We make it halfway there before I flip down the visor and look at myself in the mirror. I'd hardly slept and hadn't showered.

"I can't go to work like this," I say to Matt.

I call in to Julian and tell him about my foot. He understands, sort of.

✳ ✳ ✳

At this point in my life, I am just beginning to experience the straightforward kind of stress that comes with needing to make rent and pay for car insurance. As for health insurance, my mom was right. Thank God she'd signed me up for a plan on my behalf. (If she hadn't, I'm sure I would still be paying for that emergency-room trip.)

By my third month in Los Angeles, my Aladdin's Eatery savings are running low. More than that, I'm worried I don't have what it takes to make it in this city. Compared to Matt's friends and all of those assistants who had interviewed me that month, I feel so timid and breakable, my foot just another reminder of how fragile I am.

Since I'm not at work after all, I can get my cast on in the afternoon. I choose bright yellow for the color and am surprised to learn that though the bone I've broken is on the right side of my foot, the cast goes from my toes almost to my knee. But once it's on, I feel so much better. I feel protected. I call Julian and tell him I'm all casted up and can go in to CAA the next day if they still need me.

"Are you sure?"

"Yes," I say. "Absolutely."

For the next two days, I wrap elaborate holiday gifts from

the talent agency to their various actor and director clients. In the afternoon, I stuff envelopes. But they're not just any envelopes. They are residual checks for hundreds of thousands of dollars, and some of them are going to people whose names I'm extremely familiar with. It seems crazy to me that they'll let just anyone do this. But then, someone has to do it, right?

It's the end of 2004, before every cell phone is also a camera, so Matt and I have a bunch of actual Kodak-printed photos from this era, many of which involve me happily posing in a way that best highlights my bright-yellow cast, which Matt signed at the very top in thick capital letters and an exclamation point: *MATT!*

And all I can say is thank God for being young and naïve; that the woman who read my eye didn't also read my palm and give us a forecast of the road that lay ahead. Because, although our Hollywood experience wasn't going very well so far, and while we might not have moved out there just to be unemployed and laid up, you can't tell from these photos. No. We look as hopeful, as optimistic, and in my case, as parasite-eyed as possible.

Chapter 12

Starting from Scratch

Between the last days of 2004 and first weeks of 2005, I get my broken foot in the door temping full-time at a production company in Hollywood; we find an affordable two-bedroom apartment in centrally located West Hollywood; and so that I can stop relying on Matt for rides to work, with a gracious loan from Bruce, I buy a five-year-old Toyota Echo from a woman in Glendale who is marrying a guy who "isn't going to have his wife driving around in a five-year-old Toyota Echo."

Meanwhile, having given up on finding work through temp agencies, Matt finds a job through a friend of a friend as an occasional assistant to the guy who writes lyrics for Barry Manilow. His name is Marty Panzer. Mr. Panzer lives, works, and chain-smokes out of his Sunset Strip one-bedroom apartment, the walls of which are adorned with many gold records as well as a giant-size oil painting of his mother.

Mr. Panzer doesn't drive, so a large part of Matt's job consists of chauffeuring him around in his Hyundai. Another part of his job includes heating up Mr. Panzer's Lean Cuisines. At the end of each workday, Matt gets a check for $125 as well as a directive to either come back the next day or not.

* * *

It doesn't take long living in Los Angeles to realize you spend the vast majority of your time surrounded by extremely ambitious, successful people, their assistants, and their possessions.

Our new apartment is located one block away from an auto mechanic shop that exclusively services super-high-end cars like Rolls-Royces and Bentleys. And because of the general overabundance of cars as compared to garage spots in Los Angeles, Matt and I find ourselves parking on the street in front of or behind a $300,000 car on a daily basis.

When you're surrounded by such blatant success, it's difficult not to be fueled by it, to be pushed by it. Yes, I wanted to be a writer and, most likely, a comedy writer, but if I were truly living the dream, I would also be a comedy *performer.*

That winter, I sign up for improv classes at the famous Groundlings theater, which is less than a mile from our new apartment and is where *Saturday Night Live* cast members like Maya Rudolph and Kristen Wiig started out.

As for Matt, he and his old friend Geordie, who just moved out to Los Angeles as well, team up and begin working on an idea for an urban fishing show. Geordie is an avid fisher from New York City, and of all the Saturday morning fishing shows he watches, he realizes that none of them is doing anything different from the others and certainly none touches upon the fact that there is actually great legal fishing in most major cities throughout the world. You simply need a permit and to know where to go.

Together, Matt and Geordie come up with a concept for a new kind of fishing show that could find a home on the Resort

TV Network or even ESPN. They call it *Urban Angling with Brooks Hoffstadt*—Mr. Hoffstadt being a comedic yet informative fictional character (played by Geordie) who while traveling to various cities (London, Paris, Chicago, etc.) on business, always finds time to sneak away and do a little fishing. Geordie has a small budget for this project, and they decide to shoot the pilot episode themselves on location in Central Park (the lakes of which, in case you didn't know, are stocked with a variety of fish including smallmouth bass).

At the same time, Matt's work with Mr. Panzer comes to a close. As he explains to Matt, he's looking for his own personal Michael J. Fox. "You're not Michael J. Fox," he declares. Unable to argue with this, Matt accepts his last check and continues to search for work on Craigslist.

One position he ends up applying for is described as a *blackjack banker*. He goes on the interview and is hired right away. Though the job sounds strange and includes two weeks of intensive training, which he's told not everyone makes it through, it is *paid* training and it is blackjack. He takes it.

What is a blackjack banker, you're wondering? As we discover over the next two weeks, it's actually quite complicated.

Gambling laws are different in California than those in other states—one difference being that California only allows games that are player vs. player, not player vs. house. For example, in Las Vegas—which allows games that are player vs. house—in a game of blackjack, the dealer acts as the house, so if the dealer busts, he or she pays out all of the players at the table who didn't.

In California's specific brand of player-vs.-player blackjack, however, one of the players must act as the house, and if he busts, he has to pay out the other players at the table, which could very well be impossible if he has only twenty bucks in front of him and owes each of the other five players twenty bucks.

This is where Matt's company enters the picture. They hire and train people like Matt to arrive at a blackjack table with a bulletproof case of $100,000 in chips and act as a player who agrees to be the "all-time banker" for eight-hour shifts at a time.

Matt's first shift is at the Hollywood Park Casino in Inglewood from six p.m. to three a.m. on a Tuesday, with an hour break at midnight for dinner. And if success and ambition abound in West Hollywood, the complete opposite can be said for the Hollywood Park Casino, which on a weeknight is mostly filled with drunks and gambling addicts.

As we know, the house always wins (unless you happen to be in Vegas with your non-gambling girlfriend who forces you to quit while you're up), so Matt's company always won and Matt got paid an hourly wage. Sounds like a weird job, but hey, if you'd been unemployed for months and you like blackjack, it just might work.

But probably not.

* * *

Growing up with two doctor parents, you learn not to worry about your health. Nothing is ever a big deal to them, as displayed by Billy's and my respective broken feet, which we were basically told to shake off.

So, when Matt calls me from his car about a week after quitting his blackjack banker job (as he realized he didn't want to be the one taking money from gambling addicts at two o'clock in the morning) and tells me he thinks he is dying, it's really hard for me to believe. He was running an errand and had to pull over, thinking that he was going to die right there in his car. He's less than three minutes away, so I convince him to get back in the car and drive home so that I can see him before he dies.

When he arrives back at our apartment, he won't sit still; I can hardly get him to look at me. His skin is clammy and he's pacing from room to room asking if he should call 911. I tell him he's fine, that he's young and healthy and breathing and that there is no way he could possibly be dying. But he won't be stopped. And so I stand in our living room, which is empty, save for our recently purchased IKEA futon, and listen as he calls himself an ambulance.

I know he isn't going to die, that he's probably just having a panic attack, but at the same time, I don't know anything about panic attacks beyond the way the two words are thrown around in casual conversation to connote a certain kind of freak-out.

When the paramedics arrive, I mostly just feel strange and slightly embarrassed about having these men in our sparse living room. And to be completely honest, when Matt asks one of them, "Am I going to die?" I have to suppress a giggle.

But of course, it isn't funny.

They take him via ambulance to the emergency room at Cedars-Sinai, which is a few minutes from our apartment, and I follow behind in my new-to-me silver Toyota Echo—our second emergency-room visit in three months.

*　*　*

I know a lot about panic attacks now. I know how we humans are all wired differently, how some of us will always be more anxious than others. I know how your mind can find ways of expressing itself in the body, how perhaps being twenty-three years old and going from feeling that your dreams are within arm's reach to presently identifying as an unemployed (and seemingly unemployable) ex–blackjack banker within a matter of a few months might cause moments of panic, or physiologically speaking, surges of adrenaline, which cause your heart rate to rise, which can cause you to hyperventilate, which causes a lack of oxygen in the body, which will eventually cause you to pass out, unless of course you can manage to calm yourself down or seek medical treatment before things reach that level.

But back then, I had no idea about any of this. Back then, I remember recalling that character from *Pretty Woman*, the one walking Hollywood Boulevard, shouting: *Welcome to Hollywood! What's your dream?*

Chapter 13

Learning on the Job

My temp job turns permanent when they officially hire me as a production coordinator at the end of February. It's my first full-time, salaried, *office* job, and as such, it teaches me a lot about life. Because as I discover, like so much of life, the office is a big show. First of all, there's this seemingly constant need to demonstrate my value to the company, and the easiest way to do this, as I soon find out, is by simply being there from nine to six even if I don't have enough to do to fill those hours. And because of this structure, I also quickly learn that, for the most part, efficiency is not rewarded. What *is* rewarded are things like dedication and loyalty.

The company is primarily known for producing movie trailers, but they have a new division that is producing DVD bonus features—those short little segments found on most DVDs, e.g., *The Making of One Tree Hill, Season One.* As the production coordinator on these shoots, I'm mostly responsible for making sure the talent—which is Hollywood-speak for whichever person we're interviewing (whether or not he or she seems to exhibit much talent)—has everything he or she needs to be comfortable. When we're not shooting interviews,

I'm mostly responsible for making sure that each producer has everything he or she needs to be comfortable.

We don't have a computer at home, so one April day, just a few months after being hired, I stay after six to file my taxes. My desk just sits in a hallway, so when one of my superiors walks by on her way home at around seven o'clock, she sees me and pauses in her tracks. "Oh, Amelia," she says. "It's so good to see you here after six."

I smile and shrug. "Yeah, well, this work isn't going to finish itself."

At the same time, I discover how difficult it is to stay late at work, as that postpones my absolute favorite part of the day: going home and eating dinner.

Recovering dieter that I am, I still have a few bad habits. Namely, I still believe that I don't like certain foods when in reality I *do* like them; I had just forbidden myself from eating them for so long that I started to believe I didn't. For example, when Matt and I've finally tired of microwaved dinners and takeout, and Matt offers to make pasta for dinner, I actually say the following words aloud: "I don't like pasta."

Fortunately, Matt has the strength of character to see through such a ridiculous statement and the necessary enthusiasm to teach me the joy found in a bowl of spaghetti and marinara sauce with one heaping ladleful of grated Parmesan on top. And as it turns out, I am a quick learner. Other dishes I begin looking forward to coming home to thanks to Matt? Takeout moo shu shrimp with plum sauce, grocery-store salad-bar salads with blue cheese dressing, and Hebrew National hot dogs with mustard, ketchup, diced pickles, and raw onions on top. Not exactly James-Beardian cuisine, but straightforward delicious food that I cannot deny liking.

My office job also teaches me about hierarchy, and not just

the internal hierarchy—about those people in the company who are my superiors and the few who are my inferiors (interns)—but also about the hierarchies within the entertainment industry. I quickly realize that my friends who work as assistants to producers who are producing actual movies—as opposed to the DVD bonus features I'm doing—are superior to me. Similarly, the cooler the movie one's boss is producing, the cooler that assistant is (even if at the end of the day, all of these assistants are doing the exact same thing, e.g., reading scripts, making their boss's travel arrangements, placing their calls, and so on). I am mainly working on a piece for the DVD release of Season One of the television show *The O.C.* Ergo, I am not very cool.

But one of our friends, Martha, *is*. Specifically, Martha is cool because she is the assistant to the director who is currently directing the movie *The Family Stone*, starring Sarah Jessica Parker and Diane Keaton. During the production of the movie, it turns out that Ms. Keaton's line reader isn't working out and she needs someone new and as soon as possible to run her lines with. Martha, who knows Matt's been looking for work, says she knows someone who could do it.

And, just like that, Matt, ex-assistant to Marty Panzer and ex–blackjack banker, is driving to Bel Air to meet Diane Keaton, aka Annie Hall, aka Mrs. Corleone, at her house to run lines with her *for money*: $20/hour to be exact.

Simultaneously, just like that, I am now *dating* Diane Keaton's line reader.

Simultaneously, I'm beginning to realize how stupid my job is. And at the same time, ironically, I'm hungrier to succeed at it. I'm hungry to rise up through my company's hierarchy so as to be able to rise up through the industry's hierarchy.

But in order to do so, I understand I must put in my time.

I must wait patiently for my performance review, at which time I can make a case for myself about why I'm good at what I do, but beyond that, the ways in which I'm dedicated to the work.

Of course, all the while I'm wondering if some of the higher-ranked people, who I'm basically aspiring to be, and who hand out many of my daily tasks, somehow managed to skip my position, because had they have been where I am now, they certainly wouldn't be going about things so horribly, and in some cases, so rudely. But then again, isn't that part of it? Isn't that how they weed out the weak, so that only the truly dedicated rise to the top?

One of the things I always liked about waiting tables was not knowing how much money I'd make on any given night. There was always the promise of the rare outrageously big tipper. Of course, the outrageously small tipper was much more prevalent, but I liked the suspense of collecting my tips in my apron pocket and not tallying them up until the end of the night, just as I liked going to the bank every couple of weeks with my stack of ones, fives, tens, and twenties and seeing how much it came to.

As a production coordinator, there is no suspense. Every two weeks, I make $940 after taxes. Oftentimes I take this number and divide it by the hours I'd worked those two weeks in order to discover just how little per hour I was making. (Sure, I have health insurance, but what's health insurance to a healthy twenty-four-year-old who reasons that since she's recently broken her foot, she isn't due for another medical problem for at least a couple of years?)

What's more disconcerting is that after a year, I've taken on much more responsibility, so each of the hours I'm there is almost entirely dedicated to actual *work* (as opposed to checking my e-mail, Facebook, etc.). And when I find out that one of my male colleagues who is doing the exact same job as me is making more than I am, I decide to ask for a raise. The company does reviews eighteen months after your official hire date; for me that won't be for another seven months. So, I *also* decide I can't wait that long.

I consult with Bruce, who on top of his day job at the bank and occasional stint ministering at other churches is also paid to give lectures to businesspeople titled "Ethics: The Ethics of Decision Making" and "Managing Change: Excellence in the Midst of Change." First things first, he gives me my own personal lecture on how you should never say things like: "I'm worth X amount of money." Because, and as he speaks, I can hear his cadence change into that of a motivational speaker, "Your worth as a human being can't be measured in dollars and cents. [Pause for dramatic effect.]"

Once we get through all of that, he helps me write a profes-sional letter requesting the opportunity to discuss ~~how much I am worth~~ the idea of a raise. And just as Bruce directs me, I print it out, put it in an envelope, and place it in the mailbox outside of Mitchell's (my head boss's) office.

When I don't hear from him after a week, I follow up with a friendly e-mail.

I believe there's a term for what happens next: radio silence.

I broaden my already active job search to include positions outside of the entertainment industry.

Within a couple of weeks, I'm hired to begin paid training as an SAT and PSAT tutor. It isn't a great job, as they can't guarantee a set amount of hours per week, but at this point, Matt has found an assistant job of his own. Plus, when Ms. Keaton has a role she needs to prepare for, she still calls on

Matt's services, which both of us feel is *bound* to lead to bigger and better Keaton-related opportunities. So even if this tutoring job pays much less and even though Matt and I haven't merged our finances, Matt says he can pay a bit more in rent for the time being; I decide to take the job.

The next day at work, I pop my head into my immediate supervisor's office and ask if I can speak with her. She waves me in. Her name is Gerda, pronounced in staccato: Gehr-DA. In fact, everything about her is staccato, from her short, bleach-blonde spiky hair to her Danish accent, which only intensifies her quick, confident sentences.

So when I tell her I'd like to give my two weeks' notice, and she responds kindly with a regretful, "Oh, no. Why?" I'm surprised.

I explain that I don't think I want to work within the entertainment industry, how I want more time to work on my book. (By the way, I'm working on turning my thirty fruitless postcards to Paula Pell into a coffee-table/humor book.) "Plus," I add at the end, "I don't know if you know this, but I wrote Mitchell a letter asking to discuss the possibility of a raise and he never got back to me."

"Oh yeah," she says, trying to suppress a laugh. "He showed me that."

* * *

In the months and years to come, I'll continually doubt the decision to quit my production job, as I'll discover just how hard it is to come up with $940 every two weeks. But I'll never doubt that I wasn't cut out to be a Hollywood producer of DVD bonus features or otherwise. Nor that Mitchell and Gerda really were assholes.

While I can't say that I'm a proponent of investing in hard work for the sole purpose of trying to impress someone else, there does exist the rare occasion where you can trick someone into being impressed by an effort that didn't exactly require heavy lifting, e.g., wowing your boss with your dedication to the company by staying late at the office (even if you're actually just filing your income taxes) and making linguine and clams, which is one of those dishes that always seems to impress dinner guests even though it comes together quite effortlessly. Of course, if you've never worked with live clams before, you might hesitate. But honestly, it's just a matter of doing it once and remembering two things: One, make sure to rinse the clams free of any dirt or sand before cooking them, and two, toss the ones that don't open up. Those just weren't meant to be.

(Also, I can hardly believe I once told Matt I didn't like pasta, especially given the fact that we eat pasta at least twice a week. These days, if I falsely convince myself of anything, it's that since I use so much fresh parsley in this dish, it's like having a mini salad right there mixed in with the pasta.)

LINGUINE AND CLAMS

Adapted from Mario Batali

Should probably serve 4, but Matt and I can easily finish this between the two of us

Salt

1½ to 2 pounds manila clams (you can also use littleneck clams; they're much larger, so that 2 pounds' worth might equal about 10 clams, whereas you'll probably get more like 20 manilas)

¼ cup olive oil

6 cloves garlic, thinly sliced
I pound dried linguine
I cup white wine
I to 2 teaspoons crushed red pepper, depending on how spicy you
    like things
I large bunch flat-leaf parsley
Grated Parmesan cheese (see *Note*)

Start bringing a large pot of salted water to a boil.

Give the clams a nice rinse and a bit of a scrub. This removes any dirt and/or sand, and, as a bonus, reminds you of where they came from: the ocean! Set aside.

Take the largest skillet you own and pour in the oil. Turn the heat to medium and add the garlic. Sauté, stirring occasionally, until fragrant, 2 to 3 minutes.

Drop the linguine into the boiling water.

Add the clams, wine, and crushed red pepper to the skillet. Cover and cook, giving the pan a shake once or twice, until the clams steam open, 8 to 10 minutes.

Meanwhile, give the parsley a rough chop, stems and all.

Right before the pasta becomes al dente, pull it from the heat and drain it. Add the drained pasta to the skillet and toss to coat. Add the parsley and toss some more. Divide among bowls and serve, unapologetically, with lots of Parmesan on top. (Reserve seasoning it until you've tried a bite—between the brine from the clams and the Parmesan, it may not need any more salt.)

Note: Some people find it sacrilegious to put cheese on any pasta dish that includes fish. To those people, I say: *But have you tried my linguine and clams with Parmesan?*

Chapter 14

Call Me ~~Ishmael~~ Mealy

M$_Y$ SAT tutoring gig lasts until I realize that I'll have to drive to places like Palos Verdes and Pasadena in order to do two hours' worth of work. I hadn't even heard of Palos Verdes before, let alone driven the forty miles there from West Hollywood. But at least one of us has a full-time job. Matt's working as an assistant to two agents who represent "below-the-line talent," or in non-industry speak, people like cinematographers, set designers, makeup artists, and so on.

Via Craigslist, I discover that a gym within walking distance from our apartment is looking to hire a part-time receptionist. The description says that as an employee, I will have free access to the gym and its classes. I apply that afternoon and am quickly hired for the bargain price of $8/hour. (It's almost embarrassing just typing that number, but, hey, unlimited free classes! Just imagine how effortlessly thin I was going to get.)

The gym is called Train. And it is home to every Los Angeles cliché one could think of, from the valet parking, to the too-skinny women, to the trainers who meet with their clients in between auditions, to the muscled men throwing back protein drinks, the majority of which originate from my post behind the reception desk.

"Yo, Amelia, toss me one of those chocolate Pure Protein shakes, would ya? And put it on my tab."

"No problem," I say, before chucking a canned shake up to one of the male trainers.

Sadly, Train can only give me fifteen hours a week, so I keep applying for jobs, and a little less than a month later, I find a second receptionist gig at the School of Rock. It's a rock-music school for kids, whose name may ring a bell, as the original one had been featured in a documentary film called *Rock School*, which then spawned a scripted comedy starring Jack Black. Because of all this free publicity, the school is opening a bunch of new locations across the country, including this one on Hollywood Boulevard. The job pays $12/hour, but there's a chance of making $15/hour after three months.

I don't realize how early in the process of opening the school they are until my first day on the job includes driving my boss, Carl, to IKEA to buy furniture for the office. The next two days of my job include a combination of putting together IKEA furniture and blanketing neighborhoods with flyers announcing the new school.

Once the school officially opens, however, I mostly just sit at the front desk from three p.m. until nine p.m., do some light bookkeeping, and greet the kids who come in to take their lessons from Carl or the musician friends he's hired.

The thing about Carl is, he's possibly younger than thirty, and up until this point, has been making a living strictly as a musician, having toured with the likes of Perry Farrell and recorded with Wyclef Jean. He has shoulder-length wavy hair and always wears jeans, Converse sneakers, some manner of T-shirt, and a black studded belt. In short, he's a musician first and a director of a music school second, possibly third. It's kind of like working for a high-school kid whose dad has just handed him the keys to the business.

One of the friends he hires to give kids guitar lessons is the ex-singer and lead guitarist for Frank Zappa. His name is Ike. He looks to be in his fifties, with graying hair and that kind of weathered, Keith-Richards-esque look specific to aging rock and roll stars.

On Ike's first day, he arrives twenty minutes late and then collapses onto the couch in the lobby/waiting room area, seemingly exhausted. From his supine position, he bellows to me, "Hey, sweetheart, can you run out and grab me something to eat?" Before I can even answer, he adds, "Thanks."

I look at Carl, my eyes asking, "Who does he think he is?" But Carl just shrugs apologetically. "Use the petty cash."

On his second day on the job, Ike arrives on time, but excuses himself to the bathroom, where he spends the next twenty minutes. After the lesson, he approaches my desk and uses his newly invented nickname for me, which I suppose is better than *sweetheart* but not much. "Hey, Mealy, can I get paid?"

"Oh, uhm, I don't handle payroll. The Philadelphia office does all of that—they should cut you a check in a week or so."

"I don't need all of it. I just need twenty bucks for gas."

"I'm sorry, Ike. That's just not the protocol."

At which point, Carl overhears our conversation and tells me to go ahead and give Ike twenty dollars from petty cash. "Just this once," he adds.

I find the little key for the petty cash and hand him a twenty-dollar bill.

As for my other receptionist job, I've become a bit of a persona non grata at the gym as I've had to change my schedule in order to accommodate some of my hours at the rock school, which annoys my boss, who had just hired me with that schedule a month before. Then, during one of my routine tosses of a protein drink up to one of the trainers working on the second floor, I misfire and break a large neon sign that is (was) hanging in the window. Everyone finds it funny except for my boss, a muscular Asian woman who looks exceptionally good for her age. When she doesn't fire me on the spot, I'm surprised, and to be honest, a little let down. The male trainers are too chatty for me. One of them grills me with questions about my life on a daily basis; when he finds out that I'm an aspiring writer, he starts bugging me to bring him something I've written. Plus, the clients, who are primarily wealthy, bone-thin women, aren't exactly sweethearts to wait on. ("Can someone come and wipe down my bike? It's *disgusting*.") But I need to hang on at least long enough until my raise kicks in at the School of Rock.

* * *

A few months later, Carl and I find out that after his lessons, Ike has been asking a few of the parents if he could borrow some cash. Then, one of the parents tells me that Ike called her at home to ask for money. How he even got her number, I'm not sure.

Needless to say, we aren't going to be able to work with Ike anymore. We also can't work with Carl's European-born friend who apparently doesn't have the papers he needs to work in the States. One of our regular teachers, Justin, can no longer work with us either because he's going on tour with Miley Cyrus, et cetera and so on. But hey, this is a rock school, is it not? And three months in, I've gotten the hang of it as well as the three-dollar per hour raise, which finally lets me give notice at the gym.

My boss there is beyond nonplussed. "I don't know what happened. You seemed like such a promising hire and then you broke that sign."

At the same time, however, Matt and I are finally figuring out a way to balance our day jobs with our creative pursuits. A short piece I write about my paternal grandma is accepted at McSweeney's Internet Tendency. Matt and Geordie are finishing up editing the pilot episode of *Urban Angling with Brooks Hoffstadt*. I watch it and am impressed with what they've done. The show is informative, hilarious, and wholly unique. I've also moved on from taking improv classes at The Groundlings to a place called ImprovOlympic West, which feels like a better fit. I'm enrolled in the third level class there and have even formed an improv team with some of my classmates. Plus, with my mornings to myself, I've managed to finish writing my coffee table book and have begun looking into the process of querying literary agents.

For the first time in a long while, I feel like quitting my production job wasn't, in fact, a horrible decision.

Two months after my raise kicks in, I'm at Target when I get a call from Carl.

"Hey, so, I'm really sorry about this, but they've hired someone to replace you."

"Oh."

"Yeah, you've been really great, but *uhm*, they need someone who can take over more of my responsibilities and who is basically like, an accountant."

"Oh."

"Yeah, it's a bummer. But she's gonna be here on Thursday, so if you could train her a little bit on the day-to-day stuff before you leave, I'd really appreciate it."

After hanging up, I take a fresh look at the items I've collected in my plastic basket: printer ink, gummy bears, mascara, wooden hangers, toothpaste, and athletic socks. I grab the gummy bears and—to be fair—the toothpaste, leave the rest, and head to the checkout.

Chapter 15

The Squeaky Wheel Gets the Engagement Ring?

When Matt and I drove out to Los Angeles together from Pittsburgh, I didn't exactly clarify our relationship to Mom and Bruce, who may have believed that we were just two high school friends conveniently moving to Los Angeles at the same time. But over a year later, Mom and Grandma are coming to visit me, and I know it's time to properly communicate, to make sure we're all on the same page.

I practiced what I was going to say, even writing down a few different options of how I was going to tell my mom. But then, one day over the phone, I simply blurted out: "You know that Matt and I aren't just friends, right?"

"Well," she paused. "Bruce had wondered about that a couple of times. I said I didn't know."

"I know you guys would prefer that we didn't live together."

"Well," she paused again. My mom often lets sentences drift off into nothingness, and I thought this was one of those times, but then she surprised me with: "Have you found a church yet?"

"No, not yet. The churches are different here," I told her, which was true.

The Presbyterian church we went to as a family in the sub-urbs of Pittsburgh was a beauty: gothic architecture, church bells, and stained glass everywhere. In Los Angeles, the clos-est comparison I could find looks-wise was the Beverly Hills Presbyterian church, which I went to one Sunday, finding a very poorly attended and lackluster service.

But that wasn't really what she was getting at. *Have you found a church yet?* was WASP-speak for: "I'd prefer if you could find a less Jewish boy to date."

It was OK, though. I understood that change didn't hap-pen overnight. And at least I'd done my due diligence. She knew what was going on, she just needed a bit of time to digest it.

A month later, when she and Grandma come to Los Ange-les for their inaugural visit, Matt and I try to act like the nor-mal boyfriend and girlfriend couple that we are, showing them all around our favorite places. We shop; we eat; Matt gives them his famous driving tour through some of the fancy Bev-erly Hills neighborhoods. Grandma really wants to go to the Crystal Cathedral in Anaheim, so, on Saturday, the four of us get in my little car and drive the sixty miles there, to a veritable Christian tourist trap. We don't attend a service or anything. We simply take a look at the glass structure, tour the premises, and eat at the attached café. (Neither Matt nor I are impressed.)

But then one night, on a walk through my neighborhood to the grocery store to pick up dessert, Mom and I are alone for the first time on the trip, and she takes the opportunity to ask me: "So, have you met anyone special out here?"

I'm so confused by the question. Had she forgotten about our conversation, about *Matt*, whom she'd spent all weekend with? Had she misunderstood what I'd told her the previous month? Did I need to spell it out for her?

But all I say is, "No."

* * *

I don't know who to blame besides Hollywood and romantic comedies for my warped perception of how one becomes engaged to be married, but by the summer of 2006, I'm ready for Matt to propose. We've been together for almost two years and have known each other for ten. We've discussed getting married on more than a few occasions, and during these conversations, I've told him that I'd like a vintage engagement ring that "doesn't even have to have a diamond in it." For good measure, I even send him some links. I'm not bold enough to actually go ahead and ask *him*, so as far as I'm concerned, I've taken this particular task as far as I can.

If my life were one of those romantic comedies, the next few months would be summed up via a montage of various moments where I'm waiting for Matt to ask me to marry him and he is going about his life as usual. When we go on a fancy Caribbean beach vacation with his family, I think he might take me out for a picnic one day and do it there. Nope. Our two-year anniversary comes and goes. Nothing. My twenty-fifth birthday follows soon after. Still nothing. I'm getting annoyed, but I don't let myself say anything. I don't want to ruin the romance of it, the *surprise* factor.

But in late October, after receiving a phone call from one of my best friends on the East Coast who has just gotten engaged to her boyfriend of little over a year, I can no longer restrain myself. I gush my congratulations, hang up the phone, march into the living room and ask Matt, who is watching television, what's *taking* so long.

The question hangs in the air as he looks around the room, seemingly searching for a clue as to what he was supposed to have been doing while I was on the phone with my friend.

When he finally understands what it is I'm asking, he bombards me with a list of things he wants to accomplish before proposing. "I want to be set up first. I want to sell a script. I want to be able to buy you a really great ring!"

I don't think I can say the following in any higher of a pitch: "You want to sell a script first?!"

I may have only been in Hollywood for two years, but it's long enough to know that that might *never* happen.

We fight for a while, until I realize that this is one fight I'm not going to win.

And so, I do what I do best. I try to hurt Matt the way he has hurt me. I tell him I'm going to move back to the East Coast. I know I'm being dramatic, but as I explain it to him, it starts to make sense to me. "What am I doing in Los Angeles anyway? I have a stupid job as a receptionist at the School of Rock. All of my friends are actually *your* friends. And they all work in the *industry*," which I say using air quotes. "And if I have to hear one more story from them in which all of the people are referred to as so-and-so's assistant, I am going to flip out!" (Of course, I am already flipping out.) What I don't say aloud but also know is: I'm no good at improv (I quit at level three, after hitting a self-conscious streak where my face turned red at the drop of a hat); my coffee-table manuscript is getting rejected daily by literary agents; I have no family in Los Angeles and am pissing off the family I do have *because* of this relationship. In fact, as far as I see it, all that I really have is Matt, and if he doesn't want to marry me, I have nothing.

By the time the fight winds down, it's decided. I'm moving out. I call my brother and his girlfriend in North Carolina to tell them. I'm not sure where I'm headed yet, I say, but definitely the East Coast. Maybe even North Carolina. (Do they need a roommate?)

*　*　*

Twenty-four hours later, I call my brother again, this time to say that Matt and I are getting married!

I don't have a ring (nor a very romantic engagement story), but Matt and I have reached an agreement. It's November, and by the New Year, Matt promises we will be properly engaged. We even pop champagne and call his parents with the announcement.

Mazel tovs abound.

Well, for the moment. We still need to call my mom.

Chapter 16

Food Fight

My maternal grandmother's identity is wrapped up in food. She's been a member of the Mt. Lebanon Presbyterian church for more than sixty years and has worked in the church kitchen there for every single one of them, heading up countless afternoon luncheons, dinners, and other sundry food-focused fundraisers, sometimes staying late and operating the commercial dishwasher by herself long after everyone else has gone home.

Every Christmas, she fills large Macy's cardboard gift boxes with pizzelle cookies, each flavor—vanilla, chocolate, and anise—getting their own giant box. And these are just for family and friends to snack on throughout the season. For gifts, she packs tins with her lady locks cookies, little croissant-shaped puff pastries stuffed with cream, the dough for which she makes from scratch using butter-flavored Crisco.

She is a woman who has spent her life hosting, who always shows up at your door with something she's recently cooked or baked, and who has a pot of chicken noodle soup on her stovetop more often than not. As a kid, I must've eaten that chicken soup a thousand times. The sweet umami flavor of her homemade broth was so different from the sharp saltiness of the Maruchan ramen noodles our nanny made for my brother and me. And no matter the day or month, the contents of that chicken noodle soup remained the same: carrot rounds, celery half-moons, shredded white and dark meat chicken, and wide curly egg noodles.

* * *

Mom and Bruce, in my mother's words, "are not run of the mill Christians" (by which she means that they don't *just* believe in God; they go to church every Sunday, they tithe ten percent, they organize fund-raisers, they take on leadership roles, et cetera). So, while I expect some resistance from them to Matt's and my engagement, I also expect some level of capitulation, something akin to: "Well, we hope you don't lose your faith completely, but Matt's a good guy, so congrats all the same." (When Matt called my mom before proposing and asked for permission to marry me, she never *really* granted it, responding like a saleswoman who doesn't actually want to sell, "You know, Amelia's always been *extremely* difficult to please.")

But when I speak to her on the phone after the fact, all she can muster is a quiet pout, and when I push for her to congratulate me, to admit that apart from Matt's Jewishness, he's a good fit for me, she refuses. She is simply too "sad." She needs "time."

"Time?" I shout. "You've known Matt for ten years. You guys worked together to plan my surprise sixteenth birthday party!"

She doesn't respond, and with every passing silent second, I become more and more worked up. I can't believe this is the reaction I get from the person who married my father, the guy who notoriously brought his own hoagie to Thanksgiving dinner at Grandma's and ate in a separate room watching football and who of course would go on to do much worse things and who, on top of it all, was decidedly *not* a Christian.

After a solid minute of silence, I can't take it any longer.

"I don't want to talk to you until you can congratulate me," I say, and hang up the phone.

The following day, my blood is still boiling. What adds to the frustration is that I can't even fully vent to Matt, as I've told him a watered-down version: that my mom's less-than-pleased reaction has nothing to do with him, that she is simply worried about me no longer being a Christian—literally, about me going to hell.

And so I turn to Grandma for support. Over the years, I had seen her deal with hot-button issues like homosexuality in the church and my own liberal leanings much more gracefully than Mom ever had.

When she picks up the phone with her sweet and singsongy, "Good afternoon," I am expecting her to be on my side.

"Will you tell Mom how ridiculous she's being?" I say.

"I will *not*," she says, using a tone I've never heard her direct toward me, one that lacks any of her usual grandmotherly kindness.

"What?"

"This is marriage. This is serious. You're making a mistake."

One thing I've learned about myself by now is that I'm a fighter, and not in the Destiny's Child I'm-a-survivor sense of the word, but simply in the sense that I don't avoid conflict. I face it head on with gloves up and a racing heart. And in this case, I'm facing off with my eighty-seven-year-old grandmother. And if honesty is the name of the game, I'm ready to play.

"I know it's serious. I'm taking it seriously by opting to marry my best friend whom I've known since I was fifteen years old. And you know what? If Mom was *so concerned* about *my faith*, then she should have started taking Billy and me to church when we were kids and not for just a few rogue years in high school. But wait, she *couldn't have* because she married Dad, who is basically the opposite of a Christian and who believes that religion is for the weak!"

"It's not about religion, Amelia. He's wrong for you."

"Oh, OK, then. Why? Why exactly?"

But she changes the subject to my father. "I told your mother I didn't think she should marry him."

"Oh, great. So this is what you do? You tell people who are recently engaged that they're making a mistake?"

"I told her once, and I'll tell you once."

"Well, that's a really solid policy, Grandma."

Needless to say, I don't get a *congratulations* from Grandma either.

☀ ☀ ☀

Five months later, my mom, Grandma, and I are meeting in Asheville, North Carolina, to visit my brother and his girlfriend, Jenny, who recently moved there together. Though Mom never did congratulate me, she and I are still close. We talk on the phone almost daily, and eventually, we make up in the way that only family or very close friends can, by allowing the anger to fade by virtue of missing each other.

Grandma, on the other hand, I cannot forgive. She is still the horrible lady I happen to be related to who has unapologetically proclaimed divorce in my future. As far as I'm concerned, Grandma is the enemy. I've studied her forces, I know where to attack, and I'm not going to make this weekend easy for her.

I think we can all agree that when you're traveling and you go out to eat, it doesn't always make sense to take the leftovers to your hotel like it does when you are at home with a proper refrigerator. This idea has apparently never occurred to Grandma. By the time she and Mom, who have driven together from Pittsburgh, pick me up at the Charlotte airport, Grandma has already accumulated a container with half of a sandwich and a few half-eaten convenience-store snack food items, including an open bag of Fritos.

Our first morning together in Asheville, the five of us— Mom, Grandma, me, my brother, and Jenny—go out to breakfast, where Grandma orders the bagel and lox. (Matt and I often joke that Grandma's taste buds are at least half Jewish, since she also loves corned beef, hot pastrami, and macaroons.) Grandma, being Grandma, eats half of the bagel, barely puts a dent in the pile of lox, and asks the server for a container to pack up the rest. When we get back in the car, I see her add it to her growing collection of foodstuffs in the trunk.

That night at dinner, she strikes again, only this time it's a tablespoon of guacamole she couldn't finish. "I need a box," she announces to the server.

Six months ago, I would've found Grandma's Great-Depression-era habit of leftover-keeping endearing. *Oh, Grandma! How cute that she holds on to parsley stems and half-rotten potatoes.* But given the role she's assumed of divorce-whisperer, her request is simply annoying and impolite.

"Grandma, it's one bite of guacamole. Don't waste the Styrofoam," I say aloud, and can instantly feel the whole table's eyes on me. *No she didn't. Not to Grandma!*

"You don't know what it's like to be hungry," Grandma says, trying to shame me.

Only I'm not ashamed. I'm just getting started.

The next day, Mom has offered to make dinner for us and a few of Bill and Jenny's friends before we all leave to see The National, one of our favorite bands, who is playing that night.

In the late afternoon, Mom is prepping her ingredients when I hear Grandma ask her for the keys to the car; she needs to grab something. I then watch carefully as she returns with her purse, a Styrofoam container, and the announcement that she's going to make a smoked salmon dip.

I casually follow her into the kitchen and watch as she retrieves a box of cream cheese, a small container of sour cream, the aforementioned Fritos, and a bag of partially melted chocolate-covered potato chips from her purse. "Oh," she says, pleased. "I'd forgotten." With great care, she tears open a corner of the bag of the chocolate-covered chips and retrieves one with her thumb and forefinger. "I had never seen these before. Amelia, would you like to try one?"

I look at the chocolate melted up against the side of the clear plastic bag and decline. She moves on to my mother, who is *very* interested in trying a chip. And as the two of them nod in approval of their discovery, I put my hand on the box of cream cheese, which is warmer and softer than cream cheese should be. I peek inside the Styrofoam container and spot the leftover bagel and lox from breakfast thirty-six hours ago. *She wouldn't.*

Slipping out of the kitchen, I gather my brother and Jenny onto the porch, and with the flair and gusto normally reserved for scary campfire stories told with a flashlight shining up at your face, I report what I've seen.

We all come to the same conclusion: No one can eat any of Grandma's dip. It's simply not safe for human consumption.

Within the hour, Grandma emerges from the kitchen with a pale pink dip in a bowl, which she's placed on top of a plate layered with Fritos. "Would you like some salmon dip?" she asks, stopping right in front of my spot on the couch.

"No, thanks."

She shrugs her shoulders, turns a quarter degree, and approaches Jenny. "Try my dip."

"Oh, is that salmon? I actually can't. Sorry, Grandma."

My brother is sitting on the porch reading, and so we watch as she goes outside to find him. "William," we can hear her say. "I've made some dip."

"Thanks, Grandma, but I just brushed my teeth."

When my brother's friends start pouring in, Grandma greets them, shaking their hands and telling them that there is smoked salmon dip on the coffee table.

Perhaps it's the pinkish color of the dip or the way the Fritos seem to transplant the dish to the 1980s, but we don't have to tell the guests to steer clear of Grandma's concoction—the appetizer just sits there, unloved and uneaten all through the cocktail hour.

At one point, I spy Grandma take a Frito to it and carefully try a bite. I can tell she's trying to figure it out. Everyone always eats her food at church, and at Bible study, and at my mom's house when she brings over a dish to accompany dinner. So what's going on?

As angry as I still am, watching Grandma stare at her appetizer with confusion is difficult. It's almost enough to make me go over there and join her, to scoop a Frito into the stupid, pink, health hazard of a dip and tell her how great it tastes. But in the end, I can't quite do it. I tell myself that just because she's OK with storing smoked salmon in the trunk of the car for an extended period of time doesn't mean that I have to be. I tell myself that just because she's older than me doesn't mean she's right.

There isn't a table large enough for us all to sit together, so Mom serves us potluck style, setting her linguine and shrimp, Caesar salad, and garlic bread on the kitchen table. As I make myself a plate, I notice that the Fritos and dip have made their way to the buffet spread as well.

We leave for the concert shortly after dinner, and Mom and Grandma retire to their hotel for the night. But in the morning, when I open the refrigerator to grab the milk for my coffee, there it is—refrigerated at last—wrapped in plastic too, in case any of us want a few bites of dip for breakfast.

Chapter 17

Food Fight, Part II

Back in LA, after I'm let go from the School of Rock, I pick up a job at the Beverly Hills branch of Paper Source, a store that specializes in colorful cardstock, greeting cards, and craft supplies. It pays $11/hour, but you have to pay $4 a day for parking and endure the wrath of the regional manager, who occasionally drops in on the store and scolds me for sitting down while I work. (If I ever find myself the owner and operator of a retail store, there will be stools behind the register and a desk for those tasks that can be done sitting down.)

My spare time is dedicated to my second attempt at getting into graduate school for creative writing. Only this time I'm not taking chances, and I apply to a much wider range of schools. And though Matt and I are engaged, I'm still disenchanted with Los Angeles. So much so that USC is the only school I apply to on the West Coast. So much so, that in between my hours at Paper Source, I design a T-shirt in the style of the iconic *I ♥ NY* that reads instead: "I ♪ LA."

I buy the domain name IStomachLA.com, get a vendor's license, and though I know nothing about starting my own business, I convince my mom to *invest* $300 in the new company I'm starting. The cash pays for a first run of shirts and for some of the fees to apply for a registered trademark. The best-case scenario, as I see it, is to sell the idea to a company like Urban Outfitters. And the worst case? I can sell the T-shirts online when I'm in school.

In April, I find out I've gotten into a few different schools, one of which is the University of North Carolina Wilmington—one of my top choices. When I'm not accepted into USC's program, UNCW becomes my very top choice.

Before we uproot our lives entirely, Matt (who is also very close to being ready to leave Los Angeles) and I figure we should visit Wilmington for the first time. But when we do the math, we realize it doesn't make sense. We can barely afford one plane ticket, let alone two. So, instead, I go for the free option: watching old episodes of *Dawson's Creek*, which was shot there. And through the lens of Dawson's unrequited love for Joey Potter, I become completely sold on Wilmington. I imagine a sleepy little beach town with marshes, seagulls, and seafood restaurants on docks. I imagine a town where not every single person you meet is trying to do the exact same thing you are and where the dream of buying a small house is an attainable one. I send in the paperwork to enroll.

Meanwhile, the regional manager at the paper store yells (really, he yells!) at me yet again for sitting down on the job. I give notice the next day and go back to my original temp agency.

Again, they send me to CAA, the giant talent agency with all the young people in suits and the Lichtenstein on the wall, which has since relocated to an even grander edifice. Since I'm only a temp, they don't want to bother issuing me a parking card, telling me instead to use the valet parking and get it validated at the front desk each evening. So, every day, I valet my tiny little car right alongside all the Mercedes and Jaguars. In the lobby one morning, I see Joey Potter (aka Katie Holmes). For the rest of the day you can find me humming the Dawson's theme song. *Will it be yes, or will it beeee...sorrrry?*

* * *

The plan had been for me to move to Wilmington and get situated, and for Matt to follow in six months. However, when one of his and Geordie's scripts is named a semifinalist in the Nicholl Fellowship Screenwriting Competition—the most prestigious script contest in town—and for the first time since the *Esquire* film screenings, talent managers, producers, and agents are asking to meet with them, we decide that he should stay indefinitely.

I arrange to have my car transported from Los Angeles to Pittsburgh, where I'll fly in and spend a few days with Mom and Bruce before picking up my car, a bit of furniture, and an air mattress. And then, with printed-out directions from MapQuest, I navigate my way to what will be my house for the year.

In July, through the university's LISTSERV for students in the creative writing program, I'd discovered that a daughter of one of the poetry professors was looking for two roommates to fill a three-bedroom house a couple of miles from campus. Rent would be $325. (Matt and I are currently paying $1425.) I'd e-mailed her right away.

It immediately feels strange to be driving in a town with so much empty space and residential roads with 45 mph speed limits. And it feels even stranger when the directions tell me to turn right into what appears to be a very suburban-looking housing development, the kind where there's a sign announcing your particular development's name, e.g., *Willow Crest* or *Eagle's Landing*. As a bit of a spoiler of what's to come, my subdivision has been soberly deemed *Sawgrass*.

The poet's daughter is already living there, though she lets me know ahead of time that she's not going to be there when I arrive—she has left a key for me under the mat.

The moment I step out of the car is the strangest yet. The foreign sound of cicadas and the hot, humid night air hit me at the same time. In the photos, the house had appeared clean, plain, and generally inoffensive, but in person, it reveals itself as one of those charmless, white-carpeted, vinyl-sided houses with faux wood doors, bearing absolutely *no* resemblance to Dawson's family's cozy coastal split-level. I'm glad my new roommate's not there to register my disappointment.

But I'm exhausted from the drive. I set up my air mattress, call Matt, and fall asleep listening to the whir of the air-conditioning and beyond it, the sounds of the Southern night.

* * *

To ensure I can make it to our family's annual beach gathering, my mom has rented a house at nearby Topsail Beach, which is a short thirty-minute drive from UNCW's campus. Matt's flown in for the week as well, so we split our time between the beach house and my new place, where we're getting me set up.

And though my life feels unmoored, family vacation is the same as always.

When Matt and I arrive to the house in the late afternoon, Bruce, who "doesn't like the beach," has gone to get his car's oil changed. My brother and Jenny are at the beach. And Mom and Grandma, who have maintained their tradition of bringing coolers full of raw meat from home so as not to pay beach-grocery-store prices, are at work roasting two chickens for dinner that night.

Jinx, Grandma's 115-pound Goldendoodle, who looks like an eleven-year-old boy in a dog costume, is also present, currently eating chicken gizzards Grandma has hand-mixed in with his dry dog food, which she calls *gravel.* (I've never actually seen Jinx eat the gravel, just the human food she's put in around it.)

Jinx had been a gift from my uncle to keep Grandma busy after Grandpa died. Of course, no one had thought he'd get so big. Because of his size, Grandma's never been able to control him, and so he's gotten away with anything and everything. She was a pretty serious hoarder already, but after Jinx's arrival, her house has been *destroyed.* Her couches and pillows are torn apart, empty food containers are strewn in the backyard, and shredded newspapers and books with teeth marks cover the floor.

On Grandma's street, Jinx is notoriously the dog to watch out for, responsible for taking down more pedestrians than the ice-covered sidewalks of Pittsburgh. Grandma herself dislocated her kneecap because he pulled her down one day sprinting for a squirrel. But all of this is of no import to her. She loves that dog and will be damned if he doesn't share her Wendy's chicken sandwich and French fries.

Unmarried couples don't share beds under Bruce and Mom's not-your-run-of-the-mill-Christian roof, so I'm set to room with Jenny and my brother with Matt. However, since the *kids'* bedrooms are tucked away downstairs, we disregard these rules, having a good laugh at the idea of Bill and Matt, six feet and six feet two respectively, sharing one full-size bed.

My non-relationship with Grandma is the same too. We

haven't spoken since Asheville four months ago. We don't hug upon my arrival. In fact, we don't greet each other at all. There's no eye contact during dinner, and no one-on-one conversation between us.

After our meal of roasted chicken, Grandma begins boiling the carcasses for what will become chicken soup. Jinx stands by awaiting his inevitable gravel and chicken dinner. We kids grab some beers and suggest a friendly game of Scattergories.

Mom's in with a disclaimer: "You know I'll lose, though!"

"Scatta-what?" Bruce says before declining—he's got some (Bible) studying to do.

The following afternoon, Matt and I come in from our morning session at the beach, sun-soaked and hungry, tired from getting knocked around by the waves. We head straight to the kitchen to make sandwiches with the supplies we purchased the day before at the little co-op grocery store in Wilmington: turkey, tomatoes, organic mayo, pickles, and thick-sliced bread. But in the kitchen, we find Grandma on hostess duty with a ladle and a bowl asking if we're ready for soup, as if it's been decided that soup is what we're all having for lunch. I can see across from the kitchen bar that it's Grandma's standard-issue preparation. There are the telltale carrot circles, celery halves, and those wide, wavy egg noodles.

I have to hand it to her. It smells good, but I'm not ready to give Grandma the pleasure. Plus, I honestly want a sandwich, and I want to make it myself. And like a toddler asserting her independence, I tell her so.

✳ ✳ ✳

One night, later in the week, I watch as Grandma spoon-feeds Jinx one of her gravel and real-food mixtures. But Jinx, much to everyone's surprise, is refusing to eat any of it. "You always eat the marinara sauce at home!" Grandma says to him, and then to herself, "I don't get it. I just don't get it."

I can't help but think that if Jinx, who is at least twenty pounds overweight (which puts him in the obese range for his breed) could talk, he would say something like: "Grandma! Please. I love you and the food you make, but I'm not a bottomless pit here to absorb your Depression-era food hang-ups. And I get full. I am full! So, just leave me be for a little while!"

But then I suppose this is part of the reason why she loves Jinx so much, why he gets her full supply of smiles and hugs, because Jinx will never say that. If anything, he'll just lie back submissively and expose his belly for her to give a good scratch.

✳ ✳ ✳

One month later, I turn twenty-six on a weekday in Wilmington without any major pomp or circumstance. When I get home from school, I head upstairs to my room to open a package from Matt. He's on a Jonathan Lethem kick and has sent me a couple of his books. My mom and Bruce have sent me a check for $250, and last but not least, there's a box from Grandma. I open it and find a standard Grandma-style birthday card—a seventies-era image of birds sitting on branches. On the inside is a stock birthday-card greeting underneath which she's handwritten *Love, Gram*. I dig through the newspaper and find, packed between layers of bundled-up plastic grocery bags, a jar of mayonnaise, about three-quarters full.

I would have been more surprised, but it's not just any jar

of mayonnaise. It's an organic brand, and I quickly recognize it as the exact jar Matt and I had brought to the beach house now over a month ago. We must've left it there. And Grandma, being Grandma, must have collected it, brought it back to Pittsburgh, packed it up and sent it via USPS (*non*-priority) back to me, its rightful owner, four weeks later.

Grandma has sent me lots of strange things in the mail over the years—an eye shadow kit with fifty different shades to choose from, bundles of Easter seals, and cat-themed calendar tea towels from the 1990s—but this mayonnaise certainly takes the cake.

Without giving it a second's thought, I put it back in the box, walk downstairs, and throw it into the trash.

※　※　※

Though I won't ever eat Grandma's cooking as blindly or as willingly as I once did as a child, in a few years' time, our relationship will slowly return to normal. I'll stop refusing her dishes out of spite. I'll eventually even make some of her famous lady lock cookies alongside her in her own mess of a kitchen. I guess, somewhere along the line, I finally forgive her, and though she never tells me as much, I assume she forgives me too.

I also like to assume that the irony of that afternoon at the beach house wasn't wholly lost on her either; that when I wouldn't eat any of her chicken soup, Matt—whom she had so summarily rejected, whom she had so wrongly lumped together with my dad as a bad match for her offspring—had smilingly obliged her, taking a bowl alongside his sandwich and even giving her a definitive "Mmm. That's good soup!"

While I'm not exactly proud of the way I handled (and would continue to handle) my frustration with my mom and grandma, I do think that it's normal and natural to come to the point in your adult life where you don't have to eat whatever your parents or grandparents are serving up. This is my take on the classic chicken noodle soup. I've made just a few simple changes, but I really, wholeheartedly believe in these changes—the first being the crushed red pepper, the second being the mushrooms, and the third being the grated Parmesan on top. Please don't skip the Parmesan! It takes it from delicious to crazy delicious.

SPICY CHICKEN NOODLE SOUP WITH MUSHROOMS

Adapted from Alice Waters's The Art of Simple Food

Serves 3 to 4

For the chicken and broth:
2 chicken breasts (bone-in and skin-on if you've got them)
2 quarts chicken broth
½ medium onion, sliced
2 carrots, chopped
1 celery stalk, trimmed and chopped
Salt

For the rest of the soup:
Salt
8 ounces dried orzo pasta
2 tablespoons olive oil
2 cloves garlic, chopped
½ teaspoon crushed red pepper

½ medium onion, diced
1 carrot, sliced into rounds
1 celery stalk, diced
8 ounces button mushrooms, sliced
Grated Parmesan cheese

Combine the chicken and broth in a large saucepan and bring to a boil. Reduce the heat to a simmer and skim any foam from the top. Add the onion, carrots, and celery and simmer for 40 minutes—this length of time will work for both boneless and bone-in breasts. Turn off the heat; carefully pull the chicken out of the broth and let cool. Strain the broth through a fine-mesh strainer (discard the vegetables) and reserve it in another saucepan. Skim the fat from the broth and season with salt. Set aside.

When the chicken breasts are cool enough to handle, shred the chicken by hand into bite-size pieces (removing the skin and bones and discarding them in the process). Put the meat into a bowl and set aside.

To finish the soup, bring a pot of salted water to a boil. Add the orzo and cook, as long as directed on the packaging, until al dente. Drain, then rinse the pasta under cold water. Set aside.

Heat the oil in a stockpot over medium heat. Add the garlic and sauté until fragrant, 2 to 3 minutes. Add the reserved chicken broth, the crushed red pepper, onion, carrot, and celery and simmer for 10 minutes. Add the mushrooms and simmer for 5 more minutes, or until vegetables are softened.

Add the shredded chicken and cooked orzo and turn off heat. Taste and season with salt as needed. Serve with grated Parmesan.

Chapter 18

The Joy of Cooking

Though I'm probably close to the median age of students in my program, with my engagement ring on my finger and Matt living 2,500 miles away, I feel simultaneously older and younger. I'm both the mom of the group who goes home early to call Matt and watch *Six Feet Under* as well as the naïve eighteen-year-old who has arrived at her freshman year of college deeply committed to her high school boyfriend.

Perhaps this is why I'm now feeling very ready to set a date for the wedding—to make it permanent. Neither Los Angeles nor Pittsburgh felt like the right setting for the event. So in my spare time, I take solo visits to potential venues in North Carolina. One of these trips takes me to Bald Head Island, an island at the state's southernmost tip, reachable only by ferry and where the main form of transportation is golf cart. Not wanting to spend the money on a golf cart rental, though, I walk around on foot. I see Old Baldy, the oldest lighthouse in the state. I see a patch of greenery alongside the marsh just large enough to accommodate eighty to one hundred people. I see a red fox stop in the middle of one of the roads and stare at me. But perhaps what is most impressive is the oyster po' boy sandwich I eat at the little restaurant at the harbor. It's fried but not greasy, and the salty brininess of the oysters works perfectly with the mildly spicy, pale pink rémoulade sauce. This is more like the Wilmington I'd envisioned. This is where Dawson and Joey must've been hanging out.

* * *

I didn't realize the transformation as it was happening, but as it turns out, I have become a complete and total food snob.

Our little West Hollywood apartment where Matt still resides is situated within two miles of two different Whole Foods. It's also within walking distance of a Thai restaurant, a Chinese restaurant, and Urth Caffé, which serves delicious and all organic sandwiches, soups, and my personal favorite, a nori plum rice wrap. If we aren't in the mood for any of those, we could always pick up cheap tacos and burritos at nearby Benito's. And, of course, Joan's on Third, whose short rib sandwich recently graced the cover of *Bon Appétit* magazine, is a five-minute drive away. Heck, we even have a Persian restaurant on speed dial that will deliver hot lamb *kofta* and *mujadara* to our doorstep!

In Wilmington, there is no Whole Foods—not even a Trader Joe's. Instead, I split my shopping between a small co-op grocery store a few miles away and a giant Harris Teeter. And as for my takeout options? There's a Panera and a Chinese restaurant that looks so sad I don't even go inside. There's also a burrito place called Flaming Amy's that everyone raves about. Though when I try it, it only makes me think I should ask Benito's about franchising opportunities.

My two roommates are both younger than me. The older of the two, the daughter of the poetry professor, is a graphic designer and isn't around much. The other, Erica, just graduated from college in May. She's in my program, though we don't have any classes together. She's as sweet as she is tan, which is *very*. She has dyed-blonde hair and wears heavy black eyeliner and mascara. Her groceries include Diet Coke, bags of frozen, precooked Tyson chicken, and I Can't Believe It's Not Butter spray. In the mornings, I pour my bowl of organic cereal and try to hide my horror as she spritzes her white toast.

By the end of September, I realize that I'm not only a food snob, but I'm a hungry and helpless one at that. Without the occasional turkey BLT from Joan's or Matt's weekly giant-size bowl of pasta, the vast majority of my diet is comprised of things you might find in a United Airlines snack box: hummus, pita chips, peanut butter, carrots, cheese, and a few squares of chocolate. Sure, I'll occasionally find a ripe avocado and mash it up on toast or heat up an Amy's Organic pizza, but neither of these are exactly the kind of meals one can call *rib-sticking*.

Then, one day in early October, in the waiting room of the auto shop where I've taken my car to get an oil change, I pick up an issue of *Real Simple* and begin flipping through it. A full-page photo of a bowl of rigatoni pasta with broccoli, Brie, and pine nuts stops me in my tracks. The Brie is melting and seemingly covers every ridge of the rigatoni and broccoli florets. The pine nuts are glistening and toasted. And when I read the recipe, I'm surprised to find that those are the *only* ingredients: Brie, pasta, broccoli, and pine nuts. As soon as my car is ready, I take myself to the nearest Teeter.

Sure, I've baked cookies here and there, but this is my first time working from a recipe to make something savory, and I treat every direction extremely seriously, e.g., the recipe calls for pine nuts and I assume the recipe is no good without them.

So, despite my meager budget, I spend the $7.99—what seems to me an astronomical price—for a small bag of the teardrop-shaped nuts and grab the rest of the ingredients.

Upon closer inspection, I see that the list of ingredients calls for broccoli that's already been steamed and pine nuts that have already been toasted. Never having done either of these things, I have to Google how to steam broccoli (sans steamer) and how to toast pine nuts. I leave nothing to multitasking, waiting until my pot-simmered broccoli is tender before moving on to toasting the pine nuts in a dry skillet over medium flame.

The recipe tells me to chop the Brie "with rind" into one-inch pieces. Up until this moment, I've been one of those people who eats *around* the rind. I consider removing it, but again, I decide I must listen to the recipe *exactly*. Who knows what's liable to happen if I don't?

I cook and drain the pasta according to its packaging, put it back in the hot pot, and then add my chopped Brie, steamed broccoli, toasted nuts, salt, and pepper. While I stir the pasta and watch the Brie melt almost magically into some kind of one-ingredient pasta sauce, though I don't yet realize that this meal will mark the beginning of my love affair with cooking, that I will make this dish at least a dozen more times before I graduate (quickly coming to the conclusion that it doesn't need the pricey pine nuts), some part of me at least *does* realize that this is exactly what I need.

Because at the moment, my life is unsettled enough. I'm living in a ten-by-ten-foot room with a mattress, a bookshelf, and a pegboard with Martha Stewart's "Wedding To-Do Checklist" pinned on it. But there is nothing unsettling about a steaming hot plate of pasta made by yourself for yourself.

Because while Matt and I choose to live on opposite coasts in order to continue to throw ourselves at potential careers as artists against separate tides of resistance, I can at least cook myself a proper dinner. I can at least do myself the favor of boiling fat rigatoni noodles until al dente and then watching as the heat from these drained noodles melts the Brie, coating everything it touches.

BRIE PASTA

Adapted from Sara Quessenberry, **Real Simple** *Magazine*

Serves 4 (or 1 generously, with plenty of leftovers for the next two days)

Kosher salt

1 pound broccolini (about 2 bunches)

1 pound dried rigatoni

8 to 10 ounces Brie cheese

Freshly ground black pepper

Get your water boiling for the pasta and salt it. Use a big pot (5 or 6 quarts is best, as this is the pot everything will end up in).

Rinse the broccolini under cold water to clean it. Trim the very ends of the stems and then cut into bite-size (or slightly larger) pieces. I like to do this by using kitchen shears and then just dropping the cut pieces into the skillet I'm going to use to steam them.

Once all the broccolini is in the skillet, give it a couple pinches of kosher salt and add about an inch of water to the bottom. Cover the pan with a lid and heat over medium heat, checking on it after a few minutes. You want the water to be simmering but not boiling. Once it's simmering, it'll only need about 5 more minutes. You want the broccolini to be *just* tender—al dente, like the pasta.

Speaking of the pasta, dump it into the boiling water while the broccolini is steaming.

Chop the Brie, rind and all, into 1- or 2-inch pieces.

Once the broccolini is al dente, drain excess water from the pan and set aside.

Once the pasta is al dente, drain and then return it to the hot pot. Add your chopped Brie and then your steamed broccolini. Give it 2 or 3 big pinches of salt and a few turns of the pepper grinder. Mix everything together until the Brie is completely melted and evenly distributed. Taste for salt (it usually needs a bit more).

Chapter 19

Great Expectations

It's a Saturday afternoon in Wilmington, and I've written and read as much as I'm going to for the day. My roommates both seem to be out and about, leaving me the house to myself, and as I haven't made any friends yet—at least none that I feel comfortable enough calling up—I don't have plans.

I want to cook something again; it's the end of October and the air is just cool enough for a hot meal. But I don't own a single cookbook, nor do I subscribe to a single food magazine. So, I drive to the grocery store and head directly to the checkout, where I settle on a recipe for acorn squash soup from *Everyday Food*, that booklet-size Martha Stewart publication. With the recipe in hand, I gather the necessary ingredients. (This is, by the way, how I will grocery shop for at least the next three years—not on whims or driven by what produce looks good at the moment, but with a specific recipe in mind and, usually, in hand.) The grocery store also sells and rents DVDs. For $2.99, I go out on a limb and buy a copy of *The Baxter* based solely on the cover image of Michael Showalter and Michelle Williams.

Though my house lacks charm, the kitchen is bright, big,

and open to the living room. I crack a window to let in some of the autumn air, turn on some music, and get to work.

Apart from struggling to halve the squashes with a small steak knife, I find myself working through the rest of the recipe with relative ease, albeit a slow ease. I roast the squash halves in the oven until they're tender. For the first time in my life, I chop an onion and discover that they really do make you tear up. I find the biggest sauté pan we have and sauté the onion in butter. I add the squash, which I've released from its skin, some chicken broth, thyme, and half-and-half. I borrow my room-mate's blender and ladle the mixture into it in small batches, cautiously aware of the rookie mistake of overloading it. And by the time the sun has set, I've made acorn squash soup.

I put *The Baxter* in the DVD player, serve myself a bowl, bring it to the couch, and press PLAY. To be honest, the soup pales in comparison to my three-dollar movie (which is still a favorite). I don't yet know to salt as I go, that undersalted soup is one of life's most avoidable travesties. I also don't know that a soup like this could really use some homemade croutons as well as a dollop of crème fraîche on top. I don't even pair it with a large citrusy salad. But it's my second completed recipe and my first completed homemade soup. I'm simply happy that it's edible, that it exists, that I made it through.

If only I could approach other firsts in my life as openly and forgivingly.

*　*　*

Bruce isn't a very chatty person. On the rare occasion when he picks up the phone, we hardly make it through routine pleas-antries before he says, "Well, dear, let me grab your mother."

But a few days after the acorn squash soup, I'm talking to my mom when she abruptly says, "Wait a second. Here's Bruce."

And then, in the same tone he used to give the lecture on how to effectively ask for a raise, I'm told how he and my mother are going to send me a check for my entire wedding budget. This way, I can decide exactly how to spend it; I won't need to run each individual thing by them. And if I don't spend it all, the leftover money is Matt's and mine to keep. Of course, if I go over budget, that's my responsibility as well.

"Wow," I say, "thank you! That's very, very generous."

He puts Mom back on the phone, and I thank her too. Then, before we are about to hang up, she whispers to me, "Don't worry. I'll pay for your dress separately."

In chess, taking this money would be equivalent to taking the poison pawn, the pawn your opponent *wants* you to take—he or she is choosing to sacrifice material for better position. Because by taking this money, not only do I consciously and/or subconsciously feel indebted to them, but I also mistakenly see it as a form of capitulation, that they had come to accept that it was my life and that I should do with it what I please.

One of the reasons I'd chosen not to get married in Pittsburgh was to keep the inevitable head-butting with my mom to a bare minimum. And yet, with this gracious offer of theirs to not only foot the bill, but to do so in bulk and with seemingly no questions asked, I suddenly find myself talking to my mom about my various plans and ideas for the celebration. I tell her about Bald Head Island, how there's this grassy area right next to the harbor with the lighthouse in the background. And then without even thinking, I mention how I feel bad that Bruce can't walk me down the aisle.

"What do you mean? Why can't he?"

"Because of, well, *Dad*." It feels like such a strange thing to explain to her—had she forgotten about Dad's existence, which as she very well knew was currently a bit tenuous since he'd just undergone heart-valve replacement surgery? I'd spoken to him a few times since, and though he sounded like himself, it was a dialed-back, much weaker and sweeter version.

And then, in a move I thought I'd invented, Mom becomes so angry with me that she hangs up.

When I call back the next day, Bruce tells me that she still isn't ready to talk to me about it, which unfortunately leaves him to act as the mediator between us, which means that I must now explain to Bruce, my stepdad, who has been nothing but good to me my whole life, who has been nothing but good to my mom my whole life, and who of course is paying for the wedding, a fact which also stands as a tacit reminder that my own father is *not* paying for the wedding, that given all this and despite my dad's lousy track record as a parent, I would still like that he be the one to walk me down the aisle.

* * *

The beauty of my relationship with my dad is that at some point, I learned to accept him for who he is. Put another way, I learned to keep my expectations low. Very low. If he calls me on my birthday, he's good to go for the rest of the year. If he sends me an e-mail that's mostly about Neil Gaiman's *The Sandman*, but that includes one question about my life, I reread the question aloud to Matt, followed by a "Isn't that sweet?"

And the lack of expectations works both ways, which is nice. Or at least that's what I'd thought.

A month later, when I call to let him know we've confirmed the venue and date of the wedding, and he mentions that he would like my half sister Margaret to be a bridesmaid, I assume he's joking.

"Ha! Yeah, that'd be funny. And maybe Dolly can do a reading?"

"I'm serious, Amy," he says. "It would mean a lot to her."

Though I can hardly believe what I'm hearing, my response comes quickly, almost as if I've been practicing it for years. "If you had wanted Margaret to be a bridesmaid in my wedding, then you shouldn't have let Dolly actively keep her away from me and Billy when we were living together in the same house. I mean, I have *no* relationship with her. I don't even have her phone number. How would I even ask her?"

"You need her phone number? I can give you her phone number."

＊　＊　＊

But my mom and dad aren't the only ones who would like to rewrite history, or at least, to have my wedding represent a different history. Remember Grandma Morris? The one who took me to Burger King with the hopes of convincing me to move back to Saegertown over a chicken Parmesan sandwich?

Of her three sons, my dad is both the oldest and the one she seems to favor, and by *favor*, I'm referring to the fact that he is the one she is most consistently on speaking terms with. After my parents' divorce, she was quite vocal in blaming my mother (to her face) despite the evidence to the opposite (remember newborn baby Margaret?). In short, to say she's divisive is probably the kindest way to put it. My own brother Bill hasn't spoken to her since the early aughts. (And how I *envy* him.)

The previous year when I was still living in Los Angeles, she FedExed me what she referred to as her memoir, which she told me was an *amazing* story, a story I wouldn't believe and that we could "make millions" from if I sold it to Hollywood. Though, to be clear, she hadn't yet written the screenplay. What she'd sent me was thirty-five Xeroxed pages from her journal, which I did read. And though I had to admit that yes, Grandma has a flair for the dramatic—she and my grandpa were one of those couples that twice married and twice divorced each other—and sure, there was a reoccurring on-again, off-again lover named Jim, who took her to Mexico against her will (though it's not clear exactly how he did this and it could be interpreted as a vacation gone wrong kind of scenario), in the end, I did not turn the story into a screenplay, shop it around town, and sell it for millions. And when I broke this news to Grandma, she was miffed.

"Whatever. I think it's a big mistake, but…whatever."

And when I don't include Dad's name on the wedding invitations (opting for Mom and Bruce's along with those of Matt's parents, who are paying for the rehearsal dinner) since it was politically easier not to, she is really upset.

A couple of days after the invitations go out, Grandma calls me on the hour, every hour from ten in the morning until eight at night for two days straight. It's so precise it's as if she's set an alarm clock. She leaves messages that vary in content and level of melodrama. One lists all of the people whose hearts I've broken, including those of her neighbors, whom I've never met and who seem to be in the room with her as she leaves the message, "Stan and Pat are sitting here shocked. He is *your father.*" One message is just to remind me that she's been crying all day. Another informs me that my dad will *never* see the invitation since she's called Dolly and had her intercept it.

By the end of the second day, she's changed her tune a little bit, since she's come up with a solution: "You need to go to Kinko's and ask them to add his name. I know they can do this at Kinko's and I can see where there is space and where Dr. William Morris would fit."

I don't call her back.

But Matt does.

Matt, known for his levelheaded rationality, tells me he can handle this. He tells me how he'll lovingly explain the situation to Grandma, how my dad himself doesn't care about being left off the invitation, how it's just a formality anyway, but most important, how he's looking forward to seeing her at the wedding!

But Matt underestimates Grandma Morris.

He calls me as soon as he gets off the phone with her. "OK," he says, after taking a deep breath. "She's extremely serious about this Kinko's thing."

✶ ✶ ✶

At this point, my brother and Jenny have been together for five years, and in that time, I've gotten to know her and her family quite well. Her dad, Wyatt, happens to be an incredibly warmhearted Episcopal priest, and so, in the hopes of satisfying Mom and Bruce, Matt and I ask if he would marry us in a mostly Christian ceremony with just a few Jewish elements. Specifically, we're planning on standing underneath a chuppah, on Matt wearing a kippah, and on breaking the glass at the end of the ceremony. Wyatt agrees.

Everyone seems happy with this arrangement until for some reason, a mere week before the wedding, my brother tells my mom that we've asked Jenny's dad not to use the name Jesus in the ceremony. Though this is something we had discussed with Wyatt months ago and something that Wyatt had agreed upon months ago, since my mom is just now finding out about it, she is newly appalled.

When I call my brother and ask him why he would tell Mom this, especially a week before the wedding, an epic fight ensues between us, one of the results of which is that he and Jenny will no longer be doing us the favor of picking up our guests at the Wilmington airport and bringing them to the ferry terminal, a forty-five-minute drive that I didn't want my friends to have to make via taxi. (Full disclosure: We were paying Jenny $500 to act as our wedding coordinator, which is part of the reason why I thought tasking them with airport pickups would be OK, the other part of the reason being that he's my brother and she's my good friend.)

Matt and I are obviously the next choices to fill in. So, we spend the day in two different cars, taxiing groups of people— many of whom are my parents' friends—from the airport to the ferry. (Double full disclosure: The day of, my brother offers to help make the airport runs after all, but in my typical cut-off-my-nose-to-spite-my-face fashion, I won't let him. *Don't do me any favors, Bill!*)

Everyone's flights are on time. The only problem is that two of my friends, Liz and Ryan, who have come in all the way from London, have lost their luggage along the journey. The good news is that the airline locates the missing bags and we're told that they should arrive at the Wilmington airport by eight that evening.

And since I'm driving back and forth between the airport and the ferry terminal for the next five hours and I haven't seen Liz and Ryan in almost two years, they decide to hang out with me in the car as I chauffeur. And as I'm driving a borrowed SUV that seats seven, not only is there room for them to hang out, I'm happy to have the company.

By my last pickup at six-thirty, the car has become a mini-reunion of my college friends and their husbands. Everyone is so happy to see each other that no one wants to go to the ferry. They all want to wait with me, Liz, and Ryan in the short-term parking until eight when their bags hopefully arrive.

Meanwhile, my mom has spent the day cooking dinner to feed my nearest and dearest. I'd originally told her we could eat at sevenish, and when I call to tell her that the best-case scenario is that we'll catch the eight forty-five ferry, she doesn't sound too happy.

When the luggage does arrive and we do catch the eight forty-five ferry, everyone, particularly my London friends who have been traveling for more than thirty-six hours, is exhausted. They just want to shower and go to bed. I understand. I want to do the same. I tell them I'll send my mom their regrets.

I arrive at my mom's beach rental to deliver the news and find a somber scene awaiting me. The lights are dim. Bowls of dinner-party-ready food are covered in foil. I know she's going to be upset, but it's now after nine o'clock. We've all had long days. I hope she can understand.

She can't. She starts crying. "I made all this food."

But I'm not in the mood to console her. *I* want to be consoled. For lunch I had a packet of peanut-butter crackers while driving. *I* want to cry, to be taken care of, to be the kid in this scenario. I want her to offer to fix me a plate of food, to thank me for picking everyone up, to apologize for originally rejecting Matt because of his Jewishness, to apologize for telling me my own dad couldn't walk me down the aisle, to sympathize with me that Dad is who he is and that his mother is who she is; I want her to recognize the irony in the way she's been calling for all of these Christian elements in the ceremony when she herself seemed to refuse the one Christian dictum I liked best: to *love all*. And maybe, just maybe—and I know this is pushing it—she could momentarily side with me and tell me how lame it was for Jenny to bail on me after we paid her $500.

But instead of crying, I opt for yelling. "What do you want me to do? They all needed to shower. They're tired. This isn't about *you*!"

To which, she turns around, cries more audibly, and runs off to her bedroom.

But I'm not done with this conversation. I follow her, determined, passing through the living room where my aunt and uncle are working on a jigsaw puzzle.

Inside her bedroom, she's crying even harder. "We made all this food and now no one is going to eat it!"

"*I'm* here. I'll eat it! I've hardly eaten anything all day!"

She retreats to the bathroom. But she can't shake me that easily. I follow her again and watch as she slides down the bathroom wall and curls into a ball. "I can't do anything right," she says through her tears. "I can never do anything right."

She looks so sad and pathetic on the floor, head in her hands. And this is when I finally remember that my mom's not like me.

She can't go on and on, round after round of intense confrontation. I'm like the Russell Crowe character in *Gladiator*—thrown into the middle of the Colosseum taking on bad guy after bad guy until I've become a well-honed killing machine. First opponent was my mom; next was Grandma; then my mom again; then my dad; then my other grandma; then my brother and his girlfriend; and at this point, my fists seem to be permanently up, ready to fight. *Who else has something to say about this wedding? Huh? Do you?* [Swings around quickly in a boxer's stance and with chin jutted.] *What about* you?

But seeing my mom curled into a ball on the bathroom floor of this rented beach house is enough for me to call a truce already. "C'mon, Mom," I say softly, kneeling down. "I'll call them and see if I can round them up, OK?" She doesn't say anything. "I'll get them to come over, OK?"

She nods.

And soon, Mom's back in the kitchen. She tosses her Caesar salad with dressing and takes the foil off the large bowl of Ina Garten's roasted shrimp and orzo. A fruit salad with brown banana slices—clearly made by Grandma—also emerges. And soon enough, my friends and their husbands start to trickle in. Soon enough, it almost feels like a party.

* * *

Two days later, Matt and I are married.

If you look through our wedding pictures, it looks like

we pulled it off after all, that everyone came together in the end; that we managed to merge our two families' faiths into one beautiful, harborside, dare-I-say Martha-Stewart-esque celebration.

But looks can be deceiving.

Just as my Martha Stewart-esque acorn squash soup fell short on taste, if you peer a bit more closely at our wedding pictures, you might notice the careful, calculated physical distance placed between the various relatives from my side of the family not speaking to one another; you might see the tension between me and my brother, or me and both of my grandmas. And though our priest ended up not mentioning Jesus by name, you might argue that *He* won out anyway, as the photos also reveal seaside gusts of wind so strong that the chuppah Matt's mom made wouldn't stay in place, nor would the kippah he tried to wear.

And even though it's standard for everyone to comment otherwise, to gush as if the wedding day is a woman's beauty zenith, you'd see how tired and worn-out I look. My skin is thin and dark under the eyes, and my dress is a bit too loose from my first-time-ever sudden loss of appetite during those last weeks before the wedding.

When I was a beginner cook, Martha Stewart's recipe for acorn squash soup, with its simple list of ingredients and accompanying image of a pale orange purée in two matching white mugs, appealed to me. *I could do that*, I thought. And I did. Sort of.

As a twenty-six-year-old (read: beginner) bride, *Martha Stewart Weddings*, with its pretty brides, handsome grooms, happy guests, and charming DIY favors, appealed to me. *I could do that*, I thought. And I did. Sort of.

But recipes don't come with years of hands-on kitchen experience. And wedding magazines don't come with bold disclaimers on what a wedding really is: a high-stakes family gathering with multiple hosts. If anything, the disclaimer is: Get ready for the best day of your life!

But if it weren't called a *wedding*, would you really think that hosting a dinner party for ninety-six people and budgeting for it and trying to look your prettiest while doing so would be one of the best of your lives?

No.

Besides, perhaps the best day of my life is yet to come.

What about the day when quitting my day job doesn't sound impossible? What about the day we buy our first home? Or what about that one day we already had? We were in Big Sur for Sara and Sean's wedding. We woke up on Saturday to a big country breakfast, then walked the beach with our friends—it was late October and all of us were bundled up in our corduroys and sweaters. Matt and I went back to our log cabin of a room to clean up and accidentally took a nap instead so that we had to get dressed in two minutes to make it to the ceremony on that bluff overlooking the Pacific where Sara told Sean, "I give you my heart, the greatest gift I have to give," and afterward, as the sun went down, we ate dinner and drank champagne and danced in that crisp ocean-mountain air. My favorite picture of us is from that day. It's taken from far, far away. We're standing on the beach, and my back is to the camera and Matt is hugging me and someone's dog is walking by.

While I love butternut squash soup, Matt isn't totally sold on it. This pizza, however, makes us both happy.

BUTTERNUT SQUASH, CARAMELIZED ONION, AND GOAT CHEESE PIZZA

Serves 3 to 4

1 (16-ounce) ball store-bought pizza dough, at room temperature
1 butternut squash (see *Note*)
¼ cup plus 1 tablespoon olive oil, plus more if needed
1 large yellow onion, cut in half lengthwise and thinly sliced
Salt and freshly ground black pepper
Juice of ½ lemon
¼ teaspoon crushed red pepper
About ¼ cup all-purpose flour for dusting
4 ounces soft goat cheese (about ½ cup)
1 cup shredded mozzarella cheese
½ cup chopped flat-leaf parsley (optional but highly recommended)

If your pizza dough isn't already coming to room temperature, go ahead and take it out of the fridge.

Peel the butternut squash, cut it in half, scoop out the seeds, and cut it into ½-inch cubes. (This step always takes me a while, and since I'm most successful when using a rather large knife, I would caution you to do the same and not to rush. After all, how many times a year do you break down a butternut squash? Also, my peeler never seems to peel through all of that tough skin, so what typically happens is that while I'm chopping it, I end up slicing off thin slices of what's left of the peel as well.)

Preheat the oven to 400°F and set the squash aside while you get your onions started.

Heat ¼ cup of the oil in a large heavy skillet over medium-low heat. Add the onion and a few pinches of salt and pepper. Cover and cook, stirring occasionally, until golden-brown, 15 to 20 minutes. Remove from the heat and leave covered until you're ready to top your pizza.

Toss the squash with the remaining 1 tablespoon oil (and possibly a little more), ½ teaspoon salt, and give it a few turns of the pepper mill. Spread the squash onto a baking sheet and bake until soft and lightly browned, about 25 minutes, stirring halfway through. Once it's out of the oven, toss with the lemon juice, a pinch or two of salt, and the crushed red pepper. Set aside. Turn the oven temperature up to 500°F.

Line another baking sheet with parchment paper and set aside.

On a lightly floured work space, stretch and/or roll the pizza dough into a 12- by 10-inch rectangle—you're going for the size of the aforementioned parchment-lined baking sheet. (Mine usually looks more like an oval.) You'll find this task to be much easier if the dough is at room temperature. Transfer the dough to the parchment-lined baking sheet. Let the dough rest for 5 to 10 minutes (or longer if you'd like—sometimes I'll leave it for an hour or so while cleaning up or taking my dog for a walk).

Top the pizza dough first with the caramelized onions, followed by the roasted squash, followed by the goat cheese and then the mozzarella.

Place in the oven and bake until the cheese is melted and mottled brown and the crust is nice and brown, 8 to 12 minutes. Sprinkle the parsley on top and let it rest for a few minutes before slicing.

Note: You're only going to need about 2 cups of the squash for the pizza; however, this recipe has you roasting the whole lot so you can reserve the extra cooked squash for lunch the following day.

Chapter 20

A Feast of Failure

Once we've waved good-bye to the last of the guests from the ferry terminal, my appetite comes rushing back. We don't have the money for a proper honeymoon, but we *are* staying an extra night in our spacious island rental before flying back to Los Angeles together, where I'll be for the next three months.

We head straight to the restaurant at the harbor and order his-and-hers oyster po' boys with a side of hush puppies. I don't know if I'm experiencing repercussions from my unintended fast leading up to the wedding or if it's all the leftover adrenaline in my body from the trying day itself, but after lunch I'm still hungry. We go to the very overpriced grocery store and buy frozen French fries and Stouffer's French bread pizza, and even though we're leaving in the morning, Matt springs for a bottle of Heinz ketchup.

We open all of the cards we received and read through our guest book. And then, just a few hours after lunch, we eat an early dinner while watching television. The normalcy of it feels like heaven. And since we can't fathom trying to bring the top tier of our wedding cake home with us on tomorrow's connecting flights, we slice ourselves two large pieces of the white cake with lemon curd filling for dessert.

All in all, it's a great day.

Back in Los Angeles, Matt must return to work as normal. I, on the other hand, am looking forward to a relatively unscheduled summer. My graduate assistant job pays for the month of May, even though I haven't had to report to work, so my plan is to make that and my I-stomach-LA T-shirt money stretch through the months of June and July while spending the bulk of my days writing the first draft of the novel I hope will be my thesis.

But on the Friday of our very first week back in town, Matt comes home from work looking stunned. The Internet start-up where he's worked for the past year has let him go. We knew the company wasn't doing as well as they'd wanted, but still, we weren't prepared for this. (As it turned out, the company would go completely under the following month.)

After dinner, we take a walk around our neighborhood and discuss what we should do. I can tell that at least a small part of Matt is excited. He had hated the job, and though his title was technically *office manager*, he must have spent at least eight hours a week at Just Tires getting his boss's tires replaced. (Who knows what that guy was doing with his car, but his tires clearly couldn't handle whatever it was.)

"The good news is that I'll definitely qualify for unemployment and I'll have my days free to write," Matt says.

"*And* to apply to other jobs," I say.

"Of course," he says.

Last summer, right before I left for school, I'd picked up a job with the LA Film Festival selling tickets and answering phones for six weeks. I'd just gotten an e-mail from them with an offer to work it again, which I'd planned to decline, but now I'm thankful I've yet to respond.

We scramble to find a smaller, cheaper apartment to rent. Oddly enough, one has just become available across the street from where we are now. We apply and are quickly accepted. We'll move in at the beginning of the next month.

We hardly even discuss the other option, which is for him to move to Wilmington with me in the fall. We hardly even discuss it because Matt and Geordie have just commenced working on a brand-new script—this time one that their manager, Darren, "knows he can sell."

Though Darren and company weren't able to sell Matt and Geordie's previous script, "A Blueprint for Successful Living," the modern-day fairy tale/bildungsroman that had won awards and gotten them representation in the first place, they have a plan for Matt and Geordie.

They believe in their talent as writers. But it's hard to break into the business, even with strong representation. And as good of a script as "Blueprint" was, it was also quirky and strange, and as it's explained to them, studios don't want to risk buying such an off-the-beaten-path project from two unknown writers. What they need to do, Darren says, is write a "really hot spec"—spec being shorthand for *speculative script*, which basically means that Matt and Geordie would write this hot script first with the hope of selling it once it's completed.

According to Darren, something with a "super high concept" will give them the greatest opportunity to create a "really hot spec."

According to Darren, the title alone is fifty percent of the selling point. "Take *Jurassic Park* or *Alien*, for example," he says, "something like that would be perfect." Or something based on an historic event (*Titanic!*) or popular public domain work (*Pride and Prejudice!*) or character (any Greek god!).

Darren stresses that this formula will make the project easy to sell, and his bravado is mildly backed up by the fact that he recently sold a script that followed these very guidelines.

Matt and Geordie have plenty of ideas for stories they really want to tell, and so they immediately begin pitching them to their management team. What about an allegorical take on Joseph Conrad's *Heart of Darkness*, only set in present-day Hollywood; the main character is a young writer with a day job as an assistant to a heavy-hitting talent agent who tasks our hero with traveling deep into the Valley to retrieve a copy of a rare film. No?

What about a modern retelling of *The Pied Piper of Hamelin*, only Hamelin becomes *Hamelin Gardens*, a fictional housing development of McMansions, and the pied piper becomes Joe Piper, an eccentric rodent exterminator who promises to rid the development of rats once and for all. No?

OK. What about a present-day, comedic take on *Phantom of the Opera*? A community theater house is haunted by a phantom who aspires to become a director and thus, has a tendency to make head-scratching demands on the actors and production staff?

No?

OK. Modern retelling of Edgar Allen Poe's *The Murders in the Rue Morgue*?

No?

OK. A Roald Dahlian camp story centered around a cherubic, Godfather-like eleven-year-old who leads the Cabin Six Candy Cartel and controls, in abundance, the only currency in camp: candy.

No? Are you sure?

The weekly pitch sessions go on for months. But the ideas

are either, in the words of Darren: not high-concept enough, too character-driven, too execution-dependent, or too similar to ideas already in development somewhere.

After three months of this, Matt and Geordie ask to have a meeting so as to get a clearer idea of exactly what they're looking for. "If the story were a house, what kind of house would it be?" Matt asks. "Like, our house is typically the really interesting-looking one; it's well-built from foundation to roof, but small—maybe two bedroom, two bath, but when you pass by, you think that there's something cool about that house."

"We're looking for the biggest, gaudiest house on the street. The one you can't miss because it's ten times bigger than the others."

A few hundred mansion-size story ideas later, Matt and Geordie pitch them one they've titled simply *Safari*:

An elite rescue team ventures to a remote game preserve after receiving a cryptic emergency transmission. The straightforward rescue mission soon becomes the ultimate safari when the squad learns that the preserve specializes in designer game monsters customized to the hunter's specifications.

And after all these months of rejections, Darren and company flip for this one, certain they can sell it on concept alone. "It's like *Jurassic Park*, but with customized monsters!" They want to call it "Monster Safari." They say it's the sort of spec that sells for seven figures.

This is where we are when Matt gets laid off. After all these months of being in a stalemate, Matt and Geordie have finally begun writing a script again. And though "A Blueprint for Successful Living" took them years to write, they figure they can write "Monster Safari," a seemingly much simpler story, in a few months. Perhaps they'll even finish it by the end of summer.

In the meantime, we move into the smaller apartment. I report to the film festival daily while Matt files for unemployment, writes, and sends out his résumé. We eat a lot of pasta, Stouffer's French bread pizza, and Zatarain's jambalaya. (If we made a movie about those three months, it would be called *Our Simple High-Sodium Summer.* And it would have a disappointing opening weekend.)

By mid-August, the monster script is not going as quickly as he and Geordie had hoped; Matt has not found a job, and tension in our one-bedroom apartment is pretty high. So much so that I'm actually relieved to be able to escape to Wilmington, where I've arranged to move out of the suburbs and into "historic downtown" with a new roommate, Alison. The little house we're to share comes complete with a placard on the front porch officially marking it as *historic*, central air-conditioning, and a koi pond. What more could I possibly want?

* * *

I arrive at my new place just in time to say good-bye to Alison, who's off to spend ten days in Colorado with friends recuperating from her breakup with her live-in boyfriend, who just moved out. The house is tiny, maybe nine hundred square feet, but has four bedrooms and a loft space upstairs, which means that both of us get a bedroom and an office for the sum total of $350/month each. (Ah, Wilmington. Go for graduate school, stay for the reasonable rent!)

But within a few hours of my arrival, I understand why the price is so low. Downtown Wilmington is a bit hit-or-miss. And our street leans toward the latter. Before she leaves, Alison warns me that one of the neighbors is most certainly involved in some sort of drug ring, and "If you sit on the front porch for a few hours, you'll see the various customers pull up."

But that's fine. The house comes with an alarm system, and I have plenty to take care of to keep me busy. It's not until late that night when I notice that I keep scratching my legs. When I look down to check it out, I see I have a bunch of bites on my feet and shins.

Since I've never had a pet as an adult, it takes me until the following day to realize that the house is infested with fleas. Alison is hard to reach, but I get in touch with our landlord and find out that Alison's ex-boyfriend had two cats. And sometimes, she tells me over the phone, what happens is that when an animal moves out, it can leave behind fleas that have nothing to host on except the humans.

In the next week, I will learn everything the Internet has to teach me about fleas and removing them from a domicile. Did you know that fleas have hind legs that are so well-adapted to jumping that they can jump vertically up to seven inches and horizontally up to thirteen?

Thanks to an Internet tip, I take to wearing white knee socks while in the house, which keeps fleas, for the most part, from pouncing onto my skin. It also grosses me out to no end, however, when I look down and see my socks spotted with the small creatures clinging on for dear life.

I buy my first-ever bug bomb, set it off in the living room, and then sprint out of the house where I must stay for at least three hours while it does its work.

When I'm finally able to return, I set to vacuuming the entire house, hopefully collecting a bunch of dead bodies. And when I come face-to-face with my first dead roach, which is lying belly-up in the middle of our kitchen, I spend a whole minute feeling sorry for myself until I notice a couple of fleas have jumped up onto my bare legs.

Needless to say, this will be my first of many bug bombs and my first of many dead roaches.

Needless to say, it doesn't take too long before I hate Alison for leaving me in this stupid house, the historic charm of which I can no longer see. I also hate Matt for not being here to help me; and last but not least, I hate myself for not being able to handle the situation with just a tad more patience and grace.

⁂

After my fourth failed bug bomb, I finally call the exterminator. I'm so broken down and desperate that I sign up for an expensive monthly service. But I don't care. When Alison returns home, I bill her for half.

Ah, to be a flea on the floorboards and to have witnessed the difference between Alison's relaxed and restored demeanor and my own. Alison returns from her trip apologetic but calm. I, on the other hand, feel as though I'm inside of a Cathy cartoon. It will take me weeks to stop monitoring my legs for signs of them, to feel comfortable in the house.

In Alison's absence, Matt and I had speculated about how much she must have known about the fleas. She *had* to have noticed them, we both decided. So why didn't she do anything about them? Or at least warn me? But after a couple of weeks of living with her, I realize that she's the kind of person who may not have noticed them, or who if she had, could have just shrugged and carried on making her lunch. Alison's base state is relaxed and easy. She goes to yoga; she subscribes to *Spirituality & Health*; she cooks without using a recipe and makes large piles of garden trimmings, which is to say that she knows *how* to garden, which is to say, we are different in ways that fascinate me.

Despite an inauspicious start, we become fast friends, lingering over our morning coffees and nighttime glasses of wine. She makes the most delicious sweet potato black bean soup, which she serves with shredded cheddar cheese on top—imparting to me the basic lesson that all soup should be served with at least some sort of accoutrement on its surface. She roasts a chicken on top of a bunch of vegetables in a giant pot and invites all of our friends over. It's inspiring and makes me realize that Matt and I barely had anyone over to our new apartment over the summer.

Fall flies by in the way it always does when you're a student. And by December, I'm not only ready to return to Matt and Los Angeles, I'm also ready to try my hand at entertaining. I'll be there for almost four weeks, two of which we'll be dog-sitting for our friends Sara and Sean at their three-bedroom, two-bath house in Hollywood.

Before I can leave, though, I must go to the dentist.

Last year, I had a troublesome cavity, which led to multiple follow-up appointments, during which my dentist and I got to know each other a bit. It was right after Matt's script had been named a semifinalist in that big competition, and I must've overstated his Hollywood prowess because now the dentist seems to believe that Matt is something of a big shot, or at the very least, a working writer.

Up until this point, I've kept my recipe sourcing to *Real Simple* magazine and Martha Stewart's *Everyday Food*. But in the dentist's waiting room, I pick up the December issue of *Bon Appétit*, drawn in by the cover image of a towering, multilayered slice of chocolate cake with white chocolate peppermint mousse filling. Inside, I find a fancy recipe for macaroni and cheese that seems doable and that I know Matt would love.

Soon, the receptionist calls my name, interrupting my imaginary meal planning, and in another few moments I'm wearing a paper towel for a necklace and fielding questions about what Matt is writing now. I tell my dentist it's an action-adventure script. I tell him there is no hard deadline but that Matt hopes to have it done soon. He asks about Los Angeles and I tell him how the nights and mornings get chilly in winter and how the city seems to clear out for the holidays, leaving the roads eerily traffic-free. I don't tell him that Matt's not getting paid for this work and that, in actuality, he's been unemployed for going on seven months now, nor that all of our money goes into rent and plane tickets. Neither do we discuss the economic climate; how it's December of 2008, and the beginning of what people are calling the worst US financial crisis since the Great Depression; how it isn't a great time to dream or to be pursuing an MFA in Creative Writing either; how, really, it's a time to find any manner of available work and to sell dispensable things on eBay; how it's a time to have an undeniable, specific skill, like filling cavities and performing root canals.

I'm sent home with clean teeth, a new toothbrush, and a strong desire to make the cake from the cover of *Bon Appétit*. I'm not sure why exactly, perhaps because of the embellished conversation about my Hollywood husband, or the idea of having access to a KitchenAid mixer and a three-bedroom house over Christmas, or having just recently completed a semester of Intro to Cooking and Entertaining by Alison, or the issue of *Bon Appétit* itself—the beautiful images of which don't just give me the notion that I'm merely a numbered list of steps away from eating that chocolate-peppermint cake; they also subconsciously ignite the desire for the lifestyle surrounding that cake.

The overhead shot of a perfectly cooked apple pie next to a sweet-potato meringue pie whose tips are crisp and mottled brown doesn't just make me hungry for buttery crust and melted cinnamony apples. It slyly reminds me of the best things about the holidays: collapsing carefree into an oversize chair in your parents' living room, feet tucked underneath you, plate of pie slices in your hand, glass of wine on the end table, fire still going, dogs sleeping, and family members laughing, without a single flea in sight.

But whatever the exact reason is, I slip the issue of *Bon Appétit* into my oversize purse, return home to my small historic house, and keep reading. I make myself a peanut butter and jelly sandwich and begin to imagine, and then to *plan*. What if Matt and I had people over for a Christmas Day brunch? What if, despite never having made a cake from scratch before, I came out of the kitchen with this chocolate and peppermint cake on a platter? I can see it: the fire going, the Christmas tree up, our temporary miniature schnauzer by my side, our friends sitting cozily on the couch indulging in a slice of my miraculous cake. Wouldn't that be something? And something *possible* too. Not only could I make this cake happen, but I could have the cozy, moneyed lifestyle attached, if only for a day.

What I don't imagine nor plan for is the twenty-minute struggle for a parking spot in the Whole Foods parking lot on Christmas Eve, the trips to three different stores to find peppermint extract, the price of "good" white chocolate, the fact that Sara and Sean's kitchen, despite belonging to *real* grown-ups, still only has one cake pan, leaving me to estimate what half of the batter looks like, bake it first, wash the pan, then bake the rest of the batter separately. (Both of these layers, by the way, need to be to cut horizontally in order to arrive at the four total layers the recipe calls for.)

But after a day and a half, I have done all of these things. And what's more, I have done them ahead of time, so that Christmas morning, I can wake up leisurely in our temporary California king-size bed with our temporary dog in our temporary Hollywood, 1920s-era, cottage-style house with vaulted ceilings, at which Matt and I like to look around and say affirmingly: *We could have this by the time we're thirty-seven too.* Thirty-seven is because that's how old Sean is. (We conveniently disregard the fact that Sara is our age.)

Our guests are set to arrive at eleven, and so at ten-thirty, after a cup of coffee and a shower, and with Matt by my side, as he's become invested in my project as well, I finally begin assembling my masterpiece. We had registered for and received a cake stand as one of our wedding gifts, and we'd brought it over from our apartment for its inaugural use. Layer one is chocolate cake. Next is the dark chocolate ganache, followed by the white chocolate cream. Cake, ganache, cream.

Three more times, just like that, until we reach the final step— quite literally the icing on the cake.

This isn't just any icing, mind you. It's a fluffy peppermint icing I'd whisked with an electric hand mixer for eight to nine minutes over a saucepan of gently simmering water, until it resembled marshmallow crème, to which I added the extremely-difficult-to-find peppermint extract before moving the mixture to a regular stand mixer and beating for another seven to eight minutes, at which point it was just as it should be: "very thick."

But from the first moment's dollop of this *very thick* icing on the top layer of cake, I know we are in trouble—the sheer weight of all that sugar, egg, and air pushes the cake's structure into a diagonal panic. We move forward anyway, trying to ice it quickly. *Quickly!* As if covering it with icing might somehow save it from its ever-growing list. I ice and ice until we can no longer deny reality. The top layers are sliding off. It's now just a matter of catching them before they hit the ground.

For no real reason other than excitement over what I was accomplishing, Matt has been taking pictures of the process, and now, as he holds the cake in his hands, trying to slide the mass from the cake stand onto a plate, I grab the camera and take some more. It's absurd—like the plot of a sit-com. *It's Christmas morning, our friends will be here any minute now, and the dessert is in pieces.*

In the end, we decide the best option is to put it all in a large serving bowl. We scoop in the bottom layers and then the top, so that it *almost* looks intentional, like a trifle with a smooth layer of icing to cover all of the broken bits. Merry Christmas!

End of story? Not quite.

I'm enthralled with the chronology of the photos of the rise and fall of my Christmas Day cake. To click through them is like watching some strange flipbook version of a marathoner about to break the tape at the finish line and then suddenly, trip, fall, get passed, and lose. And when our friends begin to trickle in for the holiday potluck, I flip my digital camera around to take them through the entire progression. It's as if I've discovered a new scientific element. *Look! Look at what I found! This is Failure (Fa).*

Despite my twenty-seven years of life experience, I have held on to this childlike notion that life is somehow fair, that if I just work hard enough for what I want, the world will eventually comply and give it to me. (Specifically, I'm most interested in money and/or recognition for one of Matt's or my creative endeavors, though ideally *Matt's* because screenwriting pays a lot better than short-story writing.) And yet, here is tangible, unequivocal proof that if you work hard and follow the rules to a tee, your cake may still fall over and need to be scraped into a bowl on Christmas Day.

Hard work amounting to failure? My version paling in comparison to someone else's? It all feels so familiar, but what's remarkable is that it isn't painful. It doesn't feel personal. Because whether or not I can successfully make a layer cake doesn't factor into my identity.

Failure in food. Now, this is something I can work with.

Chapter 21

Arising Out of Necessity

Cake Wrecks is already taken," I tell Matt over the phone from my bedroom in Wilmington. "But what about Bon Appétempt?" I pause momentarily for his reaction. "Get it?"

"Bon App-attempt?" he says. "Yeah, I like it."

And so begins my new side project: a food blog. Going into my first post, all I know for sure, structure-wise, is that each one will begin in the same way, with an image of a magazine's perfect version of a finished recipe followed by an image of my much, much worse version. Of course, the first post will be the chocolate peppermint cake. And though I haven't picked out, nor attempted, my second recipe, I expect it to have a similarly disastrous (though possibly delicious) outcome.

My aim for the blog is that it show the inherent ridiculousness of the faux perfection found in the food magazines at the checkout line of your local grocery store. I want to show what we normal people are competing with: namely, the efforts of a team of professionals, from the chef to the food stylist to the photographer, not to mention all of their assistants. I want to show what life is like for the rest of us: messy, poorly lit, and falling well short of our aspirations.

Of course, more than anything, I want it to be funny.

* * *

The image of the orange polenta cake I find on *Gourmet*'s website wins me over instantly. It's both elegant, with glistening cross-sections of oranges adorning the top, and rustic, as the edge on the left side has browned perhaps just a bit too much and the whole thing (minus one slice) sits unassumingly on a wrinkled piece of parchment paper. Someone—the cook, I presume—has helped herself to a warm piece straight out of the oven. The rest she will slice, pack up, and take with her on a picnic in a meadow in Tuscany with a couple of her dear friends.

It's a no-brainer to make for the next blog post. Of course, I'm no longer housesitting in a Hollywood home with a well-stocked kitchen. I'm back in my humble shotgun-style house in Wilmington, living across the street from a local drug operation and next door to a nice woman named Lamonica Toaster (which I mention solely because I like to say Lamonica Toaster), and though I'm now bug-free, I still have an upstairs closet that the washing machine repairman/local handyman tells me I should occasionally check for *droppings*, as he once helped out the owner of the house with a "pretty bad vermin issue." Ah, coastal city living!

I do a sweep of the meager kitchen tools we already have, so that when I write down the list of ingredients I need to get, I also include basic items like a cake pan, a whisk, and a roll of parchment paper. The three ingredients I'm most worried about finding are quick-cooking polenta, ground almonds, and orange-flower water. At the largest nearby Harris Teeter, I find zero of the three. At the fancier Fresh Market near the beach, I give up on finding the last—convinced that something called *orange-flower water* has to be superfluous—but I find polenta and a bag of almond slivers, which I decide that I can chop into tiny bits. (We don't have, nor do I plan on purchasing, a food processor.) At the checkout line, I realize how pricy this whole endeavor has become and bid adieu to the five-dollar orange marmalade sitting in my basket, reasoning that this cake doesn't *need* the glaze on top.

My roommate is out on a date, and so after a simple dinner by myself, I begin to make my cake. As I'd expected, I run into problems right from the beginning. I make the caramel orange layer, but since I didn't spring for a pastry brush, I can't wash down any crystals from the side of the pan. I also feel very unsure of whether my caramel is "coloring evenly" or if it is dark amber enough; my attempt to remove all of the peel from the oranges and to slice them evenly into pretty cross-sections is a sloppy one at best. All of this goes into my buttered and parchment-lined pan anyway.

For the cake batter, I need two cups of ground almonds. I start chopping the slivers, but after a few minutes, I can tell that I'll never get the bits tiny enough. I decide to scoop them into a freezer bag and then beat them with a rolling pin. (We do have a rolling pin!) It doesn't take long until I feel a bit crazy—the sound the pin makes as it hits *some* of the almonds but *mainly* the cutting board is so loud, it's almost terrifying. It's also physically demanding. I realize I'm sweating through my shirt and decide I've done well enough. I mean, some of the almonds appear to be ground-*ish*.

The first step tells me to "beat butter with sugar using an electric mixer until just combined." I use the whisk and my arm until the latter feels like a dead, dull weight attached to my shoulder. But I must recover quickly, as I have three eggs to add, as well as all of the dry ingredients.

By the time I pour my batter on top of the orange caramel

layer and the orange slices, it's ten o'clock. The cake needs an hour to an hour and fifteen minutes in the oven. As it bakes, I clean up.

* * *

In Los Angeles, Matt and Geordie turn in a draft of *Safari* to their manager. Though the high-concept story is not one they would have arrived at on their own, I read it and must admit that they've made it their own. They've created an entire world specific to the story and the characters. I'm proud of them.

Over a week later, they get a brief e-mail from their manager, Darren, setting up a time to talk to them on the phone.

A few minutes into the call, it feels as if Darren has completely forgotten that he'd OK'd this concept. He doesn't like how they've created this new world. He wants them to reconceptualize the entire story so that it's "more *Jurassic Park*."

* * *

The MFA program I'm enrolled in typically takes three years to complete, but I realize now that my living in Wilmington doesn't work for Matt and me in the long run. I realize that I don't *stomach* LA after all. The truth is, I miss it. I miss the crowds and the sounds. I miss the feeling of being just one of the cogs in this big machine. I miss the grocery stores, the farmers' markets, and avocados. I miss our West Hollywood neighborhood and its jacaranda-lined streets.

I'd taken an extra class last semester on the chance that I'd want to finish early, and now, knowing this is the case for sure, I take an extra class this semester as well so that by this coming May, all that I'll have left to complete are my thesis hours, which I can do remotely from the West Coast.

* * *

To keep themselves from overthinking the story, as Darren doesn't seem to appreciate thinking much at all, Matt and Geordie hustle to get him a brand-new draft within a month. But when they turn it in, almost two weeks go by without a response. Finally, they get another one-sentence e-mail setting up a phone appointment.

Over the phone, Darren has a mountain of vague notes, but what's crystal clear is that what he would really like is if Matt and Geordie could time-travel back to 1992 and write *Jurassic Park*.

It's ridiculous. But they tell Darren they'll get him another draft soon.

And they will. Though they also start to realize they should distance themselves from the project; they need to manage their expectations.

Before they had even met Darren, they'd been working on a pilot for a kids' show set at summer camp. And as a way of distracting themselves from the frustration associated with *Safari*, Matt and Geordie reach out to a mutual acquaintance, producer/director and fellow ex-camp counselor, Will Gluck.

Will adores the camp script and immediately sets them up with his agent at ICM, who, in turn, gets them meetings with Disney. Matt and Geordie pitch the show, and it goes well. Disney is very interested. They set up another meeting. And then another.

Is it even worth mentioning that the third draft of the monster script is again shot down with notes and concerns from Darren and, that at this point, I hate Darren?

It's April, my last full month living in Wilmington. In five weeks, Matt will fly into town and help me pack my possessions into my tiny car before we begin the westward cross-country drive to Los Angeles. Apart from the occasional temp assignment, Matt has been unemployed for almost a year now. We've officially spent all of our wedding money (as well as the money I got from selling my wedding dress) just to stay afloat. And yet, our spirits are high because Matt has lined up another big meeting with Disney.

When Matt calls me after the meeting, it's by far the most excited I've ever heard him.

"They kept saying things like 'When we buy the show—' and then they would talk about the process of shooting the pilot and casting the characters," he tells me as I'm driving home from school. "They still want us to make it more 'Disney,' but I know this is it. I know they're going to buy it. OK, Geordie's calling me. I gotta take it. I'll call you back in a bit."

We hang up, but I'm so excited I overshoot the house and do a few victory laps around my neighborhood blasting the radio, singing along, and slapping my hands against the steering wheel à la Jerry Maguire.

I can't believe the timing. Matt selling this project now would more than justify our stupid setup during these past two years, paying two different rents and flying from ILM to CLT to LAX and back again. If Matt sold this project now, it would mean that I hadn't been completely lying all of the times I explained the practicality of our current living situation to friends and family—how we were doing what was best for our careers in the long run and how we had the rest of our lives to be together. Because in reality, there was nothing practical about it. In reality, we were taking a gamble; we were going for broke, not thinking about what our lives would be like if we lost.

* * *

By the time I've taken my orange polenta cake out of the oven and given it fifteen minutes to cool in the pan, it's almost midnight. All I have left to do is flip it out onto a plate. By now, Alison is home from her date and standing by for moral support. I place a plate on top of the cake pan and tell her everything I've done wrong so that we can be on the same level, expectations-wise.

But when I flip the pan, I can feel the weight of the cake shift in one fluid movement. And when I pull the pan away, a round cake with parchment attached remains on the plate. I peel back the shiny brown paper and there are my orange slices, embedded into this circular frame. I look up at Alison. Both of our faces reveal the same level of disbelief.

"A work of art is good if it has arisen out of necessity," Rilke writes in *Letters to a Young Poet.*

And while it seems a bit strange to refer to my orange polenta cake as a work of art, in a sense, it does feel that way. At the very least, it feels necessary, important. It shouldn't have worked out, but it did. And though I may not realize it at the time, in this way, it becomes a subtle testament against cynicism and for hope; that you can go about everything wrong and still end up with something beautiful.

* * *

At the next meeting with Disney in May, the energy has shifted. They're not going to buy the show. It's still too off-brand.

But, hey, they like Matt and Geordie and would love it if the two of them could come up with some more ideas for other shows, some ones with the Disney brand more in mind.

"Sure," they say. "We'd be happy to."

A VERY PRETTY ORANGE CAKE

Adapted from Gourmet *Magazine and Andrea Reusing's* Cooking in the Moment

Makes one 9-inch cake

For the caramel orange layer:

½ cup granulated sugar

2 tablespoons water

2 tablespoons unsalted butter, cut into bits

4 smallish Valencia oranges

For the cake:

½ cup (I stick) unsalted butter, at room temperature

¾ cup granulated sugar

2 large eggs, at room temperature

⅓ cup semolina flour

⅔ cup all-purpose flour

I teaspoon baking powder

¼ teaspoon salt

To make the caramel orange layer:

Lightly butter a 9-inch round cake pan and line the bottom with a round of parchment paper.

Bring the sugar and water to a boil in a small heavy saucepan. Stir with a wooden spoon until the sugar has dissolved. Let it boil, but instead of stirring, take the pan by the handle and swirl it every so often so that the caramel colors evenly. You want it to be a medium amber color, though don't stress too much if it goes darker (it'll still taste great). Turn off the heat and add the butter, swirling the pan again until it's incorporated. Then carefully but quickly pour the caramel into the cake pan, tilting it so that it's evenly distributed. Set aside.

Grate the zest from two of the oranges and reserve for the cake batter. Cut off the remaining peel, including the white pith, from both oranges, and cut each into ¼-inch-thick slices. Arrange these cross-sections in one layer on top of the caramel sitting in the cake pan. Depending on the size of your oranges, you will probably need one or two more oranges so that the entire bottom of the cake pan is filled with slices. (This way when you flip the cake, it will look supremely beautiful.)

Preheat oven to 350°F with a rack in the middle.

To make the cake:

Beat the butter and sugar in an electric mixer fitted with the paddle attachment until it's pale and fluffy. While the mixer is running, add an egg. Wait for it to be incorporated before adding the second egg. Add the reserved orange zest.

In a separate bowl, mix together the semolina flour, all-purpose flour, baking powder, and salt. Add the flour mixture, a little at a time, to the butter mixture and mix until all of it is incorporated.

Scoop the batter into the pan on top of the caramel layer and orange slices. The batter will be pretty thick, so using an offset spatula or back of a spoon, spread it out to the edges of the pan. Bake for 22 to 26 minutes, until the cake is golden brown and a toothpick inserted in the center comes out clean. Let cool for 5 minutes before flipping out onto a cake plate. Throw away the parchment paper. Ta-da! Isn't it pretty?

Eat while it's warm or at room temperature.

Chapter 22

Reconsidering the Oyster

My first time shucking an oyster is a thrilling experience. I've got my plastic-handled oyster knife embedded into the hinge of the oyster and am applying a steady pressure. Before I started, I was most concerned about slipping and stabbing the palm of my other hand—the one holding the oyster—but a few YouTube tutorial videos later, I realize that brute force isn't what's going to open this thing up; what's more important is the leverage-gaining, twisting motion, like jiggling a key out of a lock, only the lock is horizontal and my grip is a bit stronger. And then, just when I think I'm not going to get it, there's a satisfying release and clicking sound, like that of a heavy cast-iron trunk popping open.

I continue the same jiggling motion with the knife going around the circumference of the oyster until the top shell comes completely off. And there it is—the glimmering white and gray, translucent and opaque, oblong-shaped being surrounded by its own clear liquor. I bring my nose down to it and breathe in the familiar smell of seawater, or what Alice Waters calls "the vitality of the ocean."

And yet, before I tilt my head back and gulp it down, I suddenly have a moment's panic that it's a bad one, that I could very well get food poisoning and end up sick for the rest of the night.

It's strange, because just a few weeks ago, I ate oysters on the half shell at a restaurant and experienced zero moments of panic; not even a nanosecond of worry that the shucker of the oyster hadn't washed his or her hands recently.

So what gives? Don't I inherently have my own interests at heart much more than a complete stranger would? Wouldn't it be much more natural for someone who shucks oysters all night, five days a week, to let a bad one slip through the cracks than for me, someone who is shucking a dozen for herself by herself, to do the same?

Why then do I suddenly doubt myself?

* * *

Matt's and my second westward drive across the country is similar in route (I-40 for most of it) and destination (Los Angeles) but different in the feel of it. This time the trunk and backseats are full of stuff. This time we stick to the highway. We don't stop off in Vegas. We don't smoke cigarettes. This time it's not a joyride. It's better to keep moving, lest we leave ourselves enough time to stop and consider that once we arrive, we are going to be exactly where we started four years ago—namely, two more unemployed aspiring writers living in Los Angeles.

Matt has officially been jobless for a year now. The money saved from his well-paying gig at the Internet start-up is gone. We're now surviving on his unemployment checks, sporadic assignments from his temp agency, what's left of my student-loan money, and the occasional eBay sale of a designer purse or clothing item my mom bought me and I never wore. For the past four months, he's been volunteering at Cedars-Sinai, the nearby hospital, with the notion of possibly going back to school to become a physician's assistant or registered nurse, but apart from that and the occasional meeting with Disney to discuss new show ideas, Matt has nowhere he needs to report. As for me, once I've settled back in town, my only respite from our 1920s, basically un-air-conditioned apartment comes in the form of long hikes up into the Hollywood Hills.

In my yearlong absence, our apartment has become a bit cluttered and a bit bachelor-y. And when you're spending twenty-one to twenty-two hours of your day in your home, it's difficult not to want to *fix* it. (And if you're a writer procrastinating writing, well, there's no better time than the present!) So, in an effort to de-clutter our apartment and with the promise of Swedish meatballs for lunch, I convince Matt to go to IKEA with me to pick up some storage boxes.

Only before we actually leave, I overhear Matt on the phone with his dad engrossed in a discussion about launching an online pet/baby supply store. The theme I'm picking up on is that this is a good idea because people spare no expense when it comes to both their pets and their children.

Matt and his dad are very close—talking to each other daily—and very similar. They both come up with big ideas and are not afraid to delve into them with optimism, enthusiasm, and exhaustive detail. They discuss everything: books, stocks, the Pittsburgh Steelers, and yes, speculative ventures. Of course, the main difference between the two of them is that Matt's dad is a lawyer and can theoretically afford to embark on potential side businesses, whereas if Matt wanted to truly go into the online pet business, it would be a major career decision and making our rent would depend on its short- and long-term success.

Usually I love Matt's enthusiasm, but this morning, I don't. This morning, I'm pissed off that he hasn't been able to find a job for *a year* now and because our apartment is so small that when he has these animated conversations, I can hear every word. This morning, I'm wondering if this is how he spent his days while we were living apart. This morning, I'm convinced we're not even living in the same reality. I mean, am I the only one of us actually looking for a job?

The fight that ensues is the biggest of our entire relationship. It starts in our apartment, moves location to the sidewalks of West Hollywood, takes a brief intermission, is rekindled on the drive to IKEA, keeps going for the entire winding floor plan of IKEA, including, of course, the marketplace section downstairs, and persists for the duration of the drive home. Topics discussed include the idea that Disney or any other company may *never* pay him for writing; that if that's the case, he needs to decide what he wants his day job to be, realistically and in both the short and long term; and if that's nursing, then he needs to look into applying to *actual* programs instead of continuing to volunteer blindly once a week; and if it's not nursing, well, what? And last but not least, that maybe we shouldn't have gotten married after all!

That night, still upset, I exile myself to the living room. Matt tries to give me the bedroom, but I am dead set on depriving myself and hurting him as much as possible in the process.

But by the middle of the night, my anger has finally subsided. I crawl into bed and tell him I'm sorry for everything I said.

"No, I'm sorry," he says. "I get it. I've let everyone down."

And for the first time ever, I see Matt cry.

It's a horrible feeling, to know that you've made the most optimistic, cheerful, joyful, and sweetest man in the world cry.

And yet at the same time, I feel like I've been heard. At the same time, even if it's only for a moment, I see through Matt's optimism. For a brief moment, I see that he's just as scared as I am. I see how this past year has affected him, how I wasn't here to bear witness to his struggle to find work and, consequently, his slow loss of faith in his ability to do so, and how all of this led to the kind of low-probability schemes I overheard him discuss with his dad that morning.

But mostly I feel like we're finally on the same page—that he agrees the last thing we need are more big ideas. Between the two of us, we now have two completed short films, three feature-length scripts, one script for a kids' show, one shot, edited, and produced pilot episode of a narrative urban fishing show, five short stories, three nonfiction essays, a manuscript for a coffee-table book, an almost-finished novel, and a trunk filled of unsold I-stomach-LA T-shirts. We need fewer ideas and more *jobs*, preferably ones with health insurance.

* * *

Beginning when I was a kid and continuing well into my college years, whenever I told my mom and grandma that I was going to do something differently when I grew up that potentially required having more money, e.g., "When I grow up, I'm not going to drive two miles out of my way to save three cents per gallon on gas," and/or, "When I grow up, I'm not going to buy twelve cartons of Philadelphia cream cheese just because they're having a buy-one-get-one sale at the grocery store," the two of them always responded with the same three words: "Marry well, Amelia," typically followed by deep-belly laughter. The older I got, the more sexist and annoying I found it.

"You know, maybe I won't *have* to marry well. Maybe I'll enjoy a lifestyle that affords me the ability to purchase full-priced cream cheese on an as-needed basis all on my own. Did you ever think of that, ladies?"

Yet it isn't until this summer, the summer of Matt's and my second round of dual unemployment in Los Angeles, the summer I make Matt cry, that I realize how much I'd bought into the *marry-well* mentality.

Ever since we moved to Los Angeles, I had been relying on Matt to succeed. I had been *waiting* for his writing career to bloom so that I'd have the time and money for *my* writing career to bloom. While we were living on separate coasts, I barely inquired about his job search, because to be honest, I didn't want him to get a real job. I wanted him to sell his monster script or the kids' TV show. I wanted the big ideas. And what's worse is that I didn't just want his writing, his *art*, to save him, I wanted it to save me too.

Like the difference between trusting a professional to shuck my oysters and shucking my own oysters, it was easier for me to believe in Matt's talent than my own. It was easier to put the pressure on Matt to carry the family than to put that pressure on myself.

That summer was one of the hottest and worst of my life. And yet I'm so thankful for it. Because afterward, once we'd taken the pressure off Matt's art to save us, we realized we could save ourselves.

In *Letters to a Young Poet*, Rainer Maria Rilke famously implores his young poet: "I beg you, to have patience with everything unresolved in your heart and to try to love the questions themselves as if they were locked rooms or books written in a very foreign language." Well, in my version *(Letters to a Young Home Cook)*, I would beg the reader to try her hand at shucking an oyster and then to slurp it down in one go. There's nothing quite like it: the effort, the reward, the ocean!

RAW OYSTERS ON THE HALF SHELL

Serves 2

12 live oysters, rinsed and scrubbed
Plate or platter with a bed of crushed ice on top (or, alternatively, a refrigerated plate or platter with a thick bed of kosher salt on top)
Hot sauce (optional)
Lemon wedges (optional)

"He was a bold man that first eat an oyster" is the Jonathan Swift quote that opens M.F.K. Fisher's *Consider the Oyster*. And while I would agree with Mr. Swift's sentiment (though not necessarily his syntax), what I'm most impressed by is the fact that this first man managed to pry it open without watching a YouTube video tutorial beforehand.

When it came time for me to shuck my first oyster, despite all the directions I read, it was really the videos I watched of other people shucking them that gave me the confidence to give it a go myself. That said, here's my written advice for you first-time shuckers.

Place the oyster on a flat work surface, facing up (flatter side up and rounder, bowl-like side down) and with the pointiest part (the hinge side) toward you. Using a thick folded dishtowel (or wearing a protective glove), hold down the oyster with one hand. With the other hand, place your oyster knife into the hinge.

With pressure, start twisting the knife up and down, up and down. Keep doing this until you hear the hinge pop open. Once you're in there, go around the perimeter, making sure to scrape the top shell with the knife in order to free the oyster from where it has attached itself. The top shell will come clean off once it's free. The oyster should look opaque and wet and smell like the sea.

Next, sweep the knife under the oyster to loosen it from the bottom shell. (This way you'll be able to gulp it down.) Nestle the oyster in its shell onto the platter of crushed ice, trying your best not to spill any of the precious oyster liquor.

Last, you are bound to get some shell fragments in the oyster. Just clear the ones you can see and try not to stress too much about the ones you find in your mouth later. (At least that's what I do.)

They're delicious on their own, but also good with a dash of hot sauce or a squeeze of lemon on top.

Chapter 23

There's No Cream in Pasta Carbonara

As a beginner cook whose chosen educational method involves following somewhat advanced recipes precisely and meticulously, the first thing I'm struck by is how the majority of cookbook and magazine recipes gloss over many of the necessary steps or leave them out altogether. This is most egregious in the listing of the ingredients, e.g., "Two medium leeks (white and pale green parts only), halved lengthwise, then cut crosswise into ⅓-inch pieces," so that when you come to the section of the recipe that calls for leeks, it's understood that you have already washed and chopped them. It's therefore also understood that you know what a leek is and that you know how to properly wash one.

Matt's twenty-eighth birthday falls a week after the epic IKEA fight that almost did us both in. I tell him I'm going to make him one of his favorite dishes, pasta carbonara. The recipe from *Bon Appétit* calls for two leeks, ingredients I felt fine about when I wrote them down on the back of an old envelope, but now that I'm standing in the produce department holding up a leek, which is much larger than I anticipated—

more like a branch than any onion I've ever seen—I suddenly feel much less confident. "This is a leek, right?" I ask a nearby employee. He confirms my suspicion. I grab two and move on. Other ingredients that give me pause? The parsley. Curly or flat? I choose flat, remembering a recent episode of *Barefoot Contessa* in which Ina used some in her linguine with shrimp scampi. Last, I wonder why cream isn't on my list. Isn't pasta carbonara a notoriously rich, creamy pasta? But then again, I've never made pasta carbonara, so what do I know?

I arrive home and get to work, addressing the leeks before anything else. The Internet tells me to slice off and discard the root end as well as the dark-green tops. I'm then supposed to halve the remaining leek parts lengthwise, slice these halves crosswise, and place them into a bowl of cool water in order to remove the dirt. After five minutes, I'm amazed to find a layer of grit at the bottom of the bowl. Dealing with the parsley is much more tedious. I don't yet know that I love parsley, that you can eat the stems, and that as a parsley lover, I can certainly use more than the one tablespoon the recipe calls for. Instead, I spend more time than I'd like pulling the leaves off the stems, one by one, washing them, patting them dry, finely chopping them, and measuring one measly tablespoon.

Next up is another first for me: cooking bacon. Despite my using a pan that is so small that bacon fat covers much of the surface of the stovetop, this goes surprisingly well. The recipe tells me to pour off all but two tablespoons of the fat from the skillet. Novice that I am, instead of saving this precious animal fat for later uses, I pour it right down the drain in a move that I now know is referred to as a big culinary and plumbing *no-no.*

I sauté my leeks in the bacon fat, cook the pasta in a pot of boiling water, and whisk my two eggs with the Parmesan and some of the pasta water. Adding the pasta water to the eggs and Parm feels strange, but again, I trust that the staff of *Bon Appétit* knows more than I do.

The next step is the real head-scratcher. I'm supposed to add the drained pasta to the leeks in the skillet, remove the skillet from the heat, and then add the eggs-Parm-water mixture. Of course I haven't timed the cooking of the pasta properly, so my leeks have already been cooling for a while now. Second, who wants a bunch of raw eggs in their pasta? And third, I'm intimidated by the directions, which specify not to overcook and curdle the eggs or undercook them and end up with runny sauce.

Even though it's his birthday meal, I call in Matt to get some advice from a third party. His face falls. "Wait. Where's the cream?"

"There is no cream."

His eyes widen, like a cartoon character's. "I don't think I want my birthday dinner."

"OK, you know what? You're not helping."

On my own again, I decide to turn the heat back on the leeks and sauté them for another minute along with the pasta. Then, moving as quickly as possible, I turn off the heat and pour the egg-Parm-water mixture on top, stirring almost frantically for exactly two minutes, at which point I have to admit that it does *look* creamy.

I stir in the bacon and parsley, divide it between two plates, and come out of the kitchen smiling, ready to sell my dish.

"Don't worry," I say, "the eggs *totally* cooked just by com-ing in contact with the hot pasta and leeks."

But it's too late. He's seen too much. He eats half his plate skeptically before giving up altogether. "I can't do this," he says, and gets up to make himself a frozen pizza. "The uncooked eggs are all I can think about."

Happy birthday!

* * *

After our IKEA marital meltdown, life is different. Not only is Matt quite literally hitting the pavement with a stack of résumés in hand—leaving the apartment for long stretches of time every day—he has also signed up for an LSAT prep course. That decision feels sad, like we're giving up on our artistic dreams, but also strangely empowering. We may be struggling, but it's no longer as aimless. We have a *plan* now.

As for me? In between writing my thesis novel—which is due in a few months—cooking, and job-searching, I'm spend-ing my time organizing our tiny apartment into some state of viable dwelling.

One of these afternoons, I'm listening to music on my iPod via shuffle mode as I tackle organizing our bedroom/office for the second session (this time with IKEA-sourced file organizers). But soon I find myself distracted by this *mess* of papers under the desk I share with Matt. I had *just* cleared out this area. How could it have become such a night-mare already? But as I begin to go through it, it's clear what's happened.

I'd recently asked Matt if he could free up a dresser drawer for me, and while he graciously had, he had simply moved its contents to the cabinet under our desk, an area I had just emptied the previous week.

As I sort through everything, I discover a kind of time capsule of the various creative projects he's worked on since we moved to LA four years ago. There's page after page and notebook after notebook of research on topics from Django Reinhardt, the inspiration for one of the main characters in "A Blueprint for Successful Living," to Appalachia, the region where a different feature-length script of his takes place, to Stephen Hawking, the inspiration for another project that never really got off the ground, to, of course, big game hunting and mythical creatures, which they had used to write *Safari*. Then of course, there are drafts of all these scripts, some with notes that agents and executives have given them. Intermixed with all of this creative work are old time cards from temp jobs, new-hire orientation packets, paperwork on his stock options from his Internet start-up job, paperwork from filing (and refiling) for unemployment as well as a giant binder from The Change Program—basically a collection of CDs documenting various people's struggle with panic disorder, which Matt found helpful after that panic attack that sent him to the emergency room.

As I make piles of what I think can be tossed and what I think he'll want to hold on to, the song "Festival" by Sigur Rós comes on. It's a beautiful song on its own, but when I hear it, I'm reminded of the film *127 Hours*, in which it's heavily featured. If you haven't seen it, the movie is based on the true story of a young mountain climber who gets his arm trapped by a giant boulder while exploring an isolated desert canyon in Utah. He tries everything to free himself, but eventually (specifically, 127 hours later) he realizes that the only way he can do so is by cutting off his own arm.

The scene is gruesome and hard to watch, but at the same time, it's ultimately uplifting because he has finally realized, after five days, that it's not the boulder that's keeping him there, it's *his arm* that's keeping him there.

It's a nine-minute song, and as it builds and builds, I begin moving more things into the to-be-tossed pile, including a couple of scripts, which I notice have drafts of short stories and essays I've written on the other side. And suddenly, instead of feeling sad, I feel gratified to have a physical record of all of this *work*, to see it in this giant stack instead of as myriad separate digital files on a computer screen. But mostly it feels good to let go of it, to move on.

I've always lamented the fact that there is no map for how to make a living as an artist. We can major in Creative Writing or Filmmaking in college and then again in graduate school, but of course that doesn't guarantee we'll be able to make a living (or even pay back our student loans).

This is one of the reasons why I think I was initially attracted to cooking; a recipe is a kind of map.

But here's the thing: Even with a detailed map, it can be hard to pinpoint your exact location once you've started your journey, once you're on the trail and no longer just planning your route from the comfort of your own home.

When you start to cook after a lifetime of not cooking, you suddenly discover exactly what goes into a dish you've been eating at restaurants for years. And with this discovery, you can appreciate the *work* involved.

You discover that pasta carbonara doesn't have cream in it.

You discover that while there may not be a map for how to make a living as an artist, there is a map for how not to: by *not* writing, by *not* creating, and *not* trying. This stack of papers, I realize, isn't a testament to failure, but a testament to effort, to not giving up, to the work itself.

When Matt comes home that afternoon after a day of handing out his résumé, he collapses on the couch, admitting that he applied for a job at the Swatch store at the Beverly Center, the nearby mall that I find so palpably depressing, I avoid at all costs despite my love of shopping.

Knowing that he'll never even notice, I don't tell him about my momentous cabinet cleaning. Instead, I curl up on the couch with him and ask him what he wants for dinner.

This world recognizes results: clear success and epic failures. We're drawn to stories of those who made it as well as those who had it and lost it. But for the first time, I float the camera up to get a bird's-eye view of Matt's and my coordinates. And for the first time, I recognize the effort in our journey. And though we may be far from our desired destination, at least we're *on* the map. At least we're still trying.

I don't know if it's because Matt and I have grown up quite a bit since my initial attempt at homemade pasta carbonara, or if my constant repeating of something to the effect of how the eggs aren't *really* raw, how both the hot pasta and the hot pan in fact cook them, has changed Matt's mind over the years. But whichever it is, I'm happy to report that this meal is now a family favorite.

PASTA CARBONARA

Adapted from Jeanne Kelley, Bon Appétit *Magazine*

Serves 4

4 slices thick-cut smoked bacon
Salt
I pound dried spaghetti
½ cup chopped shallots (I or 2 shallots, depending on size)
I large egg, at room temperature
3 large egg yolks, at room temperature
⅔ cup grated Parmesan cheese, plus more for serving
½ cup chopped flat-leaf parsley, or more if you like
Freshly ground black pepper

Using kitchen shears, scissor your 4 slices of bacon into a dice over the top of a large, heavy-bottomed skillet so that the pieces fall right into the pan. Cook the bacon over medium heat until it's crisp, about 8 minutes. Turn off the heat. Using a slotted spoon, transfer the bacon pieces to a paper towel–lined plate to drain. If necessary, pour out any excess bacon fat (reserving it for another use) so that just about 3 tablespoons remain in the pan.

The rest of this happens pretty quickly, so I would get your eggs separated, Parmesan measured, and parsley chopped. Ready? OK.

Start cooking the pasta in a large pot of boiling salted water.

Turn the heat back to medium on the skillet with the bacon fat, add the shallots, and sauté until tender, about 5 minutes. Meanwhile, in a medium bowl, whisk the egg and egg yolks with the Parmesan.

Right before the pasta is ready to drain, scoop ¾ cup of the pasta water from the pot and add ¼ cup of it to the egg and Parmesan mixture, whisking while you add it. Set aside.

Drain the pasta and add it to the shallots in the skillet. Toss the pasta to coat it and then remove the skillet from the heat.

Working fairly quickly, pour the egg mixture over the pasta and toss until the sauce looks creamy and the eggs are no longer raw, about 2 minutes. Add the remaining ½ cup of the pasta water, then stir in the reserved bacon and the parsley.

Sprinkle with a little more Parmesan and some black pepper and serve immediately.

Chapter 24

Enjoying the Process

Despite our combined inability to get full-time jobs and the ninety-degree average temperature inside our apartment, that summer Matt and I do manage to fry our own chicken, braid our own challah, layer our own pavlova, and fail at our own semifreddo. We get into a system where I do the cooking and Matt takes the photographs with our point-and-shoot digital camera. I also finish a round of revisions on my thesis, teach myself how to screen-print T-shirts in our garage, and sell homemade envelopes on Etsy. At the end of August, when I see a job listing for a part-time sales associate at Heath Ceramics, a high-end ceramic dinnerware and tile company that just opened a beautiful new showroom five minutes away from our apartment, I say to Matt, "Honestly, if I can get this job, my life would be perfect."

These will of course become famous last words that Matt will hold me to time and time again after I do get the job one week later.

As a new hire, I mostly work on Saturdays and Sundays and stay in the windowless back room packing dinnerware orders. However, the mood at home lifts almost overnight. I have money coming in that isn't a sporadic payment from an eBay or Etsy buyer! Plus, on the days I work, Matt greets me at home with dinner already made, which, in my opinion, is enough reason in itself to have a job.

Employment is contagious. Matt changes temp agencies for a third time and within the next month, he finds semi-regular placement with a global public relations firm. It's tedious work involving a lot of data entry, but it's a job.

Matt finds himself on the Walmart account, and as I'm now in retail, the holidays take on a whole new meaning: they're about *work*. By November, my part-time hours have quickly turned into full-time ones and Matt's full-time hours bleed into overtime.

From the week of Thanksgiving until the day after New Year's, life becomes a series of transactions, of explaining gift-wrapping options, gift-wrapping, and of assuring customers that I took the price tag off. Traveling to the East Coast to be with our families is impossible, but since we're house-sitting again, we have extra space and can host my brother, who plans to visit us for a week over Christmas.

And though Matt and I may not have time to take him to the Getty Villa or to Venice's canals and the nearby shops, we are staying in this beautiful house; *at the very least*, I can host a holiday dinner party.

I have December 20th off and spend the day trying to re-create one of the menus from local chef Suzanne Goin's cookbook *Sunday Suppers at Lucques*. I peel pearl onions, braise short ribs in red wine and port, and puree potatoes to which I add so much butter I gain a newfound respect for the potato's absorption abilities. And I do all of this ahead of time. Tomorrow night is the dinner.

And somehow, with help from my brother and Matt, after

a full day of holiday retail work, I come home and begin a different kind of work. I reheat the short ribs—which Suzanne tells me are even better on day two—and potato puree. I slice blood oranges and toss them with almonds, chunks of Parmesan, dates, and arugula. I pour myself a giant glass of wine and I host my first dinner party for eight.

It's by far my biggest culinary achievement to date.

I then spend the next three days assuring customers I took the price tag off before gift-wrapping their gift.

"You'd like me to double-check? OK, sure. No prob. Let me just unwrap the whole thing and give it a quick check. Yep, it's off. OK. Now, let me just rewrap this for you. OK, great. Happy holidays!"

On Christmas Day, we eat leftover Chinese for lunch and burnt French onion soup for dinner (I didn't braise the onions with enough liquid) while watching the sci-fi thriller *District 9*. Happy holidays indeed!

* * *

Come the end of January, I'm dying for a break. And with my holiday bonus, I treat myself to a long weekend in Seattle to visit my best friend in the world, Mary Anne, whom I made up with a long time ago. She's currently a political science PhD candidate at the University of Washington and has always had an appreciation for food.

And so it's a no-brainer that we are going to make an epic meal together. For the week leading up to my departure, we send each other various ambitious-sounding recipe links. What about paella? Steak au poivre? Mussels and grilled bread with a homemade aioli?

A coworker of mine has recently lent me the cookbook

Living and Eating by John Pawson and Annie Bell. Pawson is an architect who favors minimalism; Bell is a food writer, and together, they make a case for the idea that the way we cook when we entertain shouldn't be that different from the way we cook for just ourselves and our family. Simple food done well is their goal. It's a gorgeous book I feel compelled to use as soon as possible.

Since we're going to be in Seattle, Mary Anne and I decide our entrée should be seafood-oriented. Over the phone, I pitch her the idea of making Pawson and Bell's squid ink risotto with scallops followed by a cheese course of Perail with endive. "I'm not sure how to pronounce it," I say before spelling it out to my French-speaking friend. "It's P-e-r-a-i-l."

"Oh, Per-*ay*," Mary Anne says.

I read Pawson and Bell's description: " 'The inside of this small round sheep's milk cheese with its delicate scent of meadow flowers has the same milky liquid charm as Vacherin Mont d'Or, but it's not as grand. Perail is a cheese to enjoy with endive when the company numbers just two or three.' "

"I love it. Let's do it," she says.

Upon my arrival, we grab cheap Thai food for dinner so that we can focus our energies on the next day's menu. Mary Anne has been into baking whole heads of garlic drenched in olive oil, so that will be our appetizer. To counter all that richness, I suggest an arugula salad tossed in lemon juice and olive oil, which we'll have before the risotto and cheese course. Dessert is the only thing we put off deciding on until tomorrow.

Mary Anne lives with her roommate in a little stand-alone house in a neighborhood in North Seattle, just a short bus ride to her campus at UW. In the morning, we sip coffee while scrolling through *Saveur*'s website debating desserts.

We eventually decide on a pretty-looking chocolate tart and begin making our shopping list. At which point, I realize that I didn't bring my copy of *Living and Eating*, and as their recipe for squid ink risotto with scallops is nowhere to be found online, we must tweak the menu ever so slightly to a recipe that is online. Spicy squid ink risotto it is.

If you've never spent the day with your best friend gathering ingredients for a giant two-person feast from various different markets, sans car, you really should try it.

We begin by taking a bus to Pike Place, the market made famous to me by the season of *The Real World* set in Seattle, in which a cast member (who we later find out has been having a secret relationship with one of the producers of the show!) works at one of its seafood stalls. We find arugula, endive, lemons, garlic, fresh bread, and of course, squid, though before we pay for the latter, the fish guys coerce Mary Anne into trying to catch a large whole fish, which they toss to her from the other side of the counter. (This is something they do there, which I also remember seeing in the credits of *The Real World*.) Mary Anne does *not* catch it, and we do not feel good about the way it falls on the dirty floor of the outdoor market and then is picked up (presumably to be sold).

We still need Arborio rice, vegetable stock, heavy cream, and chocolate, but we're most concerned about finding the squid ink, Perail, and the "digestive" crackers for the crust of our tart—all three of which Pike Place doesn't have. There's a cheese shop across the street, so we start there. No Perail. But Mary Anne knows of a gourmet specialty shop within walking distance. So, we walk.

Though it's the end of January, the weather is mild, almost as warm as it is in Los Angeles. The last time I was in this city was right after Dad had been given full custody of my brother and me, and we (my dad, Dolly, Bill, Margaret, Paul, and I) went on our first and last family vacation, taking a train from Pennsylvania to Colorado (because, remember, Dad doesn't fly), where we rented an RV, then drove to Seattle for the wrestling portion of the Goodwill Games. I was nine. So, in a sense, it's my first time in the city. And this is my favorite way to be a tourist: doing something I might do if I lived here.

The specialty shop has squid ink but neither Perail nor digestives. We decide to substitute with crème de Bourgogne, which Mare sells to me as "like Brie but creamier and richer."

We figure Whole Foods will have the rest of what we need. But as a postgraduate student on a budget, Mary Anne isn't very familiar with the location of the high-priced grocery store. We take the wrong bus and get lost. It reminds us of college, but instead of finding ourselves in the section of Baltimore where *The Wire* was shot on the way to get my nose pierced, we're in a very clean and safe-looking section of downtown Seattle trying to find an upscale grocery store.

By the time we do find it, it's close to two in the afternoon. Still no digestives, but we're OK with that. We grab some graham crackers instead and head home to start cooking.

Perhaps because the ingredient-gathering turned into a five-bus journey and in comparison, actually cooking them feels like less of a struggle, or perhaps because what we thought was an ultra-ambitious dinner menu wasn't exactly—like when the weather report says it's eighty-six degrees outside, but that's followed by a "feels like seventy-eight"—or perhaps because when you have a free afternoon with nothing to do but cook and you can share the many tasks with your best friend while drinking chilled glasses of white wine, the meal seems to come together almost effortlessly.

By six o'clock, we are eating baguette slices topped with roasted-to-the-point-of-melting, olive-oil-infused garlic cloves. Not too much longer after that, we serve ourselves inky risotto that smells faintly of the ocean alongside spicy arugula dressed in the award-winning combination of lemon juice and olive oil. We switch to red wine and sit down to the decadent crème de Bourgogne and endive, and then retreat from the kitchen and the table altogether for a few hours, slipping out to meet some of Mary Anne's friends for drinks and dancing.

By the time we return home, it's late, Mary Anne's roommate is asleep, and we're hungry for chocolate tart. We tiptoe into the kitchen, pull our chilled tart from the refrigerator, and then oh-so quietly, cut two triangles for ourselves.

And this is how we finish our meal, standing at the counter in the dimly lit kitchen, whispering and nodding in approval at what we've accomplished.

＊　＊　＊

The entire premise of the blog was based on comparing two finished versions with the expectation being that my version would always be worse. And in terms of aesthetics and the photography, this was objectively accurate. My version did *look* worse.

But back at home in Los Angeles, when I begin to write up the post about the dinner Mary Anne and I had made together, I know something has changed. I no longer resent the beautiful if not extremely unrealistic images of finished recipes found in gourmet food magazines and cookbooks.

Because these images are what got me in the kitchen; these images are what inspired me to start cooking, and now, a year later, I am grateful to them. A year later, cooking is no longer a novelty hobby. I must admit I enjoy it. I enjoy the whole process—from grocery shopping to eating the results, and even, on some days, in the repetitive nature of washing the dishes at the end of the night.

In his colossal *French Laundry* cookbook, which I once found adversarial, Thomas Keller writes: "These recipes then, although exact documents of the way food is prepared at the French Laundry, are only guidelines. You're not going to be able to duplicate the dish that I made. You may create something that in composition resembles what I made, but more important—and this is my greatest hope—you're going to create something that you have deep respect and feelings and passions for. And you know what? It's going to be more satisfying than anything I could ever make for you."

When I talk about enjoying the process, please don't get me wrong. I'm not talking about sitting at my laptop with a huge smile as I write or whistling as I struggle to carry all the groceries through the front door in one go. We all know that anything worthwhile takes work, no matter how much you love it. And I know that most days I would rather go to People.com and decide who wore it better than open up the Word document that houses this book. The best way I can describe what I mean by enjoying the process is to talk about making risotto. This isn't exactly new territory—a lot of people enjoy the process of making risotto— but let's talk about why for a moment. I think part of it's in the satisfaction of partaking in a process that's proven to work: you add a ladle of broth to the pan; you stir and stir until the rice absorbs it. You repeat. You see the results as the rice fattens and softens, all the while knowing that this process is feeding you—both body and soul. And with this specific risotto recipe, there's the satisfaction of your whole house smelling like Thanksgiving. I'm not sure why this is, but it's pretty amazing.

RED WINE RISOTTO

Adapted from John Pawson and Annie Bell's **Living & Eating**

Serves 4

I bottle red wine
Small bunch of flat-leaf parsley
¼ cup olive oil
I onion, chopped
1½ cups Arborio rice
2 cups chicken stock
1⅓ cups grated Parmesan cheese, plus a little extra to serve
2 tablespoons unsalted butter
Salt and freshly ground black pepper

Bring the wine to a boil in a medium saucepan. Meanwhile, wash, dry, and chop the parsley and set it aside. Bring the wine down to a simmer and keep it simmering as you pour the oil into a large saucepan over medium heat. Add the onion and cook, stirring occasionally, for 5 to 6 minutes, until softened and translucent. Add the rice and stir for a minute.

Get out your ladle and pour one ladleful of the simmering red wine onto the rice. Stir gently until it's absorbed. Continue this process, at no point letting your rice drown in the wine, until all of the wine is absorbed. Also, while you're ladling and stirring, bring the chicken stock to a boil and then down to a simmer as well. Once all of the wine is absorbed, start ladling in the chicken stock using the same technique. It should take between 25 and 30 minutes to get all of that liquid—both the wine and chicken stock—absorbed.

While the rice is still on the moist side, turn off the heat and stir in the Parmesan and butter. Taste for seasoning. Serve immediately with a healthy handful of the chopped parsley on top and perhaps just a bit more Parmesan.

Chapter 25

Crêpes Are Pronounced Krehps, and If You Make Enough of Them, You'll Get a Gâteau

After watching an episode of Julia Child and Jacques Pepin's PBS show, *Cooking at Home*, I'm inspired to make crêpes. I'm not sure how old Julia is during the filming of the series, but she's definitely older than any host of a cooking show I've ever seen before. She often gets a bit winded just standing there talking. And yet at the same time, when she and Jacques make crêpes side by side on separate burners, she keeps up with the much younger chef, crêpe for crêpe, flipping them sans spatula and with the kind of ease and nonchalance that I have when pouring myself a bowl of cereal each morning.

The two of them show me how to make crêpes Suzette as well as a gâteau de crêpes, which is essentially a stack of crepes with some sort of filling in between each layer, the entirety of which you might cover in a chocolate sauce. Julia and Jacques stuff theirs with thin layers of jam and chopped nuts, but Julia says (and repeats) that you can fill it with whatever you like. When Jacques cuts out a wedge, revealing what must be one of the top ten prettiest slices of food in existence, I know I have to make one.

(Full disclosure: I *have* actually made one before, but I cheated, using the Kenny Shopsin method of dipping flour tortillas in a mixture of heavy cream and eggs and frying them up as a sort of crêpe-imposter. It was delicious, but it also wasn't a true gâteau de crêpes, now was it?)

I like Hugh Fearnley-Whittingstall's directions on how to make crêpes. For starters, he refers to them as *pancakes*— a British thing I presume—which reminds me that that's all they are, just a French word for thin pancakes. Second, in *The River Cottage Family Cookbook*, he tells us, "Sooner or later you're going to want to toss them. Don't do it with the first of a batch. Wait until the pan is used to cooking the pancakes before you try to toss one." I like the idea of waiting for the pan to be ready. And soon enough, I'll know exactly what he means.

✳ ✳ ✳

By the summer of 2010, Matt's and my life together is as stable and consistent as it's ever been. I'm working four or five days a week at the ceramics store, and while I don't see a future there per se, it allows me the time and the freedom to cook, to post a new recipe every Sunday on Bon Appétempt, and to work through my professors' notes on my novel. Though my thesis *passed* and I now have an MFA, I also have pages of my professors' edits to consider before I try my hand at sending it out into the publishing world.

And though Matt did take the LSATs in the winter and he did well enough to get into some of the better law schools, when it looks like he is going to be offered a permanent position at the PR company where he's been regularly temping for months, we decide to postpone the application process. In his spare time, Matt has been working on his own book with Geordie, turning the fairy-tale script into a young adult novel. All the while they are still meeting with Disney to develop a new show called *Supersonic McMaverick*.

For the first time in our lives, we have figured out a way for our day jobs to support our art. For the first time in two years, we can breathe financially. And by our second anniversary, we can actually celebrate. We're doing it—for richer or poorer!

As for Bon Appétempt, I can't say that I have tons of readers relying on my weekly updates, but *I* rely on my weekly updates. Writing a novel can be rewarding, like solving some kind of lengthy word problem, but it can also feel like a drawn-out fool's errand, like a bunch of moveable and deletable words on a computer screen.

The blog, on the other hand, feeds me with not just one tangible product but two. There is the food, which is undoubtedly getting better, and then there is the blog post, which I can publish by myself whenever I feel it's ready to go out. Not to mention that the aesthetics of the site are improving, as Matt is now the official photographer.

Just as Jacques and Julia did, I brush my nonstick pan with butter and ladle the thin batter onto one side of the pan. I quickly swirl the pan around so that the batter spreads to the edges and then wait until the edges appear lacy. When I think that side has cooked enough, I double-check by pulling up the edge of the crêpe with the fork. When it becomes a bit mottled brown, I grab hold of the crêpe with my thumb and forefinger, directing it across the pan to its other side. Matt, who is standing nearby, is impressed.

"Nice work."

But Mr. Fearnley-Whittingstall is right. After successfully cooking a little stack of crêpes via this method, I do want to toss one.

In the video, once Jacques thinks one side is cooked enough, he whacks the side of the hot pan to loosen the crepe before tossing it, but I'm not that brave. Instead I grab the pan by the handle and give it a strong jerk. When the crêpe responds by slipping around in the pan, I tell Matt, "OK, I'm gonna flip it."

It's a strange feeling. Though I've never flipped a crêpe with just the flick of my wrist before, my wrist seems to know what to do. It's ready to go. It's my head that hesitates, that momentarily imagines the crêpe falling onto the burner and catching fire. But fortunately, my curiosity wins out. My wrist goes for it. The crêpe is tossed and lands perfectly on its other side. I can hardly wait to do it again.

You need a lot of crêpes for a gâteau, about fifteen, and once I've reached the end of my batter, I feel a little Pepin-esque. I'm not banging the side of the pan with the raw heel of my hand, but it no longer seems like a bad idea.

To put my own very slight twist on the recipe, I'm using apricot jam—as opposed to what appeared to be strawberry in the video—and chopped walnuts. I lay down a crêpe, follow it with a thin layer of jam followed by a spoonful or two of the nuts, and repeat. I pour chocolate sauce over the whole thing, though I heed Julia's warning not to cover the top entirely so that you can still see the brown speckles of the uppermost pancake, declaring its status as a crêpe cake.

* * *

In *Anam Cara: A Book of Celtic Wisdom*, the poet and philosopher John O'Donohue writes, "Where things are moving too quickly, nothing can stabilize, gather, or grow."

He then tells a brief story about a man exploring Africa who is on a deadline to make it to a certain destination by a certain time. The man has hired three or four native Africans to help him make this speedy journey, but after three days of intense traveling, the Africans stop. They will go no farther. The man pleads with them, telling them how important it is that he makes his deadline, but they won't budge. After continuing to ask them why, he finally gets an answer. One of them says, "We have moved too quickly to reach here; now we need to wait to give our spirits a chance to catch up with us."

I sometimes worry about what would have happened to Matt and me had things turned out differently, had he become a Hollywood director at age twenty-three like he'd planned. I sometimes worry about what would have happened had I not followed my impulse to make that giant chocolate peppermint cake, if it hadn't fallen over so spectacularly, if I hadn't started Bon Appétempt, and for the first couple of years of its life, when I would ask my mom why she refused to read it, if she had responded with something other than an indifferent: "How do you spell it again?"

Because all of these so-called failures allowed us to come up with our own definition of success.

Because all of these so-called failures gave our spirits the chance to catch up with us.

Because all of these so-called failures taught me that though writers would like readers as much as chefs would like eaters, at the end of the day, if there are none of either to be found, we can continue creating anyway just to feed ourselves.

A STRAWBERRY AND CREAM GÂTEAU DE CRÊPES COVERED IN CHOCOLATE SAUCE

Inspired by Jacques Pépin, **Food & Wine** *Magazine with Chocolate Sauce Adapted from David Lebovitz*

Serves 6 to 8

For the crêpes:

4 large eggs

1½ cups all-purpose flour

1 cup whole milk

¼ teaspoon salt

1 teaspoon sugar

⅔ cup cold water

1 tablespoon cognac or brandy

4 tablespoons unsalted butter, melted and slightly cooled, plus more for the skillet

For the strawberries and cream:

1 pound strawberries (or another berry of your choice), chopped into ¼-inch pieces

⅓ cup sugar

2 cups heavy cream

1 teaspoon vanilla extract (optional)

For the chocolate sauce:

½ cup water

¼ cup sugar

¼ cup light corn syrup

Scant ⅓ cup unsweetened cocoa powder

3 tablespoons finely chopped bittersweet chocolate

To make the crêpes:

In a medium bowl, whisk together the eggs, flour, milk, salt, and sugar until smooth; the batter will be thick. Whisk in the cold water, cognac, and melted butter.

Heat a 9-inch crêpe pan or nonstick skillet over medium-high heat and rub it with a little butter. (The batter is so buttery that you don't need much.) Add a ladle of the batter to one side of the pan and tilt the skillet to distribute it evenly. (If the batter isn't moving across the skillet with ease, it may be too thick. In this case, add another tablespoon or two of cold water to it.) Cook the crêpe until the edges curl up and start to brown, about 45 seconds, though for the first one, your pan may not be hot enough, so don't stress if it takes longer. Flip the crêpe. (As I mentioned, for the first few, I usually do this by pulling up on an edge with a fork and then grabbing hold with my pointer finger and thumb and quickly dragging it across the pan to its other side.) Cook for 30 seconds longer, or until a few brown spots appear on the bottom. Slide the crêpe out onto a plate. Repeat with the remaining batter to make 12 to 14 crêpes total.

To make the strawberries and cream:

Toss the strawberries in a shallow bowl with half of the sugar and leave for 10 minutes, stirring occasionally, until the berries are sitting in a nice syrup. Using a potato masher, gently mash the strawberries until they're pretty well macerated. Set aside.

Whip the cream with the remaining sugar and the vanilla until it's very stiff and holds peaks easily. Fold the berries and cream together and pop into the refrigerator until you're ready to assemble the cake.

To make the chocolate sauce:

Whisk together the water, sugar, corn syrup, and cocoa powder in a saucepan. Bring to a boil over medium heat. Take it off the heat and stir in the chopped chocolate until melted. Let stand for at least 10 minutes. If the sauce is at all lumpy, strain it through a fine-mesh strainer.

To assemble the cake:

Place a crêpe on a platter. Top with two heaping tablespoons (and maybe a bit more) of the strawberry and cream mixture. Spread to the edges as evenly as possible using an offset spatula or the back of the spoon. Repeat with the remaining crêpes and strawberry and cream mixture, leaving the last crêpe with nothing on top (because, of course, you're about to douse it with chocolate sauce!). Pour the chocolate sauce over the top of the crêpe tower, being careful not to cover it completely so that everyone can still partially see the beautiful stack of crêpes and strawberries and cream underneath. (You should have chocolate sauce left over, which I advise you to bring to the table so your guests can spoon extra over their slices.)

Chapter 26

Embrace Yourself, Avoid Canola Oil

Our family's annual beach vacation is a tradition that began with my maternal grandparents taking my mom and her brother to the Jersey Shore each summer, and is one that is currently upheld entirely by my mother. She handles all the arrangements herself, from booking the house to paying for the house to covering all of the travel expenses accrued by her children and their significant others to get to the house. She *lives* for these vacations, typically planning the next one while we're in the midst of the current one.

However, we no longer go to the Jersey Shore. We bounce around from beach to beach with no loyalties to any one in particular. This year, Mom has chosen Kiawah Island in South Carolina, as it's an easy drive for my brother to make from Charlotte.

And though Grandma, now ninety-one, has stopped coming along, Mom is channeling her Great Depression roots on her behalf. So much so that it's almost as if Mom was the one whose pet bunny got sold to the neighbors for dinner and who had to endure days on end unsure of when her next meal might be. Because just like Grandma would, Mom has taken it upon herself to bring as much food as she can from Pittsburgh, including a cooler full of seafood and meat—once again dodging the overpriced beach grocery store.

Bruce, on the other hand, who, remember, "doesn't like the beach" and whom I've never seen more than ankle-deep in the cool ocean water, comes because it's what Mom wants and divides his time between flying his kite and riding his bike— two activities that his body can still handle after college football, Vietnam, and the ensuing twenty or so major surgeries.

I think they are two activities that he *enjoys* too, but it's difficult to say. In my parents' townhouse, the walls of Bruce's third-floor office are covered with plaques and certificates marking his many accomplishments and awards, one of which refers to him as, "The Rock," a title given to him—as told to my college boyfriend David—because throughout his time in the Naval Academy and in Vietnam (and despite what I can only imagine was the most intense kind of peer pressure), he never got drunk *once*. And while I find this commendable, his strict teetotaling ways seem to push him even further to the fringes of our little family.

Through the years, I have watched him try to send off my (twenty-one and older) friends on their way to the airport with the leftover beer that they'd brought as a hostess gift—you know, as one typically does when they are invited to dinner at someone's house; I have seen him wave off champagne for the champagne toast at weddings, and express wariness of Matt driving home after drinking a glass of wine with a two-hour dinner.

But his nickname extends far beyond alcohol.

His demeanor is rocklike. I've never seen him angry. I've never seen him yell. But I've also never seen him laugh uncontrollably. I've never seen him shout at the television in excitement while watching football ("Get him! Get him!") like the rest of my family does. I've never seen him fawn over a perfectly cooked steak. While watching a live music performance during Mom's favorite show, *Dancing with the Stars*, he once asked Matt and me why the band felt like they had to "dress that way." Matt and I took another look at the screen to see what we were missing. The lead singer wore sunglasses, a T-shirt, jeans, a leather jacket, and neon sneakers. "Uhm, well, you know, they're artists and clothes are just another way to express yourself," I said after a few awkward moments.

He's maintained his weight at 180 pounds or less for the past forty-odd years. He lives life according to specific tenets and rules, one of which comes into play every family vacation. It's the one about unmarried couples not sharing bedrooms— a rule that, although familiar, will pose a particular problem at this year's gathering.

Matt and I take a red-eye flight from LA to Raleigh; from there, we catch an early morning flight to Charleston, where Bruce picks us up and drives us the forty minutes to Kiawah. Matt doesn't ever sleep on planes, so by the time we arrive, he's in dire need of a nap. But Bruce, Mom, my brother, and his newish girlfriend, Katherine, got in yesterday afternoon, and when we walk in the front door, they're already clad in their swimsuits, gathered in the living room, ready to hit the beach.

It's my first time meeting Katherine, whom Bill has been dating for about six months now. (Bill and Jenny broke up a few months after Matt's and my wedding, and though my brother never admitted as much, I'm sure that the wedding planner–related issues I had with her were sadly at least partially to blame.) But I'm distracted by my brother, who's pulled Matt aside to bring him up to date on the situation at hand. "We're not going to be staying long. I'm in the kids' room. Super tiny beds," he says, holding his hands six inches apart to illustrate just how tiny.

Mom notices and throws her hands up in the air, exasperated almost to the point of squealing, "I'm sorry! It said it was a four-bedroom."

There are technically four bedrooms, but two are basically masters, then there's a modest guest room with a full bed (Katherine's), and a playroom with two twin beds that do seem tinier than your average twin bed.

Bruce, who has been trained to survive in the jungle without so much as a Swiss Army knife, offers to take the room with the twin beds. "It doesn't matter to me," he says, blank-faced.

Mom shrugs, defeated.

It should be noted that Mom and Bruce don't sleep in the same bed anyway. Since Bruce goes to sleep promptly at ten p.m., and Mom likes to stay up and fall asleep watching television, they've long slept separately at home—Bruce in the bedroom and Mom taking the downstairs couch. And even though I understand that just because you love someone doesn't mean you have similar sleep patterns, it's also not something we openly discuss as a family. Thus, neither Bill nor I can point this out as a viable fix.

Plus, the minute my brother and I occupy the same space, our childhood rivalry comes alive. So while part of me understands his frustration, that it's not just about sleeping in an uncomfortable bed, it's about wanting to be treated like a grown-up. It's about the fact that while, yes, he may have struggled in the past with unemployment, debt, and a failed six-year relationship, the truth is he's doing quite well now. At thirty-one, he has a full-time, tenure-track job with health benefits as a lecturer in the English department at a large community college in Charlotte, North Carolina. He has students and colleagues who respect him, a girlfriend who adores him, and, in fact, he's looking to buy a house.

And yet, despite all of these accomplishments, in this rented beach house, his unmarried status relegates him to a child's room with a child-size bed surrounded by children's toys. All of this coupled with the never-mentioned fact that because I lived with Mom and Bruce for three years in high school, while Bill stayed the (depressing) course in Saegertown, Bill must feel at least some twinge of outsiderdom when we all get together.

All of this I get. Or, at least I try to. But at the same time, the other part of me, the little sister who grew up in his constant shadow and who just arrived after a day of traveling, wants him to chill out and suck it up.

Besides, I have my own things to prove to my family. I want them to see that I'm also doing well. I'm happily married; I'm pursuing my dreams; and, in the past year, I've created a food blog people seem to actually read. And what better way to show all of this than for Matt and me to cook dinner for everyone?

Much to Mom's chagrin, she realizes she's forgotten a few ingredients for the evening meal and needs to run to the store. Matt and I decide to tag along in order to gather what we'll need for the dinner we're going to make: what has become (at least between the two of us) his famous lemon pasta, and to go with it, an arugula salad.

Once at the store, the three of us split up; Matt's in charge of grabbing the pasta ingredients and I'm in charge of the ones for the salad.

I'm just about finished when Mom finds me.

"What do you need the olive oil for?" she asks—her eyes squinting with suspicion.

"Oh, I was gonna ask you. Do we already have some at the house?"

"No, but I have canola."

"This is for the salad dressing. We can't use canola for salad dressing."

"Why not?"

I can feel my head cock slightly to the side. "Well," I start to say, knowing what I'd *like* to say: We can't use canola for salad dressing because no recipe I've ever read has called for canola in a salad dressing. If anything, the recipes I've read call for "good olive oil," and the brand I have in my cart is definitely already a step down from *good*. But I know my mother, and I can see her jaw is already tightening.

"So, you want to get a whole thing of olive oil for *one* week at the beach?" she says.

"Don't worry, I'm going to pay for all of this myself."

She shakes her head and walks away.

I find Matt, who has a full basket of his own, and soon enough, we're in the checkout line behind my mom.

"Fancy meeting you here!" I say, smiling.

She rolls her eyes at me, but reaches for my basket of supplies. "Just give it to me."

"Mom, we seriously don't mind paying for this."

But she is already placing our items on the conveyor belt. "No, no. I'm not going to let you—coffee filters!" she says, interrupting herself, almost choking on the words.

On the drive home, Matt and I are told that we would *not* have made it through the Great Depression. "I mean, coffee filters?"

Mom makes Bill's favorite meal (steak and mashed potatoes) for dinner, and by the end of the night, after we four kids have finished a six-pack of beer and most of the white wine as well, Bill agrees to stick around until Wednesday, which was how long he had originally planned to stay.

The next afternoon, Bill and Katherine make a beer run.

"More beer! My goodness," Bruce says when he sees them transferring it to the refrigerator.

"Hey, we're on vacation, mon!" I say, holding up a bottle of Red Stripe.

But my joke doesn't even get a smile.

"Tough crowd," Matt whispers.

The lemon pasta Matt and I make everyone for dinner the following night is one of those dishes that really gilds the lily. I, for one, would be supremely happy with pasta coated in some lemon juice and olive oil with a nice handful of parsley and Parmesan, but this version adds white wine, grated Gruyère, and heavy cream, and it's always a crowd pleaser.

But as much as I'd like it to be, dinner is never much of an event with my family. And though everyone seems to like our meal, within fifteen minutes we're clearing the table.

"Well, Ame, that was pretty good," Bruce says to me. "I thank you for your efforts."

"You're welcome," I say. "But really, Matt did most of the work."

"Ah," he says, turning to Matt, and like a record needle being dropped onto a new track, begins again, "Thank you kindly, Matthew. Lemon pasta, huh? I'll remember that one."

✳ ✳ ✳

After Matt and I got engaged, and Grandma and Mom refused to celebrate the announcement, Bruce gave me a piece of advice that has stuck with me through the years. He told me, "You know what would be helpful? Is if instead of being so defensive, if you and Matt could just be yourselves and let everyone see you two as the happy couple that you are. That would be helpful for us."

People say you have to choose your battles. We could've made the lemon pasta and salad with the canola oil, but it's three years later now, and I don't regret fighting for the olive oil. I also don't regret fighting my parents over their reaction to Matt's and my engagement. Because I think certain things—big or small—are worth fighting for.

What I do regret, however? I regret the way I went about it, the way I hinged my happiness on their approval. In a perfect world, they wouldn't have just approved of Matt, they would have been thrilled for us. But at the end of the day, as annoying as it was to hear Bruce advise me to be less defensive and to instead go about my presumably happy life with Matt *happily*, in a way, he was right.

After all, you can't change your family. You can't convince them of your happiness or of your own success. You may not even be able to expand their worldview to include the idea of husbands cooking dinner, or of the simple beauty found in an early-evening beer on a screened-in porch in the dead of summer.

You can, however, make them pasta with marinara sauce, as we did on our last night there. And you can laugh when they say things like, "Hmm. I usually have this with meat" (even if they concede, "But this is pretty good too").

MATT'S RECIPE FOR LEMON PASTA

With an Introduction from Matt Himself

My mind tends to be on a bunch of things at any given time. As you might have read in Chapter 12, I'm prone to stressing out and the occasional panic attack. And cooking is one of those activities that lets me decompress and focus on the task at hand. In this way, it slows me down and relaxes me. It should be noted that I'm not a great cook and my main area of expertise is pasta sauce, but this works for me on a couple of important levels:

1. It's hard to mess up. In my experience, unlike photography, editing, or dealing with clients, you don't have to be super precise with the process. If your sauce has a sound foundation, most of the flavors you add to it will work; so if you're feeling like oregano, basil, garlic, hot peppers—anything—go ahead and throw them in there. The sauce won't mind—rather, it will reward your impulses by reflecting your creative choices in its finished flavor. Given this approach, I never quite end up making the same dish twice. Whether the sauce is based around tomatoes, olive oil and garlic, pesto, or some manner of lemon and cream, it's always a variation of a variation, and I'm OK with that in a big way.

2. Even though the making of pasta sauce can be a relatively simple undertaking, it's still *cooking*. From preparation to completion, it takes enough time that you can put on music, tune out the noise of the day, and spend some time making something. Fair warning: More times than not, the stuff I create in the kitchen is bad for you health-wise, and this lemon pasta is no exception,

but what it lacks in nutritional value, it makes up for in decadent deliciousness.

Serves 4

¼ cup extra virgin olive oil
3 cloves garlic, crushed and minced
1 tablespoon unsalted butter, cut into 4 chunks
Zest and juice of 1 lemon
Salt
1 pound dried spaghetti
¾ cup heavy cream
½ cup grated Parmesan or Pecorino Romano cheese, plus more for
  serving
½ cup grated Gruyère cheese
Freshly ground black pepper

Heat the oil in a skillet over low heat. Drop the garlic into the pan and move the garlic around a bit, maybe for a minute or two; don't let it brown. Turn off the heat and drop in the butter. Let the butter melt on its own. (*Side note*: Apparently non-chef friends whom I've chatted with have this idea that the inclusion of butter *and* olive oil to any dish is redundant. I don't agree. Yes, I'm a hyper-amateur saucier, but I've spent enough time with food to wholeheartedly believe that unless you're going for something super specific, the combo of butter and olive oil is better than one or the other. Point being, let the butter melt slowly on its own. You don't want it to brown for this sauce.)

At this point you have a pretty decent sauce. In fact, you can stop here if you want. You can add salt and pepper, toss in your cooked pasta, and call it a day. But if you're making the lemon pasta, you'll need to add the zest of 1 lemon, followed by the juice of that very same lemon. Again, at this point, if you want to skip out on all the cream and cheese, you could stop here and be done. The full lemon cream pasta recipe, however, the one reserved for indulgent occasions that you care not about your waistline, requires you to continue building.

Now is a great time to start cooking the pasta: Drop the dried spaghetti into a pot of lightly salted boiling water. Stir occasionally while you continue making the sauce.

Put the sauce back on low heat and bring it to a light simmer. Add the heavy cream. (You can substitute with half-and-half or even whole milk if you already have one of them on hand, but heavy cream works best.) Drop in the grated Parmesan and the Gruyère. Stir as the sauce is brought back up to a light simmer and the ingredients are completely combined. Season with salt and pepper. Turn off the heat.

Once the pasta is al dente, strain it, add it to the pan, and toss to coat it. Plate into pasta bowls and finish with a sprinkle of grated Parmesan cheese. You've got lemon pasta.

Amelia prefers that I serve it next to something green.

Chapter 27

Neither Magnificent nor Abominable

Just when the rest of the world seems to be cooling down, Southern California heats up. September is always one of the hottest and driest months here, and thus when we're most susceptible to wildfires. So when it finally cools off sometime in late October, when there's a hint of moisture in the air, it feels like a miracle. Fall has arrived, aka, soup weather.

And in case you haven't noticed by now, I love soup. I love making enough of it so as to ensure there will be some for the next day and, best-case scenario, the day after that as well. I love building it, putting it together, layering the flavors, adding salt pinch by pinch. It's not demanding. You can take your time. You don't have to have multiple burners going on. There's just the one pot, simmering away, only getting better with time.

And in a way, this is how my twenty-ninth year feels: stress-free and souplike, my life bubbling with potential.

My days off from the store typically come midweek, and on these precious mornings, I wake up early. I have a fairly large bowl of cereal, drink sugary and milk-enriched coffee while reading or Interneting, and then, for the next couple of hours, I revise the novel. In the afternoon, a nearby gym offers a one p.m. yoga class, which I start frequenting mostly because by one p.m., I'm ready to leave the house for a bit. After class, I grocery shop and then return home to a simple lunch of avocado mashed with lime and salt and pepper on top of baguette slices, perhaps followed by an apple and a few squares of chocolate. After lunch, I do a little more work. If it's approaching Sunday, the day I post on Bon Appétempt, I might work on the week's post. I might also screen-print some tote bags or T-shirts, as I haven't entirely given up on that side business. And then, around five or six, depending on how my work is going, I pour a glass of wine and begin prepping dinner. (In the winter months, I make soup so often that Matt will start to pitch other ideas. "What about that curry you made once? That was *fantastic*.") We eat at the coffee table, watch a few episodes of whichever HBO show we're currently renting, and are in bed by ten o'clock.

It's so simple but so rewarding that even though I complain to my mom about not being able to come home for the holidays because of work, and she responds with, "Have you thought about applying for teaching jobs?" I'm quick to brush her off.

"I need to finish my novel first."

Not only am I loath to take on a job that might steal time away from writing, but to be honest, I'm a bit proud of my artist lifestyle, of how I've prioritized what's important to me. Someone once told me that the actress/writer/comedienne Amy Sedaris waited tables well into her thirties and even occasionally did so after she'd "made it." I hold this piece of secondhand information close to my heart.

At the same time, however, I'm not exactly contently waiting around for my life to change. After *Bon Appétit* and *Saveur* magazines feature Bon Appétempt on their respective sites, I reach out to some of the staff there—pitching them ideas for columns I could write. They don't say yes, but they don't say no either. They tell me to keep the ideas coming.

In April, when a culinary essay I've written about baking with my ninety-two-year-old grandma is summarily rejected by every place I pitch it and/or send it to, I decide to post it on my blog, thinking that at least that way it's out there. At least that way it's not going to be stuck on my computer's desktop for the rest of its life.

But surprisingly, the essay gets a lot of attention from my readers. It even wins "Best Culinary Essay" in *Saveur* magazine's food blog awards. (And I have a line to add to my bio!)

By June, I have another draft of the novel that I feel is ready to go out to agents. I write up a query letter—which is literary-speak for an e-mail or letter in which you try to sum up your novel and yourself in the shortest and most blockbuster-y way possible, e.g., *Will and Margot* is the story of brother and sister, Will and Margot Hazelton. Will is a grand chess master who has recently fallen from grace; Margot is a happy newly-wed…or *is she*? And as for me? I'm the author of an *award-winning* food blog!

The very first agent I submit it to requests an exclusive of the manuscript, which means that I'll give her two weeks with it all to herself before sending out to other agents. I realize it's a long shot.

Or *do I*?

* * *

Three months later, I've received nothing but rejections, some kinder than others, but rejections nonetheless. By then, it's

September again, only this time I'm turning thirty. Of course, I knew this milestone was coming, but all summer long, with my novel floating out there in the ether, I still had this palpable level of hope. At any moment that summer, I could have received an e-mail from an agent declaring that he or she wanted to represent me. All summer long, my life had the potential to change, just like that.

I'm not one for throwing birthday parties for myself or having Matt throw one for me. I'd rather go out to a fancy dinner just the two of us. *But you're turning thirty*, two of my friends kept telling me, finally convincing me to take a mini getaway with them to Palm Springs, an easy two-hour drive from Los Angeles, to celebrate.

The trip is fun, but with these two friends, who rest in the socioeconomic brackets at least three or four tiers above me, and who have never worked a day of retail in their lives, it's easy to lose myself. On the way to Palm Springs, we stop by the designer outlets, and I watch as they spend six hundred and twelve hundred dollars, respectively, at Marni. I know this is not normal behavior, but I'm overcome, and in a moment of partial stupidity and partial resentment of my so-called choice to be a struggling writer, I buy a one-hundred dollar necklace, which as I'm being rung up I quickly tabulate equates to six hours of work at the store, before taxes.

Speaking of the store, September also marks my third anniversary working there, which means that I'm up for my yearly review, the process for which involves me giving five examples of my strengths and weaknesses in five different categories— from "Customer and Company" to things like "Show and Earn Respect."

I know that every job has a review process, that I'm actually quite good at my job, and that, all things considered, my job isn't half bad. But when I'm in the comfort of my own home filling out the review sheet, and forced to transform my general familiarity with a cash register into a paragraph on my adeptness with our specific point-of-sale operating system; or how I tend not to care about getting to know my customers into two hundred words on how I can work harder to build long-term client relationships, it's difficult to stay positive. It's difficult to see the job as my *day* job, as something I'm doing temporarily to support my art.

All I can see is: Amelia Morris, retail associate *for life*. And further highlighting this is that at the same time I'm prepping for my review, the company is overhauling their website, and they need photos and titles of every staff member.

Up until this point, the Internet has been a place I can represent myself the way I want, whether that's with a beautiful overhead shot of blueberry cobbler, in which the blueberries have melted into a deep navy blue color and the mix of butter, oats, and flour, a crisp golden brown, or in a video of me flipping a giant Swiss potato pancake in the pan to the tune of Eminem's "Lose Yourself." In the vast world of *social media*, I share the best photos of myself, delete the worst, and don't even bother to list my job at the store at all.

But soon an image of my smiling face labeling me as a "sales associate since 2009" will live on the Internet. Soon, the jig will be up.

On my first day back at the store after my birthday trip, I'm asked if I can pack up and ship the giant dinnerware order someone sold a few days ago that has been lingering in the back room ever since. Why no one else had the time to pack it up in my absence, I'm not sure, but at least in the back room no customers can bother me.

I get to work. I place thick pieces of corrugated cardboard in between the plates. I tape the stack together with thick masking tape. I find a suitably-sized box, fill the bottom with packing material, nestle in my stack of plates, cover it with more packing material, give the box a shake, add more packing material, and then—and this is my least favorite part, the one that requires the most effort—I must close the box. See, it shouldn't be easy to close the box. You want those plates to be stuffed in there. And in order to keep the box closed before I can tape it down, I have to use the weight of my knee, which frees up my hands to tear off a piece of packing tape. This is where I always start to break a sweat, and today is no exception. It's a big order, complete with serving pieces, cutting boards, and glassware. I've got at least seven or eight more boxes ahead of me.

On box four, something happens. I'm wearing my stupid hundred-dollar necklace, the clasp of which is a ribbon, and I can feel that the sweat on the back of my neck has soaked it. I take it off, saying aloud, "I'm an idiot." (This is usually Matt's catchphrase, but today it's mine.) Because today I am the idiot.

Today, I don't feel like getting sweaty in a small, windowless room. Today, I wish I had an office job like the rest of the people in my social circle. Today, I'm supposed to have my staff photo taken, and if I'm going to be outed on the Internet as a lifetime retail associate, I would at least like to appear as a non-sweaty, somewhat polished retail associate.

Today, all the disappointments of my life rise to the surface. If how you spend your days is how you spend your life, then I'm not a writer. I'm not an artist. I'm a thirty-year-old shop girl.

I sneak out the side door in order to privately cry in my car for fifteen minutes before returning to finish up the order.

In *The Writing Life*, Annie Dillard says of the novel-writing process, "The feeling that the work is magnificent, and the feeling that it is abominable, are both mosquitoes to be repelled, ignored, or killed, but not indulged." I think this idea applies to life in general.

And on days like this, when it's hard to accept the choices I've made, when all I can seem to muster is self-pity, and when I cannot swat away the mosquitoes telling me that I'm abominable, I need time in the kitchen where I can get out of my head for a moment, where I can focus on something else, something positive. On days like this, I need to make soup.

Because while I'm chopping onions and sautéing them in a bit of olive oil until they're fragrant and soft, when I'm peeling potatoes and the skins are piling up in the basin of my sink, I can see—even if it's only momentarily—the beauty in the effort. I'm reminded once again that success is in *the work*.

CORN, CHILE, AND POTATO SOUP

Serves 3 to 4

2 pounds medium Yukon gold potatoes (about 4)
3 tablespoons olive oil
1 large onion, chopped
Salt and freshly ground black pepper
4 cups chicken broth
½ cup water
1 to 2 canned chipotle chiles in adobo (see *Note*)
2 avocados
1 to 2 limes
1 (16-ounce) package frozen corn (not thawed)
Tortilla chips
Shredded cheddar cheese (optional)

Rinse, scrub, and peel the potatoes. Chop them into 1- to 2-inch pieces. Set aside.

Heat the oil in a stockpot over medium heat. Add the onion and give it a few pinches of salt and a bit of pepper. Cook, stirring occasionally, until the onion is softened, 4 to 5 minutes.

Add the potatoes, chicken broth, water, and 1 teaspoon salt to the pot. While bringing this to a boil, mince the chile using a fork to hold it steady as you chop. (Some people can tolerate chopping a chile while holding it in place with their bare hands. I am not one of those people.) Add the minced chile to the pot. Once the soup is boiling, take it down to a simmer; simmer until the potatoes are very tender, 15 to 17 minutes.

Meanwhile, slice the avocados in half and remove and discard the pits. With the avocado skin-side down on a cutting board, slice the flesh into strips, and using a spoon, scoop out the slices into a bowl. Sprinkle with salt and pepper and cover with the juice of half a lime. Set aside.

Using a potato masher, mash the potatoes right in the soup—just until coarsely broken up. Add the frozen corn and simmer for about 2 minutes more, until heated through. Turn off the heat. Add the juice of the other half of the lime.

Ladle into bowls and top with a nice heaping of tortilla chips, avocado slices, and, optimally, shredded cheddar. Serve with wedges from the remaining lime.

Note: One minced chile lends a nice smoky spiciness that shouldn't overwhelm anyone's palate. Two makes it *pretty* spicy.

Chapter 28

Bringing It All Back Home

It's the week of Thanksgiving, and therefore, the week of our annual sale at work, when people go from being customers to panicked consumers. And maybe because the mornings have finally turned cold enough that I need to flip the heat on, or maybe because I know I have a long day ahead of me and I feel like indulging myself a little, I decide to have a piece of toasted baguette with butter and jam for breakfast, the same thing that Matt usually has.

I change my morning routine so infrequently that when I twist open the jar of apricot jam and see bits of white, cold butter mixed in with the pale orange preserves, I'm instantly and oddly reminded of my dad. This is the way the jar of jam always looked in Saegertown. And for a brief moment, I picture him standing at the kitchen counter trying to spread squares of butter that are too substantial for the heat from the toast to melt them, before resorting to smashing them down, crushing the bread in the process. The layer of jam he smeared on top was always just as excessive.

Meanwhile, I take a bite of my own toast and find it lacking in both components. This is typical of me. I seem to always err on the side of *not quite enough*. When Matt and I sit down to a pasta dinner, I tease him about his mountain of Parmesan compared to my much more sensible couple of tablespoons, but then halfway through the meal, I take a bite of his and find it undeniably more delicious than my version.

And for a fleeting moment, I seem to better understand my father. I see him as someone who doesn't hold back, who doesn't restrain himself or his hardly conventional opinions (ranging from how the US government attacked itself on 9/11 to how he won't see *Zero Dark Thirty*, as "everyone knows Osama bin Laden died in 2003"), who continues to smoke and maintain a cheeseburger-and-pizza-centric diet well into his sixties with seemingly little concern as to his deteriorating health and his family's history of heart failure.

* * *

A month ago, the future had looked promising again. A literary agent whom I queried about my novel contacted me, interested in having me put together a proposal for a food memoir loosely based on Bon Appétempt. Not to mention that for my combined birthday and Christmas present, Matt and I booked a trip to Paris for two weeks. (In order to spread out paying for everything, we wouldn't leave until late March.)

However, once the holidays hit, my outlook takes a turn. Once again, I struggle to see beyond my ten to six-thirty existence of "I'm sorry, but we can't extend the sale price to you after the sale has ended."

Now that I'm thirty, I've also become very aware that I only have so many "good years" left to get pregnant. The fact that I'd like to have two kids feels particularly troublesome, especially considering what I've heard my dad say in passing over the years, that though most women should be fine to get pregnant up until the age of forty, thirty-five is technically when fertility starts its rapid descent.

During my morning search for the prized all-day parking spot within a three-block radius of the store, I begin to imagine a simpler life. Back at our apartment, after dinner, I retire early to the bedroom, streaming episodes of my favorite TV show of all time, *My So-Called Life*, which is set in Pittsburgh. And suddenly my vision of a simpler life has a specific setting. I begin to think about moving back home. I begin to think about the wide suburban streets I rode my bike on as a kid. I begin to think about buying a little house and getting pregnant and being able to call up my mom or Matt's parents to see if they can swing by and watch the baby while I run a few errands.

I think about how much fun it is when Matt and I go back to visit now, how we stay at his parents' house—the one he grew up in and in the basement of which we shared our first kiss—and quickly revert to our teenage habits, staying up late watching movies, eating pickles and hard pretzels, and going to sleep without properly gathering our plates and putting them in the dishwasher. In the morning, before his parents leave for work, Matt is lightly scolded for leaving empty glasses everywhere and we're left with a handwritten list of reminders: *If you go out, make sure both dogs are in their crates and the fire is turned off* followed by the perennial: *And don't let the cat out!*

Matt's dad is famous for repeating himself in a way that calls attention to the fact that he *knows* he's repeating himself. And we kids are famous for playing into the need to have these things repeated to us. "Why, Dad? Why shouldn't we let the cat out? She's clearly very curious about the outdoors," Matt will say, feigning confusion and gesturing to Autumn, the calico cat, who spends much of her day sitting and staring through the window of the front door, her tail sweeping the floor from side to side.

"Because," his dad will say, "she might like it!"

And as I daydream, I realize I'm a lot like Autumn. I'm staring out the window, pondering a different life. However, unlike Autumn, I could open the door and step through it if I really wanted to, couldn't I?

We can't go home for the holidays because of our work schedules, but like we've done in years past, we book tickets to Pittsburgh for mid-January. And while Matt knows I'm discouraged with the state of my noncareer, he doesn't know that I'm so discouraged that I'm planning on using this trip to secretly consider what it would be like if we lived there again.

We arrive at the Pittsburgh airport, and as I walk from the baggage claim area to my mom's car, which is waiting for us curbside, the freezing wind blows right through the winter coat that had worked just fine in LA and comes to rest in my bones, where it will remain for the rest of the night.

Matt and I have our own traditions with our families our first night back at home, so while Matt and his parents eat chicken wings, pizza, and what they jokingly (and lovingly) refer to as "sweat sandwiches" (as the guy who makes them is known to work up quite a sweat no matter the time of year), Mom, Bruce, and I head to Grandma's to pick her up and take her out for sushi.

Since my last visit, Grandma has cut sugar out of her diet

because of her failing kidneys, and though Mom warns me that she's lost a lot of weight and is teeny tiny now, I'm still not ready for the change. We pull into her driveway and within a minute, she is making her way toward the car, her thin legs emerging from below her wool coat like sticks.

After dinner, Mom drops me off at the Bookmans, where Matt and I usually stay when we're both home. But once I'm inside the house that's become so familiar to me over the past fifteen years, it hardly feels usual; Matt's parents are in the process of selling and moving to a smaller loft space down-town. There's hardly anything left in Matt's bedroom apart from a bed, a desk, and an icy draft coming from one of the windows.

In the morning, Matt and I eat breakfast with his parents before heading over to my house in the afternoon, where my brother and Katherine have just gotten in. They've driven up from Charlotte to spend the weekend, and Mom has taken the opportunity to arrange for us to sit for professional family photos, something Bill and I haven't done since we were kids and something that does create family unity in that Matt, me, Bill, and Katherine immediately become united against Mom because we can't believe she's actually making us do this.

That night, all of us, Grandma included, have dinner at the Bookmans. Matt's dad builds a fire, Matt's mom makes chicken Parmesan, Matt makes garlic bread, and my mom arrives with her classic Caesar salad. I do nothing more than clean a few mushrooms and pour red wine. And half-way through, I realize it's the big holiday dinner I'd wanted all season long, with people talking over one another, dogs abounding, and my brother and Matt making obscure Fantasy Football references. By the end of the night, the color has returned to my face and the circulation to my feet.

The following day, my dad is planning to drive from Saegertown to take us kids to an early dinner. I haven't seen him since the wedding four years ago, and then all of a sudden, there he is at Mom and Bruce's door, hands in the pockets of his brown leather jacket as if it's an alternate Sunday night in 1993 and he's arrived to pick us up and return us to Saegertown. And before I can stop myself, the first words out of my mouth are, "Dad, you're so fat!"

At the wedding, he had been a few months removed from heart valve replacement surgery and at least twenty to thirty pounds lighter. And as he didn't completely reek of cigarettes that weekend, I guess I'd hoped that he'd not only quit, but that the major surgery had inspired him to start taking better care of himself.

But clearly that's not the case—when I go to hug him, the smell of smoke is pervasive.

"Geez, Amy," he says, laughing, "we can't all be fit and trim Angelenos."

"I'm sorry. You just—you don't look *healthy*."

"What do you want from me? You know my dad died at sixty-two, and look at me at sixty-three! I'm doing *way* better than him," he says, and laughs again.

Matt's at a hockey game with his dad, so dinner will be just the four of us, and since Dad curiously bought himself a yellow Mini Cooper for his sixtieth birthday, we opt to take Katherine's Jeep. From my spot in the back, it's uncomfortable seeing my brother in the driver's seat and Dad in the passenger's; it doesn't suit him to just sit there, to not have his eyes firmly on the road and the wheel in front of him.

We head to one of Dad's favorite pizza places, Beto's, where they famously serve any toppings, even the cheese, uncooked. So, if it's a cheese and pepperoni pizza you want, you get a hot slice of pizza topped off with cold, shredded mozzarella and cold pepperoni.

Dad took us here all the time as kids, but I haven't been in years and am fully prepared not to enjoy the two squares with extra cheese I order, especially as I see that they're served to me on a Styrofoam plate. But honestly, it's not bad. The bottom layer of cheese ends up melting because of the residual heat, and I find the mixture of textures and temperatures bizarrely pleasing.

Dad orders four slices with extra cheese and pepperoni as well as a full pizza to go, which he'll bring back with him to Saegertown. But I'm not sure what's more disappointing: the idea of Dad eating an entire Beto's pizza himself, the ensuing conversation, or the nasty cough he displays throughout the meal.

After mostly talking to Billy about some of his old Saegertown classmates and, yes, ex-wrestling opponents, Dad turns to me. "So what's going on? You have an agent now?"

I'd recently mentioned this news to him over e-mail.

"Yeah, I do."

"And is he from the William Morris Agency?" (My dad enjoys the fact that there is a talent agency with his name.)

"No. *She* is not."

"But isn't the William Morris Agency, by virtue of its name, the best? Shouldn't you ask to switch?"

At which point, my brother jumps in. "She's working on a

memoir, Dad. So, we all have to be on our best behavior from now on."

"Oh God, remind me not to tell Dolly. You know, she's not doing well. I doubt she'll make it through the year."

"Why? What's wrong?" I ask.

"She can hardly breathe and she's basically blind."

The topic of my potential book doesn't surface again.

We do, however, discuss Dad's new online chess "clan," the Chessperados.

After dinner, we head back to Mom and Bruce's. Dad comes inside too, though he never makes it past the foyer. Mom greets him there and they talk shop for a bit, about the current state of medicine and Mom's struggle to get used to electronic records. It's always both odd and reassuring to see them standing side by side chatting—Mom with her arms crossed and Dad with his hands in his pockets, his shoulders subtly slumped.

We say our good-byes. I give Dad an awkward hug, and in the most serious voice I can muster, I tell him to take care of himself.

*　*　*

A few days later, Matt and I arrive back in Los Angeles on a late flight. By the time we retrieve our car at the Crowne Plaza hotel's long-term parking and drive home, it's eleven p.m., which of course feels like two a.m. We're hungry but too tired to do anything about it. I open my suitcase only to retrieve my toothbrush. I brush my teeth and crawl into bed. Compared to Matt's childhood mattress we'd spent the past five nights on, ours feels like something you might get at the Four Seasons.

In the morning, we wake up early and starved, but there's nothing to be had for breakfast—no cereal, milk, or even bread for toast. The nearby store doesn't open until seven. I search the pantry and realize that we have maple syrup, and that if we substitute half-and-half for milk, we can have pancakes.

And when I relay this information to Matt, he offers to make them.

"Sure," I say, already back in bed. "If you insist."

※ ※ ※

My first-ever culinary hero, Kenny Shopsin, has a chapter in his cookbook (*Eat Me: The Food and Philosophy of Kenny Shopsin*) dedicated to pancakes, in which he explains that if you heat the griddle properly beforehand, and if the griddle is well-oiled, and if you pay attention, not undercooking or overcooking the pancake, "you could use boxed pancake mix or Aunt Jemima frozen pancake batter, and your pancakes would turn out just as good as mine." (A few sentences later, he then admits that he actually uses Aunt Jemima frozen pancake batter at his restaurant.) In other words, good pancakes are all about how you handle the batter, not the batter itself.

On that early morning back in Los Angeles, I'm reminded of this while eating the ones Matt has cooked quite perfectly.

Pittsburgh is a beautiful city, which, for better or worse, is responsible for much of my constitution. But after our recent trip, I can't say I'm ready to pick up and move there; I can't say it would be a solution to my career problems or that life there would be any easier.

All I can say for sure is that for the moment, it feels really good to be home.

Truth be told, if we're talking pancakes, I prefer savory ones. Matt and I love to have these shrimp and scallion pancakes for dinner alongside a salad of mixed greens and diced avocado tossed with store-bought ginger and soy sauce vinaigrette.

KOREAN-STYLE SHRIMP AND SCALLION PANCAKES

Makes 8 to 10 pancakes

For the pancakes:

1 cup all-purpose flour

2 large eggs, lightly beaten

1 tablespoon grapeseed oil or another neutral oil, plus more for the pan

1 bunch scallions, dark and pale green parts only, cut into 3-inch pieces

1 pound peeled shrimp, chopped into 1-inch pieces (depending on the exact size of the shrimp, each one is chopped into 2 or 3 pieces)

1 small jalapeño, sliced into very thin rounds

For the dipping sauce:

2 tablespoons rice vinegar

3 tablespoons soy sauce

A few pinches of Korean red pepper (or Italian crushed red pepper)

To make the pancakes:

In a large bowl, mix the flour, eggs, and oil with 1 cup water until a smooth batter is formed. Stir in the scallions and shrimp. Let the mixture rest for 30 minutes to 1 hour.

Place a large cast-iron skillet over medium-high heat and thinly coat the bottom with oil. Once the oil is hot and lightly smoking, use a slotted spoon to scoop out as many 4-inch-in-diameter pancakes as you can. (The slotted spoon is important here, as you want *just enough* batter to hold the pancake together.)

With the bottom side of the pancakes cooking, use a fork (to protect your fingers) to lay one or two of the jalapeño rounds on top of each pancake. (You may not end up using the entire jalapeño.)

Cook until the bottom is browned, about 3 minutes, then flip and cook for another 3 minutes, occasionally pressing down on each pancake with the spatula, which helps to make sure you don't get any pancakes with uncooked batter in the middle.

Repeat with the remaining batter, adding additional oil halfway through if needed. (You may want to place the finished pancakes in an ovenproof dish and throw them in a 275°F oven just to keep them warm.)

To make the dipping sauce:

In a small bowl, mix together the vinegar, soy sauce, and red pepper. Serve the dipping sauce alongside the pancakes.

Chapter 29

Our Many Lives

Friends of friends have a one-bedroom apartment in Paris, which they occasionally rent out to people they know for the extremely reasonable price of $400/week. Back in September, Matt and I did the math. If we bought our tickets six months in advance and I used the frequent flyer miles I've had saved up for years, we could afford to go for two solid weeks.

And so, at the end of March, almost six months to the day from my thirtieth birthday, we board a nonstop flight from LAX to Charles de Gaulle. We're going to Paris! Is there a better sentence in the world? Or a better feeling than that of the beginning of a vacation? Of leaving your regular life behind, of becoming someone else—someone a little more cultured, a little more Parisian—for a bit?

It's a six p.m. flight that arrives in Paris at two-thirty p.m. the following day, though of course we're still on Pacific Standard Time, so it feels like four a.m. We're tired, but I really want to take public transportation from the airport to our apartment, which, in my previous travels, I always found to be a great introduction to the city. We take the RER train into Paris, but instead of switching metro lines and getting off at Saint-Germain-des-Prés, we decide to get off at Saint-Michel.

On the map, it looks close enough and we figure it will be nice to walk a bit. And it *is*. It's sublime. The sheer history of the city hits you right away with its architecture, although our excitement begins to wane about fifteen minutes into the walk (as we're doing it avec two suitcases on rollers and two large duffel bags).

The place we're renting is located in the 6th arrondissement, on Rue Guisarde, a street so tiny it's more of a passageway. It's an attic apartment reachable via five flights of the oldest, most narrow spiral stairs I've ever seen. The landing in front of the front door is barely big enough for Matt, me, and our two suitcases, but when we open it, it's love at first sight. The 345-square-foot one-bedroom apartment is both charming and modern, with ancient wooden rafters along the ceilings and views of rooftops from almost every window.

We drop off our luggage and immediately head back out. We pick up a pair of ham and cheese crêpes and do a small grocery run. But by seven p.m., Paris-time, I can't keep my eyes open. I know I should stay up longer, but I've been dealing with a recurring case of insomnia for the past few months—some nights finding myself not able to fall asleep until five in the morning—and so when that feeling I've been longing for, that straightforward sense of falling asleep naturally and without a racing heartbeat, comes, it's irresistible. I take it. (Of course, I also wake up at two a.m. local time, ready for breakfast.)

Our first few days are a blur of unpasteurized double-cream cheeses, wine, *crêpes sucrées*, booking dinner reservations for later in the trip, and long, meandering walks to museums.

And by the end of our first week, I've come down with a specific brand of nausea. All of a sudden, my body wants nothing to do with butter, cream, or cheese, aka the building blocks of French cuisine. When it first hits me, dry toast and tea are the only things I want, though the following day, avocado, rice, and hot sauce sound appealing. We seek out a Korean restaurant in our neighborhood, where I happily eat *bibimbap* with lots of chili paste mixed in.

Unfortunately, the next night we have dinner reservations—which we'd made the previous week—at Les Papilles, a very French restaurant that came highly recommended. It's a place where you're not given a menu. You simply show up and are served that night's specific three courses. This sounded awesome last week, but now it seems much less so. But Matt is really excited, and I know that if we cancel, we most likely won't be able to get a table another night.

So I put on my boots and we circle down the five flights that spit us out onto Rue Guisarde. It's chilly and slightly raining, and our route takes us through the Luxembourg Gardens. It's so Parisian and beautiful that by the time we arrive at the restaurant, I *almost* feel like eating. It's a tiny place (though every Paris restaurant seems tiny compared to our American standards), and the same man who took our reservation last week walks us to our seats. Once seated, he explains that they serve wine by the bottle only, and whatever we don't drink, he kindly says, he can cork and we can take home to enjoy. I know we should choose a red, but a crisp, citrusy white sounds like a cure-all to me, and so from the wall to our right, we have this kind Parisian gentleman help us choose a white wine that will go with the night's menu.

I take a sip, and it seems to work. I think I'll be OK.

Our first course is beautiful. The waiter serves us two wide shallow bowls with crisp lardons, golden croutons, and chopped asparagus steamed just to al dente resting in the middle. He then sets down a soup tureen filled with a creamy kelly-green broth and ladles it into our bowls. Though I know that everything is cooked to perfection, the aroma is that of butter, cream, and bacon, and I'm not even tempted to taste it. Matt, on the other hand, goes back for seconds.

When a different waiter comes to take away our plates, he must see the relief on my face. *Yes, please take away the stunning bowl of soup!* "You don't like?" he asks in English.

"No, I did," I say, nodding, unconvincingly.

"We *loved* it," Matt says. *"Parfait."* (Matt and I are both the type of people who hate to make others—particularly strangers—feel uncomfortable. When Matt is handed a sample of something at the grocery store, I always laugh at his over-the-top response: a thumbs-up coupled with, "I'm going to shop around but I'll definitely swing back and pick this up on the way out.")

In between courses, the warmth and coziness of the restaurant starts to feel stifling. I ask Matt to hand me his phone so that I can pretend to take a call outside just in order to breathe in the cold fresh air for a bit.

The next course is even prettier. It arrives in individual-sized oval copper pots. And when the lid is lifted away, we discover a crispy-skinned chicken breast and leg topped with a few sprigs of thyme. Underneath are more perfectly handled vegetables and al dente ziti in a pale green pesto-cream sauce.

Pasta and chicken sound OK, but the sauce is so rich that I can't eat more than a few bites. I transfer some of my portion to Matt's copper pot so that this time the waiter is less suspicious when he collects our dishes.

The next course, the cheese course, is enough to make me

want to cry. In my regular, non-nauseated state, I dream of cheese courses, which evoke a different way of life—a less practical, more indulgent, kinder one. So when, on a rectangular piece of slate, from left to right, we're introduced to a slice of soft Brie-esque cow's milk cheese with a delicate white rind, a quenelle of house-made orange and fig fruit paste, followed by a red stripe of ground chile, I do my very best to enjoy it. Unfortunately, I can only show my appreciation by taking a photo of it with Matt's iPhone.

Our last course is ice-cold chocolate mousse—the kind of chocolate that has all sorts of notes to it. It's rich but clean-tasting, sweet but bitter, chocolate with a touch of vanilla. (All this I get from my one spoonful.)

I've never experienced a more beautiful meal, and I've never been happier to get the check.

To add insult to injury, that night my insomnia returns, and with it all of the anxieties I'd hoped to leave in Los Angeles—you know the ones, e.g., my career prospects or lack thereof, this book proposal I'm working on, and, of course, my newly ticking biological clock.

And so, instead of lying there in the dark with negative thought after negative thought just like I would at home, I get out of bed and move to the couch, where I can turn on a light, read, and not resent (quite as much) the way Matt just falls asleep and stays asleep.

I pick up one of the books from the apartment's collection. It's one I remember the owners recommending when they'd given Matt and me the keys, Adam Gopnik's *Paris to the Moon*. It's a memoir that focuses on the five years Gopnik lived in Paris with his wife and young child. And perhaps because the very first sentence mentions rue Saint-Sulpice and I can actually see the top of Saint-Sulpice from the living room windows, I keep reading well into the dead of the night.

＊ ＊ ＊

As I recover from my bout with what I can only diagnose as a case of too much French food for my typically Southern Californian/Mediterranean-fed gastric system, Matt comes down with a horrible cold. It's so bad, I turn to Rick Steves's guidebook to find out how to say the words cough and fever so that I can explain his symptoms in French to a pharmacist.

We are supposed to leave that afternoon for a day trip to Reims, where champagne is produced and where you can take tours of the production process and, you know, drink lots of champagne, but Matt is in no shape for travel. Instead, he spends the day sipping miso soup made from a packet and nonironically reading Dan Brown's *The Da Vinci Code*. As for me, I walk to our neighborhood café, laptop in hand, and enjoy checking my e-mail and reading the Wikipedia pages on Saint-Sulpice, Josephine Baker, Musée de l'Orangerie, and everything else I've wanted to look up for the past ten days. We spend a few days like this—not really touring the city, just living in it.

Once Matt is feeling better, we make it to Versailles, which we love, though our tour is so crowded with other people we find ourselves rushing a bit through each room and are almost relieved once we realize we've seen everything and can go back home. On the train back, we discuss what we should do that night. We still have a few restaurants we want to try.

"Or we could pick up stuff at the grocery store, I could make huge bowls of pasta, and we could watch the end of *Ronin*?" Matt says in a way that makes clear that he knows that that's probably what we *shouldn't* do. Because, well, we're in Paris, and we're both finally feeling better. We should probably do something we can't do in Los Angeles, right?

∗ ∗ ∗

There's a paragraph in the beginning of *Paris to the Moon* I go back to again and again. In it, the author seems to almost warn the reader about what his book is really about, that though yes it's about Paris and a specific five-year period—from 1995 to 2000—it is really mostly "about life spent at home."

"Life is mostly lived by timid bodies at home," he writes, "and since we see life as deeply in our pleasures as in our pains, we see the differences in lives as deeply there too. The real differences among people shine most brightly in two bedrooms and one building, with a clock ticking, five years to find out how and why. Not just how and why and in what way Paris is different from New York, but how [one] might end up feeling about the idea of difference itself—about the existence of minute variations among people: which ones really matter and which ones really don't."

∗ ∗ ∗

On our last day, I type up a list of my favorite moments from the trip so that I won't forget them. Our first fancy dinner at L'Epi Dupin, and specifically their carrot ginger soup, makes the list. The dance exhibit at the Pompidou (and our impromptu snack at the museum restaurant where we accidentally ordered an apple tart with ice cream when we thought we were ordering French fries) makes the list. Our evening walk down to the Seine to see the Eiffel Tower lit up makes the list. And, surprisingly or not, our pasta night "with the exciting conclusion of *Ronin*" makes the list. (For some reason, we found *Ronin*, which is decidedly *not* a comedy, to be hilarious.)

Versailles and all of its gilded furniture doesn't make the list.

The expensive macarons we got at the famous patisserie Pierre Hermé don't make the list.

Our dinner at Les Papilles doesn't make the list (though the walk home in the rain does).

Matt and I may not have done Paris to the max, or the way we maybe thought we were supposed to do it. And back home, we may not have been doing Los Angeles the way we thought we were going to. We certainly weren't leading lives as outwardly and objectively successful as those of our many friends.

But if life is "mostly lived by timid bodies at home," we are *mostly* doing great. At that part of life, I know we excel. And though this may not be as easy to share at dinner parties with strangers ("What do you do?" "Well, I love cooking dinner for my husband and myself and then eating it while watching *House Hunters International*."), I'm realizing that that's OK.

In fact, that's what the whole ballgame is about.

When we came back home to Los Angeles from Paris, this is exactly what I wanted to eat. *Note:* This dish may seem like a real pain to make, but once you've purchased the kombu and bonito flakes at an Asian grocery or a well-stocked health food store, you're practically halfway there!

MY RELATIVELY SIMPLE MISO RAMEN WITH A POACHED EGG

Makes 2 large portions or 4 more reasonably sized ones

For the dashi:

8 cups water
One 3-inch square kombu (sea kelp)
¾ cup bonito flakes

For the rest of the soup:

½ cup yellow miso paste
1 9.5 ounce packet dried ramen noodles (see *Note*)
White vinegar
2 to 4 eggs (1 for each bowl of soup)
1 (18- or 19-ounce) block extra-firm tofu, cut into ¼-inch cubes
Half a bunch of scallions, green tops thinly sliced
Sriracha sauce
Toasted sesame oil

To make the dashi:

Pour the water into a stockpot. Place the kombu in the cold water. Turn the heat to high and heat until it just begins to boil. Turn off the heat and fish out and discard the kombu. Stir in the bonito flakes and let it steep for 5 minutes. Meanwhile, prepare a large bowl with a fine-mesh strainer on top. After the 5 minutes, strain into the prepared bowl. Pour the strained liquid back into the stockpot.

The rest of this happens pretty quickly. So you probably want to make sure your tofu is chopped and your scallions are sliced. Ready? OK!

Bring the strained dashi to a boil.

For timing purposes, get a saucepan filled with 3 to 4 inches of simmering water in order to poach your eggs.

Place the miso paste in a small bowl. After the dashi has come to a boil, scoop out 1 cup of it and add it to the bowl with the miso. Whisk until smooth and completely combined. Set aside.

Dump your dried ramen noodles into the boiling dashi and cook according to the package directions while you poach your eggs.

To poach the eggs:

(Truth be told, I overcook my poached eggs all the time by letting the water go from a gentle simmer to a violent simmer. But maybe you'll have better luck?) Add a tablespoon or two of white vinegar to the simmering water. Crack an egg into a small bowl and kindly coax it into the simmering water. Start timing! 4 minutes at a gentle simmer will give you a poached egg with a runny yolk, which is exactly what you want. You're probably poaching at least two eggs, so using a slotted spoon, scoop your finished poached egg from the simmering water and place in a bowl of warm water to keep it warm while you poach your next one.

To finish the soup:

Once the ramen is cooked, turn off the heat.

Pour the miso and dashi mixture into the broth with the ramen. Stir until it is incorporated. Stir in the tofu cubes and sliced scallions.

Divide the soup among bowls, topping each with a poached egg. Serve with sriracha and toasted sesame oil.

Note: I use a brand of ramen called Hakubaku that's sold at my grocery store, but if you can't find ramen, you can substitute dried spaghetti. I've done it before, and though I'm sure it's hugely frowned upon by the ramen community, it still makes for a delicious noodle.

Chapter 30

Be Careful When Hammering Your Life into Shape

I'd gone to Whole Foods planning to pick up ingredients for linguine and clams, but as I stand there shivering in the produce department on an unseasonably cold, gray day by Los Angeles standards, I decide that what I'd really like is Manhattan clam chowder, something I've never made before.

Though it's 2012, I still don't have a smartphone; I can't Google a recipe. But what I do have is a husband at work with access to the Internet. I call Matt and ask him to please find a Manhattan clam chowder recipe online and read off the ingredients to me. He kindly agrees but with the proviso that he's at work and is not available for a million follow-up questions. (He knows me too well.)

I buy the majority of what he tells me to: littleneck clams (as the smaller ones, manilas, aren't available), bacon, celery, onion, white wine, a can of tomatoes. I skip the chorizo and instead grab some halibut. Why? Because I'm feeling confident. I'm making soup. And soups, I've discovered in the short history of my cooking life, are hard to mess up. Why halibut specifically? Because it seems like a nice, if not familiar-sounding, fish that will hold up in a soup.

I go about my day off as I normally do, and then, at five o'clock, I pour myself a glass of white wine, turn on some music, and begin making my inaugural chowder. The recipe doesn't mention anything about potatoes, but I have some on hand and, well, who doesn't like potatoes in their clam chowder? I put them in a pot of water and bring them to a simmer, waiting until they're just fork-tender. I drain them and allow them to cool for a bit while I get the bacon ready to fry.

As I'm frying the bacon, I remember this amazing bacon potato hash I once made. Impulsively, I slice the potatoes with their skin still somewhat attached and toss them in the bacon fat.

Unfortunately, while my heart is in the right place (a starchy vegetable cooked in animal fat), within a few minutes, it seems that I may have overloaded the pan with potatoes, because the flesh doesn't seem to be crisping up the way I'd like. Plus, the skin has come off some of the potatoes and adhered itself to the pan. And worst of all, I realize that since I'm going to throw these potatoes in the soup, it doesn't matter if they crisp up because it's not like they're going to stay crisp while suspended in broth.

The recipe tells me to remove the cooked bacon from the pan and to use the bacon fat to cook some minced garlic, to which I'm supposed to add white wine and water in order to steam open the clams. But the potato skin is so stuck to the pan that I end up using a slotted spoon to remove the bacon to one plate and the potatoes to another before I pour the leftover grease into another pan entirely.

In the fresh pan, I sauté the garlic in the bacon fat and add the white wine, water, and finally the batch of littleneck clams. Once the clams have steamed open, I pull them out one by one and place them into a bowl. As for the liquid, I'm supposed to strain this off into another bowl. At this point, there is the smallest bit of counter space left to work on, and as I'm straining the hot liquid, I pour too slowly and lose at least a cup to the side of the pan, the counter, and—bonus!—the floor. Next, I avoid that section of the floor as I remove the clam meat from the shells, chop them up, and reserve them in another bowl.

I take a time-out to clean up, during which Matt comes home from work.

"Wow, it smells great!"

"Don't come in here!"

"Why?"

"What time is it?"

"Uhm, about six-thirty."

"Six-thirty!"

I resentfully move on to a new pan—this time an enameled cast-iron stockpot—and melt some butter and add the onion and celery. (This is where I would have added the chorizo I didn't buy.) I cook the onion until it's translucent, then add a bit of flour. Next up is the clam broth, which I must bring to a simmer. Then, in goes my large can of tomatoes, sugar, pepper flakes, and thyme. Here, I'm supposed to cover and cook at a low simmer until the broth is flavorful, about twenty to thirty minutes, adding the reserved bacon and clams at the very end, but then I remember I have that stupid halibut in the refrigerator that I haven't done anything with yet.

I bring the broth to a simmer and add the halibut, which I've chopped into bite-size pieces. This seems to work, as the halibut is clearly cooking, only it has brought the level of the liquid to within an inch of the top of the pot. If I want to add the potatoes and clams to this, I'm definitely going to have to transfer the soup to a bigger stockpot.

As I do so, the red broth leaves its splattery mark. I'd love to add the emptied pot to the sink, but alas there's no room. Finally, I add the potatoes and chopped clams to the newer, larger pot, and, with a sense of great defeat, announce that dinner is ready.

Oh, but there's one stipulation. "I work tomorrow," I tell Matt, "and since this was such a nightmare to make, this *needs* to last us for two meals."

✳ ✳ ✳

Five months later, at the beginning of September, I send my agent the latest draft of my book proposal. I'm proud of myself, not for having done the work but because I feel like I haven't rushed the process, that I've applied her notes, revised it from top to bottom, given it room to breathe, and then revised it one more time.

What has perhaps helped me be patient is that Matt and I have had a great summer. I've gotten a job teaching a writing class one day a week through a private Los Angeles writing school, which allows me to change my schedule at Heath so that I only have to be there three days a week. And because of the videos we've made together for Bon Appétempt, Matt has not only stumbled into freelance work as a shooter/director, but his job at the PR firm has evolved such that he is now shooting and directing web spots for his agency's major clients. In other words, he is getting to do the work he's always wanted to do. But the most exciting change of all is that in June, we bought a small house in Echo Park, a windy, hilly neighborhood in east Los Angeles, and almost immediately followed it up with the acquisition of a small dog we named Mavis.

So that by September, the life I've always wanted seems to be coming into focus. By September, I begin to think that maybe that brand of T-shirts Matt's dad sports on occasion is right: Life *is* good.

But when my agent gets back to me via phone, it becomes clear that we're not even remotely close to being on the same page—no pun intended, as a pun would imply an air of light-heartedness, and by the end of our hour-long conversation, I'm the opposite of lighthearted. I'm both defeated and worked up. I'm also in a T-shirt, shorts, and sneakers, as right before she called, I was about to leave for a hike with Mavis.

But now it's almost eleven o'clock. It's hot and the sun is high in the sky. Mavis, who is still very much a puppy, doesn't hike well in the heat. But she's pawing at my legs, seemingly asking to go with me, so against my better judgment, I grab her and head for Griffith Park anyway.

Why do I want to write this book? The answer to which I'm supposed to *think about* rings in my head as I walk.

Why do I want to write this book?

I know what I'm supposed to say. I should quote Annie Dillard or Rilke about how if I'm really a writer, then that's just what writers do. We *write*! And if the recognition comes, the recognition comes.

But what I want to say—No, what I want to shout is: *I'll tell you why I want to write this book! Because I want to have a book—out there in the world and not just on my computer.*

Because, at the end of the day, I'm still struggling to drink my own Kool-Aid. Because, though I tell myself differently, part of me still believes that my job as a shop girl *does* define me.

Because part of me believes, despite what Anne Lamott tells me, that publishing this book *will* bring me happiness, or at the very least, a certain level of respect and/or recognition from those people who have made me feel small, who have made me feel undeserving and dispensable: from the customers at the store to my coworkers and bosses (present and past) to my dad and stepmom. Specifically, I want my dad to hear the news and think: *Hmmm…maybe I underestimated Amy. Hmmm…maybe I should've paid a little more attention to her when she was a kid.* Likewise, I want my stepmom to be worried: *Oh, shit. She's writing a memoir? Maybe I picked the wrong eleven-year-old girl to have told that she wouldn't amount to anything.*

Sometimes I find myself envying Mavis because she seems the very opposite of tortured. She plays. She eats. She searches for morsels of food on the kitchen floor. And on walks, if it's too hot outside, she finds herself a shady patch and sits down, sometimes only five minutes in. When she does this, I usually respond by jumping up and down, trying to get her going again. "C'mon, Mavis! Let's go! Weeee! This is fun!" And sometimes it works.

But today, after my disappointing phone conversation, I don't even bother trying. Today, I scoop all eleven pounds of her up into my arms and say, "You know what? I don't blame you."

* * *

When I first started Bon Appétempt, though it was a side project and something I wanted to do for fun, I also felt adamant about sticking to the structure of beginning each post with *their version*, which was always an image of the completed recipe as it appeared perfectly and beautifully in a magazine or cookbook. This was then followed up by *my version*, which was always, of course, a very flawed image.

But after the first year, this structure began to stifle me. I would find photo-less recipes I wanted to try. Yet not wanting to break the template I created, I wouldn't. Eventually, though, I gave in.

And once I did, I was off and running. I attempted Julia Child's photo-less recipe for mayonnaise. I re-created the butterscotch *budino* from one of my favorite restaurants. I let Matt do a guest post on the roasted pumpkin seeds he makes every Halloween. And after a weekend in Big Sur, we simply posted a series of photos from our trip—there was no recipe at all.

So, two and a half years into the life of the blog, when I came across Swedish pop star Robyn's music video for her song "Call Your Girlfriend," in which she mesmerizingly dances with abandon in a giant warehouse space in one long take while wearing floral leggings with a faux-fur long-sleeved jacket for the entire length of the song, I not only know that I want to re-create it for the blog, but I know that I *can*—that it technically falls under the realm of a *bon appétempt*.

But wanting to shoot a music video of me dancing for three solid minutes in floral leggings in at least somewhat of a choreographed fashion, I soon learned, is a very different experience from actually doing so. When my friends and I began the shoot, I felt like an idiot wearing extremely unflattering clothing and too much eye makeup. But then, the more takes we did and the more my friends screamed at me to "go crazy!" the more I let go.

And ironically, not only does this become the second most popular post of my *food* blog's lifetime, but also, of all the things I've accomplished (not *too* much, but you know, I did graduate Phi Beta Kappa from Johns Hopkins, have had a few small publications to my name, married a nice fellow, etc.), it was *this video* that pushed my dad to e-mail me that he was proud of me—words I'd learned not to expect from him; words I thought were reserved solely for my brother, and even then, only within the confines of the sport of wrestling.

Sometime shortly after that September phone call with my agent, it begins to dawn on me that I've seemingly forgotten about Bon Appétempt's expectation-less, founded-in-fun origins. Back then, the kitchen and the blog were safe places for me to explore, to play, and to *fail* if need be. I wasn't trying to prove anything or impress anyone.

And now what? It's a few years later, and just because my soup didn't come together as easily as I thought it might, I become upset and beat myself up about it? It reminds me of my obsessive dieting in college—putting such severe expectations on myself, not being able to live up to them, and then hating myself for it.

In the next couple of months, I start to come to terms with the fact that I cannot *will* this book to happen any more than I can will Mavis to walk when she doesn't want to, any more than I can will certain recipes to come together flawlessly and effortlessly.

I can work hard. And I can do my best. And sometimes that's when I'm happiest, when I have a project and I know I'm putting in the necessary time and effort. But that's just one facet of who I am. There's another part of me that needs more space to properly thrive, that needs room to spread out— to do things I want to do just because I want to do them, and, if necessary, to look stupid in the process. I need to reserve the right to make a simple meal that doesn't even require a recipe, one that isn't for the blog or because Matt requested it, but merely because that's what I'm hungry for.

This is one of the first meals I made without a recipe to guide me. It's a staple meal of one of my coworkers who hails from Panama. And so, with nothing more than her description of how she sautés some garlic and onion, then adds rice, beans, and coconut milk, and lets it all simmer together in the pan until the rice is cooked, I went home and made it. She told me to serve it with avocado slices and lime, but Matt and I usually also add salsa and often wrap everything in a tortilla. Sour cream doesn't hurt either.

RICE AND BLACK BEANS IN COCONUT MILK WITH AVOCADO

Serves 4

2 tablespoons olive oil (or, if you have it, coconut oil works really well here)

1 onion, sliced

2 cloves garlic, minced

1 teaspoon salt, plus more for seasoning

Freshly ground black pepper

1 (13.5-ounce) can light coconut milk

¼ cup water

1 heaping cup white basmati rice (or another kind of white rice of your choosing)

1 (15-ounce) can black beans, drained and rinsed

1 teaspoon ground cumin

8 corn tortillas

2 avocados

1 to 2 limes

Sour cream

Your favorite store-bought salsa

Heat the oil in a wide skillet over medium heat. Add the onion and sauté for 4 to 5 minutes, until softened. Add the garlic and sauté for 2 to 3 minutes more. Add a few pinches of salt and pepper.

Preheat the oven to 250°F.

Add the coconut milk, water, rice, and beans. While it's coming to a boil, add 1 teaspoon salt, the cumin, and a few more pinches of pepper. Once it's boiling, cover the pan with a lid, bring the heat down to a gentle simmer, and simmer for 16 to 18 minutes (if you're using a type of rice other than white basmati, check the package directions as the simmering time may vary). After it has cooked, let it rest with the heat off and lid on for another 10 minutes.

While the rice is resting, wrap your tortillas in foil and warm them in the oven.

Slice the avocados in half and remove and discard the pits. With each avocado half skin-side down on a cutting board, slice the flesh into strips, and using a spoon, scoop out the slices into a bowl. Sprinkle with salt and pepper and cover with the juice of half a lime. Set aside.

Just before serving, juice the remaining half of the lime and pour over the rice. Stir to distribute and season with salt and pepper. Serve the rice and beans with the tortillas, avocado slices, extra lime slices, sour cream, and salsa. (Matt likes to wrap everything up in his tortilla, whereas I like to have it there on the side to scoop up bites.)

Chapter 31

Figuring It Out for Yourself

At the end of November, as usual, Matt and I both have work the days leading up to Thanksgiving as well as the day after, aka Black Friday, aka retail's biggest day! For the fourth year in a row we won't be able to travel home for Thanksgiving, which, to be fair, isn't necessarily a bad thing.

During these past four years, we've been able to build our own little Thanksgiving traditions. One of these is simmering mulled wine in the early afternoon and drinking it while we cook. Matt typically takes charge of the gravy and the bird while I handle the side dishes and dessert. The hardest part is finding the time to do the giant grocery trip beforehand.

After work, all I want to do is sit down, spend some time alone, and try to forget about how just a few hours earlier a pair of registrants purchased all of the remaining items on their registry, how they paid with $1,800 cash, how between packing up all of their items, marking them off the registry, and double-counting the $1,800, I somehow forgot to give them their $63 in change, how I then went on my lunch break (it was almost three p.m. at this point, so I firmly blame this giant mistake on low blood sugar), how they came back fifteen minutes later to explain they hadn't gotten the cash back, how I wasn't there to confirm my mistake, how things got a bit heated between them and my assistant manager, how my assistant manager had to remove the cash drawer and count it in the back room to discover that, yes, we were $63 over, at which point, I returned from lunch so that I could first hug my assistant manager, who was trying not to cry as she counted, and then, second, hand the money back to the registrants and apologize for my error.

But this year, two days before Thanksgiving, I come down with the worst case of strep throat of my life. It's the kind of sore throat that makes you realize what an asshole you've been for taking for granted the ability to swallow your own saliva with neither pain nor fear.

When my mom doesn't answer her landline or cell phone, I track her down at the office and have her confirm my diagnosis. She technically can't do so without a throat culture, but she kindly calls me in some antibiotics anyway. After calling work to let them know I can't make it in and picking up my meds at the pharmacy, I tuck myself into bed with my laptop. Last Thanksgiving, we'd watched back-to-back documentaries on different people's journeys up Mount Everest. Remembering this with great fondness, I begin my Netflix search there, hoping a new documentary might have come out in the past year.

Sadly, there isn't anything Everest-y I haven't already seen. This leads me through the entire selection of Netflix's sports-documentary subgenre, which eventually spits me out onto YouTube, where I find someone has posted the entire two-day broadcast of the 2008 Women's Gymnastics Olympic Trials competition. I saw it live, but that was four years ago. I'm more than happy to rewatch it now.

To me, the two achievements—summiting Everest and making the US Olympic gymnastics team—share a lot in common. Both rely so much on a person's drive and work ethic, and yet, simultaneously, so much hinges on specific arbitrary circumstances, like the weather for the climbers and one's age for the gymnasts.

To set the 2008 gymnastics scene for you, only six girls (all of who must be sixteen or older) can make the Olympic team. You might think that this means the top six finishers at Trials would be the ones named to the team. But only the top two all-around competitors automatically make it. In 2008, they're Nastia Liukin and Shawn Johnson. (By the way, Johnson, of all of the celebrities I've run into here in Los Angeles, is the only one I've felt compelled to approach and tell what a fan I am. We were both shopping at a health food store and at five feet six and thirty-one years old, I towered over her both in height and age as I sang her praises and lamented the fact that her knee injury had kept her from trying to make another Olympic team at age twenty in 2012. When I was finished, she timidly said, "Thank you." I stood there for a moment, waiting for something more but realized that was it, then returned to grocery shopping feeling like a low-level creep.)

The rest of the team is chosen by the suits, namely USA Gymnastics, which is headed by Márta Károlyi, the National Team Coordinator for USA Gymnastics, who needs to make sure that among those six girls, she has four who are solid on beam, four who are solid on floor, four on bars, and four on vault. In the end, this means that the two teenagers who actually placed fifth and sixth at Trials in the all-around don't end up making the team, as they simply don't fit into Márta's puzzle.

To come so close and *not* make it. Can you imagine?

Once I've shaken myself from my gymnastics trance, I realize that if I can somehow get out of bed and to the grocery store, I can accomplish the dreaded Thanksgiving grocery run at two p.m. on the Tuesday before Thanksgiving instead of on Wednesday, the day before Thanksgiving, which has to be the busiest food-shopping day of the year. And since my mom said that I should start to feel better within twenty-four hours, maybe by tomorrow, I can even prep a few dishes ahead of time.

In a way, my strep-ridden, sweatpants-and-hooded-sweatshirt-clad trip to Whole Foods is simpler than it would've been under healthy circumstances. Had I been healthy, I would have been rushing and distracted. I would have been annoyed by the fight for a parking space and the throngs of humans surrounding the normally unloved russet potato bin. But in my fevered state, I cannot be distracted. It takes all of my energy to just be there, list in hand, shopping.

I drive home and after unloading all of my bags, I'm completely spent. I sleep the rest of the day.

By Thanksgiving Day, however, I am feeling better. Not great, but hungry. Although it's not my typical kind of hunger; the potential dreaminess of a perfect meal doesn't entice me. I'm hungry for the day itself, for the ritual of it, for this tradition Matt and I have created over the past four years.

There are no demands on us. And since it's just Matt and me, we needn't bother changing out of our pajamas or setting a time dinner needs to be ready by. We eat breakfast, lingering over our coffees. We take Mavis for a neighborhood stroll. Matt watches football, the sounds of which—the whistles from the referees and voices of the commentators I know so well—are actually comforting. We occasionally check in on the Macy's Day parade and are surprisingly entertained by the song and dance numbers.

And sometime in the early afternoon, we begin to cook.

Instead of stuffing, I make a savory bread pudding with ham, mushrooms, radicchio, and Gruyère. I take it right up to the final step so that all I will need to do is bake it for about forty-five minutes before dinner. And instead of cranberry sauce, I unmold the cranberry-maple jelly I made last night, which just spent twelve hours in the refrigerator.

As for Matt, he's in charge of roasting two small chickens with lemon and garlic as well as the Brussels sprouts. But these dishes, like the mashed potatoes and gravy, can't be made too far in advance.

Thus, the rest of the afternoon is spent on dessert, an apple tart. I mix the tart dough in the food processor, work it into a ball, cover it in plastic wrap, and then put it in the refrigerator so all that butter in the dough can re-solidify.

Meanwhile, I peel, core, and slice two pounds of apples. It takes a long time, but it's satisfying to see my pile of pale-yellow crescent-shaped apple slices grow and grow. I preheat the oven and flour my work surface. I unwrap the dough from its plastic and roll it into a thin flat circle. I consider whether my circle is fourteen inches in diameter and decide that it's very close. Then, remembering the beautiful accidental tarte aux pommes we ordered in Paris with its spiraling circle of apple slices, I layer my own slices. My pattern starts out perfectly, but by the end has lost its way. I remind myself that this is a rustic tart; I'm not even baking it in a tart pan. I'm simply folding the edges of the dough over on itself. And once I do, I coat it with melted butter and a sprinkling of sugar.

When it comes out of the oven forty-five minutes later, it's a sight to behold.

The whole dinner is. From the table, which I've set with all of my best linens and dishes (accrued over the years at Heath), to the individual chocolate turkeys I've placed at both of our place settings to, of course, the food.

And though my appetite isn't fully restored—my plate holds just a sampling of each dish on it—Matt's exuberance is enough for the two of us. His plate is comically towering with food and un-photogenically completely covered with gravy. He's holding his fork in one hand and knife in the other when he looks up at me. "Well?"

It's that moment that only happens before certain meals when we know how hard we've worked and how seldom we eat such bounty.

And so we pray. Matt leads off with the Jewish version, the *baruch*. And I finish with the Christian one I grew up with. *Thank you, God, for this food. Bless it for our use. Amen.*

And then, at long last, we eat.

* * *

Almost exactly three months later, my agent thinks my book proposal is ready to go out to publishers. She sends it to a couple of her contacts on a Friday so that, that Saturday, while it's *out there* in the hands of the deciders, Matt and I are eating dinner with two of our oldest friends at Taix, one of the oldest restaurants in Los Angeles—opened in 1927 and where some of the servers are over eighty years old. The chicken is always dry, but the pommes frites are fantastic, and so is the semicircular booth the four of us are sitting in. And while scooping out New England clam chowder from a terrine in the middle of the table, Matt says, "Oh, guys. Amelia's book proposal is out to publishers."

"Oh, yeah?" says Neal. "How do you feel? Are you nervous?"

"Well, yeah, I'm nervous," I say, "but at the same time, I'm—you know—life is going to keep going no matter what happens." As I say it, I check my theory for holes, for leaks, for cynicism. But no. I seem to actually believe it.

When the proposal does sell less than a week later, I'm both surprised and ecstatic. I hadn't expected to hear something so quickly. It had taken me over a year to get those forty-plus pages together. I had gone through so many drafts, and then all of a sudden, just like that, that part of the journey was over.

The news is hardly more than a few minutes old when we do what we always do when we have good news. We call Matt's parents.

Matt's parents are the kind of people I hope everyone has access to when they have good news to share. They are such positive, effusive people that it's truly more fun to hear their reaction to any good news than to hear the good news yourself. (I once snapped a vacation photo that caught Matt in midair as he was diving headfirst onto a hotel bed. When Matt's mom saw it, she responded with an enthusiastic, "Aw, that's great, Matt!")

And when we tell them, they don't disappoint. They cheer so loudly over the phone I feel like some kind of Olympic champion. (OK, fine, I feel like an Olympic *gymnastics* champion.)

When we eventually hang up, we're still on a high. And

since Matt's working from home today, we have time to continue to celebrate.

"Let's call your brother!"

We call my brother.

"Let's call your mom!"

We call my mom. (She knew it, by the way. "Aw, Sweetie. I knew someday somebody would recognize your talent.")

"Let's call your dad!"

"I dunno."

"What do you mean? C'mon. He's going to be thrilled."

"I dunno. Maybe let's eat some breakfast first."

In the late afternoon, we pour ourselves some sparkling wine. And after some more prodding from Matt, and despite *knowing* my dad—that he's the opposite of Matt's parents, that he's your classic know-it-all downer—I'm still excited enough that I cave.

"Put it on speaker!" Matt says from across the room.

I do, and when my dad picks up, he sounds genuinely happy to hear from me, "Oh, Amy! I was just thinking about you!"

I feel encouraged. I launch right in. "I have some good news."

"Oh, yeah?"

"Yeah," I say. "I sold my book proposal."

"You sold your book proposal? Oh my God. I thought you were going to tell me you finally finished reading the second book of *Game of Thrones*. You haven't, have you?"

"No."

"HBO released the trailer for season three. I sent you the link, right? I was hoping you would have finished book three by now. It's just, look, I applaud HBO for their efforts, but they cannot—they simply *cannot*—capture everything that happens in the books. Take Daenerys for example. Her storyline is..." And he's off and running.

Matt is meanwhile frowning and motioning for me to take the phone off speaker. I top my glass with more sparkling wine and head outside, listening to his thoughts on where the show has gone wrong.

* * *

You don't know this when you set out to achieve something. (Or, at least, you don't *want* to know this.) But once you achieve it—and I think those who have summited Mount Everest and made Olympic teams would agree with me—you start to realize that life really *is* about the doing as opposed to the results. At the very least, it's the way we spend the majority of our time. On Thanksgiving, this equates to being in the kitchen with Matt, my dog, music, and perhaps the occasional halftime update from Cris Collinsworth and Al Michaels. It's about the quiet satisfaction that comes from having done the work that no one really acknowledges, but at the same time no one can take away.

And while it seems to be true that publication very well may not change your life or solve your problems, I can tell you this. The *promise* of publication may cause you to drink to excess.

By the time I hang up with my dad, it's not even six o'clock and I've finished off my second glass of sparkling wine and moved on to my third. At which point, our friend and neighbor comes over with his dog. The three of us congregate outside underneath our carport, where we can finish the bottle while our dogs play in the adjacent backyard. It's February in Los Angeles, so the weather is perfectly chilled. All you need is a sweater and a light jacket. Without hesitation, we move on to a bottle of red wine. It feels like college. We don't worry about dinner. We don't worry about having to wake up for work in the morning. At least for the night, we don't worry about anything.

Chapter 32

2013

In January, Matt changes our health insurance plan so we can have better options were I to become pregnant. In other words, for the first time in our lives, we're not avoiding pregnancy. That said, it's not a great time to get pregnant. We've just begun to get paid for doing what we *want* to be doing. By now, Matt's day job description has totally morphed so that now most of his responsibilities include shooting and directing ads and videos for his agency's clients, which is great. But these shoots often require him to travel across the country for long stretches of the week. And of course, I can't imagine that standing on my feet for eight hours a day and lifting heavy ceramics will be very comfortable if I'm six or seven months pregnant. Plus, I'm still teaching one day a week; PBS's online counterpart, PBS Digital Studios, is interested in adding the cooking videos Matt and I have been making to their network; *and* I need to write a book.

But I'm thirty-one and have heard too many stories about couples just a few years older than me struggling to conceive. Right now may not be an ideal time to start a family, but I can see that there probably never will be.

⁂ ⁂ ⁂

On the first Sunday of May, I wake up and am almost positive that I'm pregnant. My body is sore and simply, oddly, no longer feels like mine alone.

That same day, in a few hours, in fact, my mom is set to arrive at the airport, but before I go to pick her up, Matt runs out to buy a pregnancy test. Overly responsible girl that I am (future child, please take note), it happens to be my first pregnancy test ever, and when I take it, it instantly reads as positive.

"It says to wait for three minutes, but I think I'm pregnant," I say to Matt, showing him the double line.

"Oh, you're pregnant," he says, looking at it. "You're definitely pregnant."

My mom is an obsessive needlepointer. She always has a major project going on, whether it's a pillow or a purse or a Christmas stocking. My brother and I have shared many laughs over one project in particular: a poster-size *Babar the Elephant* rug/wall hanging she completed for either his or my first baby almost five years ago now. You would think that maybe she would have stored it away until one of us was actually expecting a child, but no. Instead, for the past five years, it has sat strangely draped over an antique chair in her and Bruce's living room. It's so haphazardly situated it's as if she picked it up from the finishers, came home, and, unable to put away all of her hard work, decided to rest it on the chair for the time being. But Babar and his friends have remained there, awkwardly and proudly, ever since.

In short, I know my mom will be thrilled when I tell her our news. But Matt and I decide it will be much more fun if we can catch her reaction on camera. My mom is nothing if not a good sport, and even though she's been up since five o'clock in the morning and has just flown across country, when I tell her we're going to shoot a quick Bon Appétempt video back at home, she's up for it. And when I tell her I'm pregnant on camera? Well, she's very excited. For me, for Matt, for herself, and of course, for Babar.

But just a few days after my mom leaves, I experience some uncharacteristic bleeding. When I call my doctor, she tells me to come in as soon as possible.

I do, and while I'm relieved when she confirms that the fetus is still there, she isn't very reassuring. "There's about a fifty-fifty chance of making it to twelve weeks," she says, at which point miscarriages are rare. "And until then, I want you to take it easy. No walking your dog, no yoga. No major stress."

"But yoga is a huge stress reliever for me."

She just shakes her head and wags her finger.

I had just chosen this doctor at the beginning of the year, and I hadn't liked her very much before she'd told me all of this scary, seemingly overly cautious information. But now I definitely want a second opinion.

As soon as I get home, I call my dad and tell him everything in a couple of breathless sentences, leaving no space for celebration—not wanting to celebrate if this baby isn't going to stick around.

Dad practically guffaws at what my doctor has told me before launching into three very *normal* reasons why women might bleed early in pregnancy. And then, most reassuringly of all, he says, "Look, if a woman's going to miscarry, she's going to miscarry. But is walking your dog or going to yoga going to cause it? Absolutely not. See, this is one of the many problems with medicine today. Doctors are *so scared* of being sued. So they're extra cautious. Babies are *packed* in there, and apart from exposing them to radiation or drinking the water in Saegertown, there's not much you can do to hurt them. Oh, and don't use your microwave. Got that? No radiation, no Saegertown water, and no microwaves."

He's being his classically weird, opinionated self, and I know that as always, I should take his advice—gynecological or otherwise—with a grain of salt, but his calm, confident dismissal of my doctor's orders is exactly what I needed to hear and exactly how I wanted to hear it.

By my twelfth week, I have a new doctor and a confirmation that the baby is doing just fine. Plus, in those five weeks, my dad and I speak more times than we have in the past six months combined.

* * *

While I was ready to know that Matt and I were physiologically capable of making a baby, it seems another thing entirely to act as a host to a life growing inside my body.

I mourn the loss of the daily glass of wine or beer that usually accompanied me while I prepped dinner, as well as the loss of my regular appetite, embracing saltines, oatmeal, and pickles instead.

At the same time, the idea of motherhood suddenly looms large. I feel a strong urge to find a therapist in order to work out all of my emotional shortcomings so as to not hand them down to this helpless thing that is going to completely depend on me.

And when I casually mention to Matt that I think Mavis

Bon Appétempt

has put on some weight and that we should be more careful with the amount of treats we give her, he looks at me like I'm crazy. "She's definitely *not* overweight," he says, picking her up as if to protect her from me. "You know, I don't want you projecting your own weird weight issues onto our dog."

As he says it, a deluge of fear rushes to my head. *Oh my God. What if I try to micro-manage my teenage child's weight? Oh my God. What if I'm going to be one of those horrible narcissist parents who can't separate their child from themselves and who will therefore judge their child as harshly as they judge themselves and the kid grows up to be as critical of those he or she loves as I am?*

* * *

It's August, and we have a major ant problem. I'm stuck in the house waiting for the exterminator to arrive between our allotted window of eleven and two. But it's OK, because I have writing to do as well as a bag of dried pinto beans and a basket of multicolored cherry tomatoes.

It's the peak of summer, and I cannot read one more article on what to do with all of the tomatoes my garden has been producing. For one, despite having ample room for a garden, I haven't gone further in the planning process than to occasionally consider starting one. And second, all the articles tell me to slow-roast my glut of tomatoes—something I've always wanted to do yet simply haven't. But after having come across the image of a bowl of glistening beans topped with puckered, shiny slow-roasted cherry tomatoes in Deborah Madison's cookbook *Vegetable Literacy*, I decide I must change this. And with the knowledge that I would be housebound today, I picked up the necessary tomatoes and pinto beans last night.

Ms. Madison's recipe calls for black beans and a pressure

cooker. But I prefer pinto and wouldn't use a pressure cooker even if I owned one. What I've got is a small space of countertop that hasn't been overrun with ants. I want to opposite-of-pressure cook. I want to slowly simmer some humble beans in even humbler water for hours until they soften and their skins crack.

I start by slicing an onion into thin half-circles, pausing to remove an ant that has found its way up my forearm. I spend a few minutes checking my body for others. Seemingly free and clear, I continue chopping three cloves of garlic until they're almost minced. I have some thick-cut bacon in the refrigerator, and though the recipe doesn't call for it, I feel like it would be a huge mistake not to include a few slices. Using kitchen shears, I scissor three strips of the bacon over my four-quart enameled cast-iron pot. I turn the heat to medium, letting the bacon render its fat and become nice and golden. I add seven cups of water, the pinto beans, the onion, garlic, cumin, two jalapeños, a bit of cinnamon, and a few large pinches of salt. I stir and breathe in the aroma of the earthy cumin and smoky bacon. I turn up the heat and wait for it to come to a boil. While I wait, I clean up, rinsing about ten to twenty ants down the drain in the process. Once it's at a boil, I turn the heat back down to a simmer and put the lid on top. The only thing that separates me from delicious, spicy, pinto beans is *time.*

While it's simmering, the exterminator arrives.

I briefly tell him about our problem, and he goes outside to inspect the situation. After about twenty minutes, he knocks on the door. "Wanna come check out what I found?"

I don't. But he's looking at me expectantly, almost proudly. "Sure," I say, and follow him outside.

"Yeah, there's a big colony right here." He points to a spot in the ground near the front entrance. "Also, found a coupla black widows."

"Oh."

"And over here," he says, now from underneath the deck, "I found a whole slew of 'em lining up and entering the house through this crack. *Aaaand,* there's another black widow." He looks at me for a response.

I nod.

"You guys get a lot of skunks up here too, I bet, huh?"

I nod again. "Yep." It's like watching *Ramsay's Kitchen Nightmares*—everything you never wanted to see about what goes on in a commercial kitchen, except it's our own backyard.

Back inside, I sign some paperwork, and Ron tells me the kitchen should be ant-free in two to three days. "The product does work," he says on his way out. "You just have to give it some time."

Alone again, I check on my beans and give them a stir before starting, at long last, on my first batch of slow-roasted tomatoes. I set my oven to 300°F. I toss the multicolored orbs in a bowl with a bit of olive oil and sea salt before spreading them in a single layer in a shallow baking dish. I place them in the oven and take a look at the clock. The recipe tells me to give them an hour, maybe more.

With my tomatoes roasting, my beans simmering, and the ants in-the-process-of vacating, I'm a relatively free woman. It's only one o'clock in the afternoon and dinner is basically taken care of.

* * *

In mid-August, Matt and I are at our second-trimester screening, where they do an ultrasound and take a close look at the baby to try to see if everything's progressing normally. This is where they will officially tell us the sex. At our last ultrasound, the doctor had told us she was a girl, but then he had followed that up by saying he was only about seventy percent sure.

As it turns out, he was seventy percent wrong. The technician tells us it's definitely a boy and shows us the evidence to prove it. We're both surprised. But what surprises me most is the sense of relief I feel.

In the ten weeks between ultrasound appointments, Matt and I had traveled to North Carolina to join in on my family's beach vacation. And it's only now, as I lay on my back with the technician showing me all of the various parts to our baby *boy* that I realize how closely I'd been tracking my relationship with my mom—both how hard I am on her as well as the ways in which I want to parent differently.

On our first day there, my pediatrician mother's back and shoulders are already extremely tan. But by midweek, she is reddish-brown, the color of a crisp piece of bacon. If she isn't at the beach, she has found herself a sunny spot on one of the house's decks. "You know, I'm going to take a photo of you and send it to your dermatologist," I threaten at one point.

"Oh, c'mon. I'm wearing fifteen!" she says, referring to her sunscreen's SPF.

If she's inside, she's never without a can of Diet Coke, her latest needlepoint project or crossword puzzle, and a blaring television. And I can't help but think how ironic it is how much time she spends talking about and arranging these familial gatherings and then how little of her seems present once we're all there.

And without even realizing it, I have begun to fear something more specific than motherhood. I've begun to fear having a daughter just like myself—a daughter so quick to criticize and slow to hug, a daughter who might someday point out my own bad habits, which come to think of are fairly similar to my mother's. At home, Matt and I eat the majority of our meals while watching television, and when we're done eating, with the TV still on, I turn to my phone and play digital Scrabble for the rest of the night, or if it's my turn to clean up, I turn on a podcast—basically avoiding single-tasking at all costs.

But now that I know it's a boy, I immediately feel less pressure. Because certainly (or so I've convinced myself) our little boy will take after Matt—openhearted, loving, optimistic, and quick to hug.

✻ ✻ ✻

When Matt comes home from work, I scoop out the pinto beans into two wide, shallow bowls. I top them with the glistening cherry tomatoes, a couple spoonfuls of sour cream, a drizzle of hot sauce, and a bit of chopped cilantro. Along the side of the bowl, I tuck in a pair of folded tortillas. I bring them upstairs, where we eat at the coffee table while watching The US Open. Tonight, it's the young American, Isner, versus the wily Frenchman, Monfils. It's an exciting match. After winning the first two sets, Isner drops the third to Monfils. Though at the moment, the excitement is stemming from the crowd itself. Despite the New York City location, the mostly American crowd has been won over by Monfils's exuberant personality and has begun to chant, "Monfils! Monfils!"

And in a fairly unorthodox move, Isner has opted to take a very long bathroom break. While we wait for him to return, the commentators talk about the crowd. They say they've never seen anything like it. One of them reports that he saw Isner on his way to the locker room and that he looked *extremely rattled*.

"Poor Isner," I say. "To be cheered against in your own country."

Matt shrugs. "Eh, they just want a good game."

"Yeah, but it's the *US* Open. It's rude!"

I look over at him and notice that he's stopped short of finishing his first bowl of beans, which is rare for someone who almost always has seconds.

"You didn't like it?" I ask.

"Eh," he says, shrugging. "It's *a lot* of beans."

I know it's a lot of beans. It's a lot of delicious *beans!* I want to say, but Matt's attention is back on the television. Isner has returned from his epic bathroom break and Matt has joined the crowd in chanting, "Monfils! Monfils!"

"Oh, c'mon. It's the *US* Open! How would you feel if you were Isner?"

But Matt just looks at me with a wide grin and continues to cheer, "Monfils! Monfils!"

*   *   *

By October, I'm six months into my pregnancy. The baby has received good reports at every doctor's appointment, and talking with my dad about it is no longer reassuring. For one, he's old school and doesn't believe in ultrasounds. He doesn't think I should get a flu shot. He doesn't think I should get a Tdap vaccine. He basically doesn't think I should be doing much of anything that's standard practice nowadays. He's also mentioned three times how he's going to take a train out to LA in early January to meet the baby. I don't give the idea too much thought until this third mention, when I realize he's being serious. "Would you stay with us?" I ask him, trying to sound nonchalant.

"Yeah, sure," he says.

"OK." I try not to sound panicked, but at the same time, I can't imagine what that would even look like. Would he come clean with his smoking or would he continue to sneak cigarettes behind my back multiple times a day? Speaking of which, what would he do *all day*? Does he have a laptop? Or would he take over one of our computers in order to keep up with all of his online chess games? What would he even *eat*?

"You'd have to come after Mom leaves is all. I think she's planning on staying a couple of weeks."

"Oh, Becky gets first rights?"

"Well, yeah."

* * *

Those who have shared a kitchen with me are well aware that I like everything done in a certain way. Before beginning any recipe, the sink must be free and clear of dirty dishes; I wash up in between steps, never touch a cabinet knob with buttery fingers or, worse, raw-chicken fingers—something my mom did on a recent visit and got scolded for. Ideally, I clean as I go so that when whatever I am making is ready to eat, so too is the kitchen (for another round of *spotless cooking* with your host, Amelia!).

Similarly, though this book isn't due until December 1st, with the baby due January 7th, I set a deadline to turn it in a month early, at the beginning of November. That way, perhaps (just perhaps!), I can fit in the edits before the baby comes.

This means that when my ninety-four-year-old grandma

(my mom's mom) comes to visit for a few days at the end of October, I'm not only seven months pregnant, but I'm in the home stretch of writing my first draft.

In the past year, Grandma has slowed down a lot. She now needs a cane to walk and supplemental oxygen to breathe. She's also recently moved to Taos, New Mexico, to live with my aunt and uncle, which is the reason she's able to visit me now. Aunt Martha and Uncle Bob have a conference in San Diego to attend, and they decide to drive her to LA and drop her off with Matt and me while they continue on.

And though I'm initially concerned about taking care of the trifecta that will be Grandma, the baby, and myself, I realize it's a rare opportunity and must take it. What I forget is that my aunt and uncle play things a bit faster and looser than my immediate family does. They're supposed to arrive on a Wednesday around dinnertime, but at seven p.m., I get a message that they're running late. When they finally arrive, it's almost midnight. After everyone hugs everyone and we get Grandma inside, Uncle Bob explains they can't chat long. They need to make it to Venice, where they're staying the night with Martha's sister so they can get an early start tomorrow; but first we need to "quickly go over Grandma's equipment."

For the next ten minutes, Matt and I receive a crash course on how to operate and troubleshoot oxygen machines, both Grandma's portable and stationary ones, the latter of which is the size of an oven, though it's thankfully on wheels. Once Uncle Bob has explained everything to us, he says, "OK, great. We'll see you all next week!"

"Sunday night?" I say. Their original e-mail inquiring about the visit had simply specified *a few days*, and I assumed the conference would end on a Sunday.

"No, not until Wednesday," he says.

"Oh."

Ultimately, however, everything works out just fine. Grandma is surprisingly self-sufficient. She knows how to hook herself up to the stationary oxygen machine, which she uses to sleep at night, and she basically ignores the portable one during the day. In the morning, I make her toast with butter and jam. Matt goes to work. And I write for a few hours while Grandma reads and rereads the past six issues of *Martha Stewart Living*. Thanksgiving is just four weeks away, and she takes a particular interest in planning her side dishes for the upcoming holiday.

In the afternoon, she comes to the park and sits on the bench while Mavis and I walk. When I have to run to the grocery store, she's happy to push the cart. And when I need to recipe test a batch of lemon and fennel shortbread cookies, she's the one grinding the fennel seeds with a mortar and pestle. One afternoon, I take her to the Griffith Park Observatory, where she poses (with Mavis) for a few photos with the Hollywood sign in the background.

Bob and Martha have cut sugar and carbs out of their diets, and much to Grandma's chagrin, they've tried to do the same with her. But enacting the age-old "our house, our rules" clause, we indulge her (and ourselves). We make pizzas and pastas all week long and finish each meal with scoops of ice cream for everyone. On her last night with us, Matt makes her a full-blown sundae with chocolate sauce and a cherry on top. I have a photo of her with it; she's smiling so wide you can tell she's laughing.

Bob and Martha pick her up a day early, on Tuesday.

I turn in my book six days later, the following Monday.

That same day, my mom arrives in Taos on a visit she's planned for months.

On Thursday, Mom calls to tell me that she's a little worried. Grandma took a fall, and though she didn't break anything, she doesn't even want to get out of bed today.

On Friday, when I check in, Mom tells me how she keeps clutching at her heart and saying her chest hurts. But still, she doesn't want to go to the hospital.

On Saturday, Mom calls to tell me that they've set up hospice care for her and that the nurse doesn't think she'll last the week. Mom puts the phone up to Grandma's ear and lets me talk to her for a bit. Grandma doesn't say anything back, but I can hear her laugh when I tell her how Mavis peed out of excitement all over my shoes that afternoon.

On Sunday, she's too tired to talk.

With both of her children by her side, she dies early Monday morning.

❉ ❉ ❉

I hadn't spoken with my dad since my birthday at the end of September, so when I see that he's calling me two days after Grandma died, I figure Bill has told him what's happened and I don't pick up. Dad and Grandma were practically archenemies, and the last thing I want to hear is him crack a joke at her expense. But when I listen to his voice mail message hours later, he sounds honestly sad and offers me a sincere condolence.

I try him back the following morning and catch him at a restaurant waiting to pick up his hoagie. "Yeah," he says, when I thank him for the nice message. "I'm really sorry. You know, she'd made it this long. I thought for sure she could have held out until the baby was born."

He can't talk long because he's on his lunch break, but speaking of the baby, he wants to get me something. He asks me what I need, and I tell him I'll e-mail him the link to Matt's and my registry. We hang up. I tell him I'll call him on Thanksgiving.

Grandma's memorial service takes place in Pittsburgh a little less than two weeks later, on the Saturday before Thanksgiving. As I'll be thirty-four weeks pregnant and my doctor doesn't recommend traveling out of state after thirty-five weeks, I decide not to make the cross-country journey. After all, I feel lucky to have spent a week with her so close to the end. I feel as though I got to say good-bye.

But when I call my brother after the service to ask how it went, I have a few pangs of regret. He's at Mom and Bruce's with Katherine and my cousin Rob, whom I haven't seen in years. They've ordered pizza and calzones from Grandma's favorite Italian restaurant and are about to sit down to eat. The service was beautiful and the church was filled with at least two hundred people. "Oh, and Dad showed up," he says.

"What?"

"I know," he says, laughing. "Hold on, here's Mom."

"Yeah, Ame," she says. "It was really nice. He said that he knew they hadn't been the greatest fans of each other, but he felt he had to come to pay his respects."

The following morning, I'm pouring my coffee when I just miss a call from my brother. Though it's seven-thirty a.m., which is early for him to be calling, I don't think too much of it. He's probably just hit the road to drive back to Charlotte

and wants to tell me something he couldn't in front of everyone else. I call him right back.

"Hey," I say.

"Hey," he says. "I got a call from Margaret this morning."

Margaret never calls either of us, but I know that she's also
pregnant, about eighteen weeks along with her first baby too.
Oh, no, I think. Something's happened to the baby.

And then he says: "Dad died."

"What?" I say it so loudly that Matt asks me what's wrong
from the bedroom.

But I can't respond to him because Bill has continued talking, giving me the details he learned from Margaret, that he'd
apparently been watching a movie last night and never came
up to bed, that Dolly went downstairs to check on him and
found him there, already dead. "I guess it was a massive heart
attack."

"But you just *saw* him."

"I know," he says, and I can tell he's either crying or trying
not to cry. "He looked like shit, but he was there."

But I don't cry. Not yet. I save most of that for two days
later when the Moses basket he bought us off our baby registry arrives with the attached note: *Happy Babyday. I can be "on
call," you know!*

* * *

Dad's funeral service is set for the Saturday after Thanksgiving, exactly one week after Grandma's. After getting permission from my doctor to fly, I book my ticket to Pittsburgh,
leaving Friday. Because of work, Matt can't come with me.

I haven't been to either Saegertown or Meadville in seven

years, and for Mom, who has offered to drive me the two hours there (and wait for me in the parking lot, as she doesn't feel comfortable coming in), it's been even longer.

Everything feels remotely familiar, from the Sheetz gas station right off the Meadville exit where we stop to use the bathroom, to the Dairy Queen across the street where Mom often took us kids for an afterschool Oreo Blizzard before we got on the highway back to Pittsburgh on those every-other-Friday trips. I know all these places—I've even been to the funeral home before, but still I have to use my phone to navigate us there. On our way, we pass right by the YMCA where I took gymnastics so seriously three days a week for so many years.

There's a long hallway leading to the reception room where the service will be. He'd opted to be cremated, so in lieu of a casket, there hangs a poster-size fabric tapestry printed with a photo of him, which is surrounded by stock, almost pixelated images of his interests: chess pieces, that winged symbol for medicine and/or health care, some books on the Civil War, and album covers from a couple of his favorite bands—The Moody Blues and Cat Stevens. At the top it reads, *William "Bill" Morris* and then underneath in small font: *Came from God, 1948. Returned to God, 2013.* I can't help but think Dad would've hated that wording. *I* personally hate the quotes around *Bill.* It would be one thing if people called him Petey or another name not immediately associated with William. But *Bill?* The quotes make it feel jokey, fake.

The service is at two p.m., but I arrive there at noon in order to be there for the receiving hours. Bill and Katherine are already there, having driven straight from Charlotte the previous day. And though both Bill and I spend a little time with Margaret and Paul and offer our condolences to Dolly, without planning it, we find ourselves in the hallway receiving people while Dolly and her kids do so in the main reception room.

The wrestling moms and hospital nurses remember me, but it's been seventeen years since I lived in this town, and I can see the confusion on the faces of the rest of the people as they try to figure out who I am. Some people who know that Margaret is pregnant but maybe haven't seen either of us in years look at my nine-month pregnant belly and say, "Margaret?"

"Nope," I say. "She's the other pregnant daughter. I'm Amelia."

"Oh."

One man asks me flat out, "And how do you fit in?"

"I'm his daughter," I say. "From his first marriage."

Margaret, who took on the role of intermediary between Bill and me and Dolly, had asked me if I wanted to say anything at the service, and though part of me did, a bigger part of me wanted to assume my role as the little sister, leaving Bill to speak for the both of us.

But when the service finally begins and I sit there listening to what everyone else has to say, I start to think that maybe the quotes around Dad's name are appropriate. Dolly's brother, Denny, speaks first and goes on and on about how Dad wouldn't accept mediocrity, how he *fought* mediocrity. But how and from where, I wonder. Behind his computer in the safety of his study in Saegertown, Pennsylvania, population one thousand? And what's so bad about mediocrity anyway? Denny wraps up by saying that he has yet to mention my dad's dedication to his family but that he's sure his kids will speak to that. This is my brother's cue.

But when Bill gets up there, he doesn't. Instead, he speaks highly of Dad's work as a physician, his talent as a chess player, and his intellect. I *sort of* know the guy he's talking about.

Margaret is next, and the "Bill" she describes is one who wouldn't miss a soccer game. Whether it was an away game or at home, high school or college, he was there in the stands. The "Bill" she describes is one who advocated for her when she hadn't gotten into her top elective, the chess club, for a second year in a row. He is someone with whom she watched movie after movie. But above all, he is someone who was a simple and straightforward presence in her life.

The rest of the people who speak are not immediate family. They are doctors, nurses, and patients. They have stories highlighting his skill, his sense of humor, his strong (and usually controversial) opinions, and the overall high quality of care he was dedicated to giving. Though I don't really know this "Bill" either, this is the one I enjoy hearing about most.

* * *

It's January 1, 2014, and I'm six days away from my due date. In the past few weeks, Matt and I have been busy preparing for the baby's arrival. The car seat is installed. The crib is built, above which hangs a multicolored mobile. Mom has sent me the Babar rug, and it cheerfully lies on the floor. I've prewashed and put away all of the new baby clothes and swaddling blankets I received as gifts. I even have a package of diapers and baby wipes. The room looks picture-perfect.

As long as you don't open the closet, where we've haphazardly stashed baby gear we know he won't need until he's older, Matt's camera equipment, our winter coats, the leaf to our dining room table, a wooden oversize chess board, yoga mats, boxes of my old journals, and other various possessions in need of a proper, or at least better-organized, home.

I'd been meaning to deal with this closet for months now—nine months to be exact. I'd wanted a clean start, for everything to be *just so*. But as I stand in the nursery, I have a moment's acceptance of the mess.

Besides, I think, with the arrival of this baby will come the departure of anything being *just so* again; my picture-perfect nursery will soon come to life with piles of unfolded clothes, burp cloths, and swaddle blankets. It will go from static floor model to being lived in.

And as I stand there, I catch myself thinking of my dad and of death, of how when you die, everything comes to an abrupt standstill.

Whatever task you had put off until the next day or week or month, you won't get to. Any unpaid bills or unwashed clothes are left for other people—the survivors—to take care of. And the tasks that other people can't handle remain undone, forever.

Later, when I logged on to Dad's favorite chess site, I saw that he was in the middle of five different games, having moved as recently as the afternoon of the day he died.

* * *

After more than ten years of writing and ten years of rejections, I'm aware I've developed a certain comfort level with failure, with the notion that I'm getting the raw end of the deal, that my talent is being overlooked. I know that I fall quickly and easily into a defensive mode, from where I'll mechanically stick up for myself, or the dinner I just made, or a random American professional tennis player. It's easy for me to paint myself as the victim, to think that I may never get the validation that I want.

What's harder to admit is that maybe I already have.

What's harder to admit is that just because my dad and I didn't have a traditionally close relationship or one similar to those of his other children doesn't mean that we didn't have a meaningful one, one that because of the distance between us, pushed me to work harder and do better, one that because of the distance between us made it all the sweeter when he told me he loved me or wrote to me that he was proud of me.

I like to think that if he had lived long enough to read this book, there might have been this new understanding between us, that he might have finally *gotten it*—why I was angry with him for so many years and how he'd hurt me. Maybe he would've even apologized. But to be honest, I can't hear those words coming from his mouth.

What I *can* hear is him poking fun at the book's cover design or correcting me on some trivial point. I can hear him jokingly comparing it to *The Lord of the Rings*: "Well, you didn't create your own Elven language, but it was a decent read."

What's sometimes harder to accept is that I'm actually doing well, that I have carved out a beautiful life for myself. And that sometimes, I don't need to keep fighting.

Annie Dillard writes: "At its best, the sensation of writing is that of any unmerited grace. It is handed to you, but only if you look for it. You search, you break your heart, your back, your brain, and then—and only then—it is handed to you."

You search, you break your heart, your back, your brain,

and when it *is* finally handed to you, in whatever form it arrives, whether it's a bowl of slow-simmered spicy pinto beans or your dream job or what looks like the beginning of a family with someone who loves you despite the countless times you pushed him away from ages fifteen through twenty-two, there is one last step. To claim it, to believe it belongs to you.

SLOW-SIMMERED PINTO BEANS WITH SLOW-ROASTED TOMATOES

Adapted from Deborah Madison's Vegetable Literacy

Serves 4

- 3 slices thick-cut bacon, chopped
- I pound dried pinto beans, rinsed
- 2 teaspoons ground cumin
- ¼ teaspoon ground cinnamon
- 2 teaspoons dried epazote (A slightly tangy herb often used in Mexican cooking. I get mine either at a store that specializes in spices or at a Mexican grocery. I recommend using it, but if you can't find it, don't worry. Your beans will still taste great.)
- 2 jalapeños (I whole and I slit down the middle lengthwise)
- 3 cloves garlic, chopped
- I onion, cut in half lengthwise and thinly sliced
- I lime
- Salt

To serve:
Slow-Roasted Tomatoes (recipe follows)
Sour cream
Corn tortillas
½ lime, cut into wedges

Place the bacon in a large saucepan over medium heat and cook until browned, stirring, about 7 minutes. Add 7 cups water, the beans, cumin, cinnamon, epazote, jalapeños, garlic, and onion. Raise the heat to high, bring to a boil, then reduce the heat, cover, and simmer, stirring occasionally, until the beans are tender, 2½ to 3 hours. Add the juice of 1 lime and 1 teaspoon salt. Taste for seasoning (it will probably need another teaspoon or more of salt).

Note: Time is your friend with this dish. If I'm making it in the afternoon for dinner that night, after 2½ hours, I'll probably take it off the heat, go take Mavis for a walk, run an errand, etc., and then come back to it half an hour before I want to eat to finish up.

Serve with slow-roasted tomatoes and lots of sour cream on top as well as with corn tortillas and lime wedges on the side. (Matt would tell you to heap on a few spoonfuls of shredded cheddar cheese as well.)

I make these tomatoes while the beans are simmering and then leave them at room temperature until I'm ready to use them.

SLOW-ROASTED TOMATOES

1 pint cherry tomatoes
Olive oil
Sea salt

Preheat the oven to 300°F.

Toss the tomatoes (leave them whole) in a bowl with a few drizzles of olive oil and a few pinches of salt until nicely coated. Pour into a shallow baking dish in a single layer. Roast for about 1 hour, until the skins get crinkly and puckered.

Epilogue

Three days after my due date, following a long walk around my very hilly neighborhood, a trip to the grocery store, three cups of raspberry leaf tea (rumored to help induce labor), and a dinner of rice and black beans in coconut milk (see page 261 for the recipe), I finally went into labor.

And the following morning, around eleven a.m., Matt's and my son, Teddy, was born.

A week later, my mom came to stay with us for ten days. And whenever I would say something about how cute the baby is or how much I love him, she would say, "Just wait until he smiles at you," followed by a guttural sigh of longing.

I didn't know this (as I didn't know most things about newborns), but apparently they don't start smiling at you (on purpose at least) until they are about six weeks old. Well, tomorrow marks six weeks, and today he stared at me and smiled for a solid thirty seconds, during which my eyes welled with tears of extreme joy.

Don't get me wrong. These six weeks have been hard. Each day has involved doing something I'd previously never done, from giving birth, to breast-feeding, to burping a baby, to recovering from giving birth, to putting a baby in a car seat, to finding a pacifier your baby deems acceptable, to operating a breast pump, to taking your dog out to pee while the baby is inside hopefully sleeping and not suddenly crying, and so on and so forth.

And all the clichés about having a baby seem to be true: Matt and I are tired; our household chores have doubled; our piles of clean laundry may never get put away; and we're both unsure if we'll ever again have the pleasure of a relaxed dinner together instead of one spent in alternating shifts of eating and baby-holding.

But I've found that there are other truths too—ones no one had told me. Like, it will take just a matter of minutes for me to miss his face, that when he wakes up screaming to eat at three a.m., that though I'm exhausted, I'm almost relieved and instantly calmed upon seeing his big eyes and flailing arms; that I will feel a quiet yet powerful satisfaction in caring for him—in learning how to calm him down, in anticipating his needs, and in realizing how I hardly blink an eye anymore when he pees (amazingly) straight up in the air while I'm changing him; and that I will find a deep-seated happiness in seeing how much other people love him, in watching Matt play with him or read to him and my mom melt with joy when he's in her arms.

During these six weeks, I've found myself thinking about my dad often. In the mornings, I think about how he would disapprove of me reheating my cold coffee in the microwave. I think about him when I'm staring at Teddy's face and wondering what color his eyes will settle on in a few months, if they'll become brown like Matt's and my mom's or if they'll turn greenish blue like mine and my dad's. I wonder if he would've held him for long periods of time or just a few moments here and there, and *how* he would've held him: if he would have cradled him in his arms close to his chest or slightly farther from his body, placing his head in one open palm and his back in the other. I wonder if he would've sung to him the songs he sang to Billy and me—"Here Comes the Sun" and that weird Three Stooges' "Alphabet Song."

And though I'm not sure exactly what I believe in when it comes to an *afterlife*, I like to think of Grandma just getting settled into her new digs, catching up with Grandpa, and then bumping into Dad in the hallway: "*Bill?* What on earth are you doing here?"

"Oh, hey, Ruth. Yeah, I just got here, which *means* I outlived you by almost two weeks. So technically, I won," Dad might kid, before the two of them got to talking, inevitably landing· on the subject of Teddy—empathizing with each other that they didn't get to meet him and agreeing on his adorableness.

During these six weeks, I've realized that everything I was worried about in terms of failing as a parent has for the most part been replaced with simply doing the best I can.

When we first brought Teddy home, the nights were particularly difficult, because—as he sleeps in the Moses basket my dad gave us at the side of our bed—any sound he made required one of us to flip on the light and make sure he was OK. But you can only keep up that kind of vigilance for so long. Soon enough, your own needs begin to resurface. Soon enough, you simply need to sleep.

And soon after that, a few of your *wants* emerge as well.

For me, this has meant finding time to make dinner (even if it involves chopping a few cloves of garlic and an onion at three p.m. only to sauté them hours later), to manage to bake a cake brimming with chocolate, dates, and pecans, to take myself and Mavis for walks (with Teddy strapped to my chest), to squeeze in productive writing sessions (while Teddy sleeps next to me on the couch), to let my mind wander to thoughts of book number two and baby number two, and sometimes even to let myself dream; specifically, of moving the family to Paris for a few years and/or of renting a cabin with friends and shooting a Bon Appétempt movie. Of course, both of these ideas feel completely out of reach and highly impractical, which is sort of how I felt about that chocolate peppermint cake.

Acknowledgments

First and foremost, I want to thank the readers of my blog. Without all of you, this book would never have happened. I especially want to thank those who, through their thoughtful comments on the site and occasional e-mails, became more than just readers but cheerleaders and friends. Whether you knew it or not, your digital messages often served as tangible proof I actually *had* readers, which translated into quiet encouragement to continue the blog (and to continue writing in general).

I want to thank my agent Amy Hughes for calling me three years ago and proposing the idea for this book as well as for her continued support through this whole process, not to mention other important processes, e.g., childbirth and child-rearing.

I want to thank my editor Emily Griffin, who encouraged me to write the kind of book I always wanted to write and who took so much care not only with this manuscript but also with *me*. I like to joke with my writing students about how writers are naturally fragile, self-conscious, sensitive creatures, and during the writing of this book, I was all of these as well as pregnant, and then *very* pregnant and grieving. I couldn't have asked for a better or more understanding person to help me shape this book.

Acknowledgments

I want to thank Wendy Brenner—my professor and thesis director while I was at the University of North Carolina Wilmington—who has always encouraged my writing, both fiction and non-, and who has been a reader and supporter of the blog from the very beginning. I also want to thank her for convincing me to watch the 1948 classic film *The Red Shoes* during a time period when I was feeling particularly down and out. She wrote to me, "the MOVIE is insolent and...you (Amelia) have to be insolent (defiant) to be an artist of any kind." It was exactly what I needed to hear at the time.

I also want to thank my other writing professors who believed in me enough to allow me to believe in myself (if even for a few fleeting moments). I'm referring to you: Rebecca Lee, Lucy Bucknell, and Stephen Dixon.

I want to thank my fellow "food bloggers," or perhaps better-put, this creative, supportive community I've found myself in; specifically, Tim from Lottie and Doof, Luisa from The Wednesday Chef, Kimberley from The Year in Food, Sarah from The Yellow House, and Kelsey from Happyolks. Each one of you and your sites have been sources of encouragement as well as inspiration.

I want to thank my friends, coworkers, and bosses at Heath Ceramics. Although the job might have brought me to tears on more than one occasion, the people I worked with made me smile way more often. Plus, I found daily inspiration in the company's dedication to the *art of making* as well as the beautiful ceramics.

I'm a demanding friend. (Or, as my friend Liz once kindly put it, "Amy is complicated.") I want to thank my close circle of friends for their support. Mary Anne, Raena, Sonya, Liz,

Acknowledgments

Kara, Tim, Corinne, Jodi, Neal, Sara, Sean, you guys have been there for me time and time again, and I can't thank you enough. Thank you also to those of you who served as trusty recipe testers. Your feedback was invaluable to this self-taught home cook.

Of course, this book really wouldn't be possible without its main topic, my family. They say, "you can't choose your family," but if you could, I bet very few people would choose someone who was writing a memoir in which you were a main character. Yet my immediate family has been nothing but supportive of this project—from my kindhearted stepdad to my loving and enthusiastic in-laws (aka Mombers Dadbers) to my amazing siblings-in-law (Andrea, Adam, and Fave) to my late grandma, my culinary guardian angel, and, of course, my late father who supported this book in his own unique way.

I especially want to thank my mom and brother, who helped me write this book by picking up the phone when I called (just about daily) while on a walk in the late afternoon after a morning at my computer. When Matt asked my mom for permission to marry me, and she famously warned him that I'm *extremely* difficult, she was *extremely* right. With that in mind, I also want to thank my mom and brother for loving me despite all of my many flaws *and* all of the instances I've taken the time to point out theirs. The truth is that no matter what I might say (or write), I love them with my whole heart.

Of course as much gratitude as I owe to all of the aforementioned people, I am most indebted to my husband and best friend, Matt, without whom I would have given up the blog long ago; without whom this story wouldn't be worth telling.

Acknowledgments

To be on the receiving end of Matt's specific, highly energized, and openhearted brand of unconditional love is a very special thing. And to watch it in action with our six-week-old son is possibly even more special. Just for introducing me to this kind of love, I'll never be able to thank him enough.